The
Servants'
Story

The Servants' Story

Managing a Great Country House

Pamela Sambrook

AMBERLEY

Dedicated to the memory of Freddy Stitt, Staffordshire County Archivist and William Salt Librarian from 1956 to 1985, who died in September 2016, aged 93

First published 2016

Amberley Publishing
The Hill, Stroud
Gloucestershire, GL5 4EP

www.amberley-books.com

British Library Cataloguing in Publication Data.
A catalogue record for this book is available from the British Library.

ISBN 978 1 4456 5420 1 (hardback)
ISBN 978 1 4456 5421 8 (ebook)

Typesetting and Origination by Amberley Publishing.
Printed in the UK.

Contents

Part Three

Appendices

Acknowledgements

My sincere thanks for help in so many ways go to: my good friend Linda Barton for continued support, enthusiasm and help with research; and to two other friends, Rose Wheat and Paul Anderton, for patiently reading through my drafts. For advice about Napoleonic studies I thank Malcolm Cook of the University of Keele; to Peter Brown for questions about accountancy methods and other advice; to the other members of the Staffordshire History Group who have given me great encouragement; to Nigel Tringham, editor of the Victoria County History of Staffordshire; and to Chris Copp, Melanie Williamson and Howard Dixon of Staffordshire Arts and Museum Service and Staffordshire Pasttrack. I thank all the staff of Amberley Publishing, especially Annie Campbell and Aaron Meek for their great patience with me. I also thank my friends and family for understanding my frequent disappearances for long periods.

My acknowledgement of permissions to reproduce images and sincere thanks to those who helped find them go to: *Country Life* (8); David Cooke and Alan Myatt (4, 10, 12, 17, 27, 29, 35); Jayne Morley (24); Jonathan Neale (7); National Portrait Gallery (32); Newcastle-under-Lyme Borough Museum (18, 22); Paul Anderton (33); Robert Metcalfe (6); Staffordshire and Stoke-on-Trent Archives (9, 13, 14, 16, 19, 20, 23, 30, 31); Susie Clowes (11, 28, 34).

Preface

This book has its origins in something amazing which happened in 2006. It is based almost entirely on one set of archives, the Sutherland Collection, the family papers of the Leveson-Gowers, who originated in Staffordshire, Shropshire and Yorkshire. Through judicious marriage they rose to the title of the Dukes of Sutherland, owning a large part of the Scottish Highlands as well as estates in the north of England and the Midlands. For a time they were the largest private landlord in the United Kingdom and one of its richest families.

None of the three main houses built and occupied by the Leveson-Gowers in England in the 1830s survive in their original use. Trentham, their country house in Staffordshire, exists only as a sad, mouldering ruin set in its restored gardens and a busy shopping area. Lilleshall Hall in Shropshire is full of youth and vibrancy, now a National Sports Centre. The great pile of Stafford House, the family's London home from the 1830s onwards, is today known as Lancaster House and is occupied by the Foreign and Commonwealth Office.

By bizarre contrast, the paperwork generated by the family and their employees survives largely intact. The historical archives are huge, covering ten centuries. Some are housed in Shropshire Archives and the National Library of Scotland, but the largest part was eventually stored at Trentham and was thus deposited on loan to the Staffordshire County Record Office in 1959. In 2003 it was offered for sale by private treaty at an asking price of just under £2 million. Over the next couple of years, the Staffordshire and Stoke-on-Trent Archive Service raised this amount and more with the help of the Heritage Lottery Fund (half-donor) together with hundreds of other supporters – the Friends of Staffordshire and Stoke-on-Trent Archives, local authorities, historical societies, businesses, womens' institutes and private individuals who were simply interested in history – most of them living locally, in the Potteries and the wider county. It was an amazing effort and a real tribute to everyone concerned – the people of Staffordshire.

The collection is still housed in the record office at Stafford and is also accessible on its own website (www.sutherlandcollection.org.uk) and through the Staffordshire Record Office's online catalogue: Gateway to the Past.

I used only a tiny fraction of the archive in the preparation of this book, which is published as a very inadequate and long-delayed tribute to all those staff and donors who worked so hard ten years ago to keep the collection intact and accessible.

Introducing the Sutherlands

The Leveson family were medieval sheep farmers and wool merchants in Willenhall who acquired estates in Staffordshire and Shropshire after the dissolution of the monasteries.

In 1689 a marriage into the Gowers, a family of Yorkshire squires, united the Levesons with estates in Yorkshire.

In 1785 the marriage between George Granville Leveson-Gower, the 2nd Marquess of Stafford, and Elizabeth, Countess of Sutherland and Baroness Strathnaver, brought the huge estates of Sutherland into the family. The countess, who was sole heir to her father, had inherited her titles and estates in her own right, having taken her case through the House of Lords.

The 2nd Marquess was an MP for Staffordshire seats from 1778 to 1798. Between 1790 and 1792 he was ambassador to Paris. He was given the title of the Duke of Sutherland in January 1833. He died in July 1833, after which his widow became known as the Duchess Countess.

In 1803 the 2nd Marquess inherited from his uncle the Duke of Bridgewater the annual income from the Bridgewater Canal Trust. When combined with income from land and industrial investments this reputedly made him the wealthiest aristocrat in the country outside of the royal family. It is also said that he was the largest private landlord in terms of acreage.

The 2nd Duke, also George Granville, inherited from his father in 1833. He married Harriet Elizabeth Georgiana Howard (Duchess Harriet), Mistress of the Robes to Queen Victoria. He also succeeded to his mother's title of 20th Earl of Sutherland on her death in 1839.

The 2nd Duke's eldest son, George Granville William, succeeded to the dukedom in 1861. He married Anne Hay-Mackenzie (Duchess Anne).

The archives used here are of two types. On the one hand there are administrative records of the households, which are similar to many commonly surviving in other country-house collections – wages books, accounts, cellar books, meal books, bills, rentals and reports on tenants, as well as some rarities including the porters' lodge books and the estate savings bank records. These illustrate what it was like to live at Trentham as an employee. What were the rules and regulations of this highly complex community, what were the rewards and how did the hierarchy work?

On the other hand, there is also in the archive a vast collection of correspondence, much of it between sub-agents and the chief agent in London, James Loch. Some of these provide excellent sources for addressing questions of relationships, character, behaviour and punishments, all part of the management of an estate. As such they are particularly valuable. The intimate details and feelings of servants are available to us from other houses in later periods in the nineteenth and twentieth centuries, when sources from oral history and memories have been used to construct servants' biographies and autobiographies; but for earlier decades in the nineteenth century, beyond the reach of reminiscence, written evidence of this personal quality is much harder to come by. In this respect the servant world of the 1830s is usually a hidden story – except when people such as James Loch and his clerks were at work.

My original intention was to organise each chapter of the book into narratives of individuals, put together largely from the correspondence. This has proved to be possible for a number of people and families. As these developed, however, it became obvious that some preliminary explanations were required, some background to the household in which the stories are set, that other formal world of rules and regulation. The dual nature of the sources is thus reflected in the structure of the book. After an introduction to some of the questions raised by the correspondence, the three chapters of Part One set the context of the servant households, dealing with management structure, household systems, wages, accommodation and other rewards. In Part Two more personal stories are developed, based on the real experience of individuals working for the Sutherlands, each of which are portrayed within a slightly different context or theme. Part Three recognizes that it would be absurd not to include some description of the two major correspondents, William Lewis and James Loch, insofar as they are revealed by their letters. Overall, it is hoped that the reader will be taken on a journey from the general to the personal.

Though they are an exceptional source, the Sutherland letters have their problems for the historian. Most of the stories are revealed by correspondence between a few men and fewer women who were fairly senior in the hierarchy of the Sutherland administrative system. This means we see events through the eyes of managers rather than the more junior staff, of whom we catch only occasional glimpses. Day-to-day work practices are illustrated only by occasional oblique references. Housekeepers and clerks were middle managers as well as skilled servants in their own right, and it was this level which seems to have taken much of the day-to-day stress of running such a high-level project.

Another general problem is presented by the fact that the land agents referred on to Loch details of incidents taking place in the house only when things went seriously wrong, or when some scandal or misdemeanour occurred. This makes for interesting reading but no doubt gives a skewed picture of the wider context. This is no reason, of course, to discount them, but it must be borne in mind when assessing the whole picture.

One practical issue has been that the Sutherland archive presents an embarrassment of riches. The collection of surviving correspondence, for example, is huge, though the digitised catalogue helps. For this reason references relating to the individual letters have been included in the endnotes to each chapter, for the assistance of family and local historians.

Thanks to the digitisation of family history sources it has been possible to link data from the archives to local and national records such as parish registers, censuses and birth, marriage and death registrations. Thus it is possible in many instances to place an employee in the context of their family origins and their family futures. This has helped enormously in drawing a rounded picture of the individuals concerned. Since access to census and parish records is now relatively straightforward through family history websites and record offices, no references to these have been included in the endnotes; name, date and place are usually enough to find them on family history websites.

The sections contained within a frame are specialised, 'optional' extras. A list of members of the household mentioned in the text – a sort of dramatis personae – will be found in Appendix I.

A downside to any study of servants before the middle of the nineteenth century is that there are likely to be no visual images of them. This is true here, with the single exception of the estate's chief agent and manager, James Loch. Rather than importing paintings or sketches from other households, I hope that people's characters will occasionally live through their words, written down almost two hundred years ago.

Of the thousands of people and families connected with the Sutherlands over a long period, only a tiny selection is represented here, purely for reasons of space; apologies are due to those who may be disappointed. The people I have written about were chosen not because they were in any way 'better' or 'typical', but because their story is accessible, interesting and at some point is brought into what feels like the true light of history – albeit sometimes a dim and flickering light.

Pamela Sambrook

Introduction

We begin with a story about an old woman and a young man living on the Shropshire estate of the Leveson-Gowers, a story which is perhaps unimportant in its own right but which illustrates well a number of points which lie at the heart of our study.

Sarah Tungate was just an ordinary country-house servant. She was born in 1772, probably somewhere near the east coast of England, and seems never to have married; her title of 'Mrs' was the courtesy often given to older single servants. Having gone into service she must have done well, for she was listed in a wage record which dates from around 1817 as the still-room maid in the London house of George Granville Leveson-Gower, the Marquess of Stafford, who later became the 1st Duke of Sutherland. By 1822 she had left London and was employed at what later was called Lilleshall Old Hall, the Marquess's modest country house in the small Shropshire village of Lilleshall.[1]

By 1830 when she was aged fifty-eight, Lewis, the agent then in charge of the Marquess's estates in England, reported that Mrs Tungate was unwell and that she herself felt that the heavy work of baking and brewing was getting too much for her. The old hall at Lilleshall, little more than an overgrown farmhouse, had been superseded in 1829 by the larger new hall, today known as Lilleshall Hall, built a couple of miles away (see Illus. 1). There was probably no debate about whether Mrs Tungate was physically fit enough to work at the new house. Lewis felt 'she has failed much of late and will not live many years', and again, 'I fear she won't be a long liver she appears to me to be dropsical. She eats little or nothing.'[2]

The Marquess's man of affairs and chief agent in London, James Loch, replied to Lewis's letter of concern. Mrs Tungate was to be given what was in effect semi-retirement; she was to stay in the old hall where she felt at home, relieved of her heavy duties, her salary continued and a maid provided to look after her. Since the old hall was surplus to family requirements it could be useful as accommodation for unmarried staff and visitors to the estate, for whom Mrs Tungate could act as housekeeper. This worked well, for when Lewis or Loch needed to visit Lilleshall they usually preferred staying at the old house rather than the new hall. Another part of the old hall accommodated a young clerk and his wife, the cashier in the Lilleshall agent's office.[3]

Mrs Tungate was to prove Lewis wrong, for eleven years later, in 1841, she was still living in 'semi-retirement' in her home in the old hall, still being paid both her salary and the wages for her maid and telling the census enumerator that she was still a female servant.

Things were to come to a head shortly, however. On 16 September 1841, the sixty-nine-year-old Mrs Tungate sent for William Smith, a polite young Scotsman who was the land agent of the Lilleshall estates, having taken over that responsibility from Lewis. He was in effect her boss, though he lodged with her in the old hall.

William Smith was born in Kirriemuir, Angus, and was in his late twenties when he came to work at Lilleshall in 1834. He was already an experienced land steward for he had previously worked for the Sutherlands on one of their estates in Scotland, but he was the first full-time resident agent to be appointed at Lilleshall for some years. For this reason, there was no established agent's house available for him, so because he was single he had to make do with lodgings in the old hall, looked after by Mrs Tungate. Though no doubt she made him comfortable this was hardly a suitable arrangement for a man of his status or responsibilities. He was promised that better accommodation would soon be made ready for him, but this was not forthcoming due to a period of stringent economies introduced by Loch.

William lodged with Mrs Tungate for seven years before finally running out of patience and writing to Loch to complain, and then only because he had found himself a wife and the couple needed their own household.[4]

For once James Loch was at a loss as to how to proceed. If Mrs Tungate was to give up work completely they would need to separate her accommodation from the main part of the house or move her altogether. Lewis, who had known her for many years, thought 'it would be better for her to leave … for <u>her own comfort</u>', but also, 'She has been a most worthy valuable servant for many years and it would be cruel to do anything to hurt her feelings.' Loch admitted, 'I must deal most carefully and tenderly with Mrs Tungate … She should of course have her salary and her maid continued. How shall I accomplish this and had we better try and settle her upon Lilleshall or Trentham or Newcastle or in town or where?'[5] Mrs Tungate accepted that she should now really 'retire' – the problem was where should she retire to?

This was the issue which Mrs Tungate had wanted to discuss with William Smith when she asked to see him. We can perhaps picture the two of them, seated at her tea table in a room looking down to the fish pond and the gentle, green hills and valleys leading up to the great mass of the Wrekin. She would be sitting very upright, in her starched and frilled housekeeper's cap, perhaps with spectacles perched on her nose, but still short-sighted, frail but nevertheless very sharp. William was trying to do his best for her. He had come back to the house from his work around the estate, perhaps damp and steaming from the rain because James Loch had forgotten to pay for a gig for him and he spent long days on horseback.

She had received a letter from Loch, which she asked William to read out aloud to her, not sure that she had understood it aright. After listening carefully, she said simply and firmly, 'No, no': she would not accept Loch's offer to convert part of the old hall into a proper self-contained apartment for her retirement, she would lodge somewhere else until she could make her own arrangements. There were to be no more discussions or pleadings. She asked William to reply to Loch on her behalf, and to refuse the offer politely but once and for all.[6] She sounds a very proud, independent and stubborn old lady, but one who did not want a lot of fuss made.

The offer which Loch had made to her was very generous. William was happy to subdivide the house between them, explaining that the old servants' hall would be adapted as a kitchen for her. She would also retain her existing sitting room, with the bedroom above, take in another bedroom over the office and the little room at the head of the stairs for her maid, giving her three bedrooms. By blocking up one passageway she would have unrestricted access to the garden. For this she would be charged no rent.

Unwilling to accept her refusal of this arrangement, William did not give up easily. He delayed sending her reply to Loch for a few days, to give her time to change her mind, for he thought he could make her very comfortable in the old hall. He began preparations to go ahead with the alterations and even arranged for Mrs Kirke to call on her. Mrs Kirke had been housekeeper at the new Lilleshall Hall since 1831 and was a close friend of Mrs Tungate. According to William's report to Loch, 'she reasoned with her in every way she could think', and even offered her the use of the front bedrooms – the best in the house – but all to no avail. Mrs Tungate's reply was that 'the place shall be clear of her very soon'.[7]

Loch and William Smith treated Mrs Tungate very kindly, searching for solutions to the problem. If she did not wish to stay in the old hall, a dairy maid was leaving the home farmhouse and some rooms could be adapted for her there; but she refused to consider this, too, and refused also the idea of a cottage either at Lilleshall or Trentham, insisting that she was going to stay for a time with her old friend Mr Lewis who was living at Groundslow, near Trentham, until she had made up her mind where to go.[8] Unfortunately at this point, in the autumn of 1841, Lewis himself was struck down with a paralysing stroke, so any thought of staying with him and his family even for a short time was out of the question.

Mrs Tungate, however, was true to her promise, for before the end of the year she had found new lodgings and moved out of Lilleshall. Both Loch and William Smith were left feeling vaguely guilty; the latter sent a note assuring Loch that if anyone asked about her or claimed that an elderly, infirm servant had been left to fend for herself, he would tell them that it was 'by her will that she left Lilleshall and that every consideration has been given her'.[9]

The lodging she had chosen was part of a large, bustling farming household on one of the Sutherlands' estates in Staffordshire. It had been known as Hanchurch Hill Farm, described by James Loch in 1820 as 'a good dry arable farm' with a large new three-storey brick and tiled house. In 1851 it was redesigned by the Duke of Sutherland's surveyor and called Hanchurch Model Farm. In the 1841 census it was tenanted by the Heatleys, a young man and his wife with three small children, two living-in farm servants and a female servant.[10] Mrs Tungate would have felt comfortable there, for Hanchurch was a hamlet close to the north-west side of the Sutherlands' park at Trentham. It was inhabited mainly by Sutherland tenant farmers, cottagers and employees – including, for example, the senior Trentham office clerk, whom she knew personally from the years when he had worked at Lilleshall, and several of the estate stonemasons working in the nearby quarries.

Her generous pension arrangements were continued for a further eleven years until her death, though the first payment was a little tardy and William Smith had to send his cashier over to Hanchurch personally to deliver it. William passed on the report of his visit: 'She is pretty well and he said he never saw one so overcome with gratitude as she was.'[11] No wonder, for her pension totalled £86 16*s* a year, plus £10 to £12 a year lodging expenses in lieu of the accommodation she had refused – all in all an extremely generous allowance for that time.

At that point we lose sight of her until September 1852, when a death certificate recorded her demise, aged eighty, at Aston in the parish of Stone, Staffordshire. The person who witnessed and registered her death was a local farmer, another tenant of the Sutherlands. She was buried in the churchyard at Trentham. It seems that the Sutherland family connection stayed with her until the very end.

William Smith was married in the autumn of 1840 to Rebecca Ann Taylor in Melton Mowbray, Leicestershire. By 1851 he and his wife were living at Little Hales in the parish of Sheriffhales, not far from Lilleshall Hall. He had two women servants and one manservant. There the couple stayed for the rest of their lives, William remaining as land agent to the Duke of Sutherland, developing the Shropshire estates through the agricultural and industrial challenges of the middle of the nineteenth century, designing estate houses, leading a comfortable life with several servants, but having no children. Rebecca died in 1873, William died in 1876 aged seventy; both were buried at Lilleshall, in his case with all honours, by the vicars of both Lilleshall and Little Hales. He died comfortably off if not rich, as probate records valued his effects at around £2,000. He had served the Sutherlands all his working life, forty-two years of which were in Shropshire.

Questions raised

Perhaps the first and most intriguing question raised by the story of Mrs Tungate's dilemma is: was she specially favoured by the Sutherlands? They seemed to regard her almost as part of their family.

Were all their servants treated so carefully or so generously at the end of their working lives? There is no doubt that obtaining a situation with the Sutherlands must have been the dream of many servants, for this would represent the very top of their employment tree. One could expect that, in comparison to most other households at the time, conditions of employment, accommodation and food would be good. In reality, though, was it a highly pressurised environment, at times a nightmare rather than a dream? Were employees tied into a system of dependence, deference and servility? Did service with the Leveson-Gowers provide assured security over a long period, of huge importance whether for a man with a young family or a single woman looking for a haven in old age? Was it a good working environment for women? Was such good fortune a means of social mobility for men, enabling them and perhaps their children to move up the social hierarchy? Were employees' expectations realised, at least by the standards of their own time if not by ours? Moreover, was it mere coincidence that both Mrs Tungate and William Smith were incomers with no local family ties? These were the sort of questions which formed the background to the initial research. The questions proved to be simple, but the stories which emerged were far more complicated.

Two hierarchies

A second point is that the picture of the two employees, William Smith and Mrs Tungate, brings together the two halves of country-house service and management. Thanks largely to television and cinema, the word 'servant' is now usually interpreted as 'domestic servant', one working within the domestic household. In early nineteenth-century law, however, the term 'servant' was used generally for anyone contracted to labour for another for a given hiring period, usually twelve or six months, often with accommodation provided. For example, a man who would later be known as an agricultural labourer was called a farm servant if he had such an agreement; in these cases the law of contract between master and servant operated. Because of the intimate nature of much of their work, however, the question as to whether or not domestic or personal servants came within the terms of the law was a point of major dispute over a long period of time, and many people on both sides were unsure of their rights.[12] Even the law was wary of intrusion into the private lives of well-to-do families. So the word 'servant' is in itself deeply ambivalent, as we can still see today in the use of the term 'civil servant'.

It is clear, however, that Sarah Tungate had been a professional living-in domestic servant of the Sutherlands for much of her working life. William Smith, on the other hand, was equally clearly not a domestic servant – he was a full-time career 'land agent' serving the Duke of Sutherland. Following the appointment of James Loch as the managerial head in 1812, the estate administration had been fully professionalised. William Lewis, Trentham agent from 1817 to 1841, sometimes referred to himself as a 'land steward', but this was an old-fashioned term in England, replaced by the name 'land agent' in the eighteenth century, a man who headed a managerial service encompassing outdoor workers, estate tenants (farmers, cottagers and commercial and industrial enterprises) plus indoor workers such as clerks and cashiers. These were administratively separate from those servants who ran the various domestic households belonging to the family, who were headed by a senior manservant called the 'house steward'. Both hierarchies worked for James Loch who struggled, sometimes ineffectually, to keep them financially separate. One of course was income-producing, the other a means of spending.

In practice the two hierarchies often overlapped at both Trentham and Lilleshall, especially during the seasonal absences of the family who usually took their house steward with them. At these times William Lewis, as the senior man on the spot, had responsibility for the whole of Trentham, including, when appropriate, the housekeeper and her domestic staff; so also William Smith headed the whole establishment at Lilleshall in the family's absence. Each set of employees was in some ways dependant on the other. Unlike households such as the Earl of Stamford's at Dunham Massey, the agent was not distanced from the house. At Dunham for much of the time the estate and farm was run by a local solicitor who employed clerks to help manage the estate, all located in the nearby town of Altrincham.[13] In contrast, the Trentham agent had his office and clerks established in a building in the service yard and himself lived in the steward's house alongside the brewhouse, wash house and home farm. The two hierarchies lived and worked in close proximity, might well have been near neighbours, and sometimes socialised together. When the family was away and the pressure of work slightly eased, it seems the housekeeper's room at Trentham Hall became a minor

social centre where the servants who were left at Trentham and
the clerks and agent could drop in for a chat. There was even the
occasional marriage between members of the two worlds.

It is this interplay of managers and servants which forms the
context of Trentham in the mid-nineteenth century. In practice,
at both Lilleshall and at Trentham, the two worlds to which
Mrs Tungate and William Smith each belonged must have formed
some sort of coherent community, albeit of a complex hierarchical
structure. One advantage of this inclusive approach has been to
bring into the light those highly professional middle managers
who have been almost totally ignored by historians, the estate
clerks. Ironically, it is they who laboriously and with great skill
wrote out most of the records used here. Learning the intricacies
of their trade and their handwriting brings the researcher very
close to them.

Trentham and Lilleshall

Thirdly, Mrs Tungate and William Smith both worked and lived
at Lilleshall, the centre of the Sutherlands' estates in Shropshire,
yet this study deals mainly with Trentham, over twenty miles to
the east in Staffordshire, on the southern outskirts of the Potteries.
The reality is that the various households of a family such as the
Sutherlands were of necessity closely linked administratively.
By the 1830s the family owned six main houses for their own
use, forming a network servicing their peripatetic, in many
ways restless lifestyle. Each house had its particular function.
In 1840 Trentham was emerging as the centre for the family's
rural hospitality, a house designed for exclusive, sophisticated
country-house parties, as well as the centre of the Staffordshire
estate administration. Lilleshall was more of a quiet, private
family retreat. Stafford House, their London house in St James'
Park, was the ultimate status symbol, adjacent to Buckingham
Palace and convenient for the Duchess of Sutherland who was
lady-in-waiting to Queen Victoria. West Hill, a country house in
Wandsworth, still with its park and farmlands attached, was a
convenient supplement to Stafford House, useful for the supply of
home-grown foodstuffs and as a quiet home for the children of the
family. Cleveland (previously Bridgewater) House was the family's
main London house before the purchase of Stafford House, after
which it became the residence for the dowager or heir. Dunrobin,

up on the far north-east coast of Scotland, was the family holiday home and the administrative centre for their vast Scottish estates. There were several other houses used intermittently by the family, such Cliveden, purchased in the 1840s, Tarbet, near Dunrobin, and many other smaller hunting lodges.

Introducing the main houses of the Dukes of Sutherland in the 1830s

1. Trentham Hall, Staffordshire was built on the site of a priory, acquired after the Reformation by the Leveson family. A new hall was built in the 1630s, substantially redesigned at various times throughout the eighteenth century and again in 1834–41 by Sir Charles Barry as an Italianate villa for the Leveson-Gowers, that is, the 2nd Duke of Sutherland and his Duchess, Lady Harriet Howard.

   Illustration 4 shows the hall as it was after Barry's rebuild, which cost £123,000. The 4th Duke gave up the house in 1905, offering it to Staffordshire County Council as a women's teacher training college; it was refused as no endowment income was offered. Stoke-on-Trent City Council similarly refused it in 1911. Demolition started the same year. Many parts of the building were sold, notably the top of the belvedere which went to Sandon. The site is now a retail centre with fine restored gardens and many other attractions, overlooked by fragments of Barry's building.

   In 1817 Trentham was visited by the 2nd Marquess of Stafford's sister-in-law, Harriet Countess Granville, who wrote to her sister:

   This is in many ways a beautiful place, and ... the neatness, the training up of flowers and fruit trees, gates, enclosures, hedges are what in no other country is dreamt of; and then there is a repose ... a freedom, and a security ... that no other destiny offers one ... nothing but trees and birds; but then comes the enormous satisfaction of always finding a man dressing a hedge, or a woman in a gingham dress and black bonnet on her knees picking up weeds.

   (Leveson-Gower, F., ed., *Letters of Harriet Countess Granville, 1810–1845* (London, 1894) vol. 2, p. 35)

2. Lilleshall Hall, Shropshire was the fourth Lilleshall house to be inhabited by the Leveson-Gower family (see Illus. 2). The first was a lodge attached to the ruins of Lilleshall Abbey which was made uninhabitable during the Civil War, after which the family moved to a timber-framed house in the village of Lilleshall, called Lilleshall Old Lodge. This was replaced in the mid-eighteenth century by another house in the village, later called Lilleshall Old Hall (see Illus. 1). Lilleshall Hall itself was designed by Jeffry Wyatville and built between 1829 and 1831 at a cost of over £80,000. It was sold by the family in 1917 and is now a National Sports Centre.

3. Stafford House, St James', London, was designed by Benjamin Dean Wyatt for the Duke of York with a loan of £60,000 from the Marquess of Stafford (see Illus. 5). The Duke of York died in 1827 and the loan was never repaid. The government bought the incomplete Stafford House and leased it for 99 years to the Marquess of Stafford for £72,000 plus an annual rent of £758. At this point it had restricted garden space and no family accommodation, which meant an extra storey had to be added, and no stables or laundry, which were rented nearby. The building and furnishing was completed in 1840 by Robert Smirke and Charles Barry, at a further cost of £203,554. In 1850 the 2nd Duke of Sutherland said he wished Stafford House had been burnt down – it would have been a great saving. The family relinquished the lease 28 years early. It is still owned by the government and is managed by the Foreign and Commonwealth Office.

      (Richards, E., *The Leviathan of Wealth*
      (London, 1973) pp. 16, 295)

4. Dunrobin Castle, Golspie, was the ancient home of the Earls of Sutherland since the thirteenth century (see Illus. 3). A central fortified keep forms part of the castle, which has been extended and rebuilt many times over the centuries. It was refurbished by Charles Barry between 1835 and 1850 at a cost of £60,000.

Looking back through the archives it is impossible to understand how one house operated without referring to the others. In particular, Trentham and Lilleshall worked closely together, especially before 1834 when William Smith was appointed. Until then William Lewis, based at Trentham, had been Loch's agent in overall charge of all the English estates. As a result of the physical and administrative proximity of Trentham and Lilleshall, both clerks and domestic servants were frequently moved between them. The unfortunate circumstances by which the two estates based at Trentham and Lilleshall became administratively separated in 1834 is explored later.

Further links were forged by the servants of the Stafford House establishment who moved seasonally between all the other houses. Some of these had their family origins in Staffordshire, and others chose to settle their families in the county despite having no previous connections there. Again, when she retired from Lilleshall, Mrs Tungate chose to lodge at Hanchurch, on the Trentham estate, not in Shropshire. Both Trentham and Lilleshall were never single isolated country houses but rather one part of a complex system. Though the intention at the beginning of this research was to focus on Trentham alone, it quickly became obvious that this was impossible, the two households and estates being so closely tied to each other.

1830s

The next point concerns the period chosen for the main study, the 1830s and early years of the 1840s. This may at first sight seem somewhat perverse. The 1830s had been a time of great upheaval for the Sutherlands' households in England, but by 1841 when Mrs Tungate was reviewing her future, things were beginning to settle down a little. The turmoil was the result primarily of family circumstances but there was also a difficult wider national context.

For the Sutherlands themselves the early decades of the nineteenth century were a time of unprecedented wealth. Income from their vast English and Scottish estates and from investment in industrial development was inflated in 1803 by the inheritance of an interest in the Bridgewater Canal Trust by the head of the family George Granville, then the 2nd Marquess of Stafford, through the death of his uncle, the Duke of Bridgewater. Early in 1833 the Marquess was given the title of Duke of Sutherland, but he enjoyed that elevation for only six months, for in that summer he died of a chill exacerbated by the long journey from London to Dunrobin. This threw all the various households into disarray: old servants retired or moved with the Dowager Duchess to Cleveland House and new servants were set on and trained for Stafford House and the new Duke.

There were further long-term financial implications of the 1st Duke's sudden death, however. Under the terms of the Duke of Bridgewater's will, the income from the Bridgewater Canal had gone to George Granville as a life interest only, well worth having for over the period of the last thirty years of his life it was reckoned the total income from the canal was some £2.25 million.[14] On his death, however, the income went not to the 2nd Duke but to his younger brother, the second son, on condition he changed his name to Egerton, which he did – becoming Lord Francis Egerton. Thus, at a time when the 2nd Duke's expectations had been raised by his family's recent elevation to a new title, his income was drastically reduced, from around £200,000 a year to some £90,000. Such a situation could potentially threaten the equanimity of the whole family.

Before his elevation to the dukedom, George Granville had finished building the new incarnation of Lilleshall Hall, replacing the old hall in 1829–31 (at a cost of over £80,000). The new house became the home of his eldest son and heir, and the old hall where Mrs Tungate and William Smith lived became a useful place to lodge visitors and employees. On his father's death, the 2nd Duke proceeded to spend a good part of the family's wealth on three of the other houses, employing a young Charles Barry to refashion Trentham (between 1833 to 1842, cost 123,000), and Sir Robert Smirke and Barry to finish the building and furnishing of Stafford House (between 1827 and 1840, cost £275,000), after which Barry moved on to remodel the house at Dunrobin (between 1835 and 1850, cost £60,000).[15] With the exception of West Hill, old houses were not sold off, but retained and staffed.

For much of the 1830s and well into the early 1840s Trentham and its gardens was a building site. The family and their personal servants spent little time there, preferring to live in London or indulge in prolonged and expensive visits to the Continent. So Trentham at this historical juncture is not a good choice for an exposition of the workings of a 'typical' country house, even if there were ever any such thing. It was, however, a typical renovation project, vastly exceeding the budget and running way over the deadlines agreed. Adopting the age-old premise that it is when things go wrong that you are shown the real characters of people and the real nature of the energy which drives them, we can see that the 1830s and '40s at Trentham is a fascinating time to reflect on. This therefore constitutes the core period covered by this book, though obviously we will look back and forwards for context, and on one occasion we take an excursion of several decades into a time when Barry's house was working as it was designed to work (see Illus. 6–8).

The Sutherland family's concentration on rebuilding their houses and living up to their enhanced aristocratic status was at odds with what was going on around them in the 1830s and '40s. As a prominent Whig family, they supported many of the important political changes introduced by the Whig government of Earl Grey – for example, the 1832 Reform Act and the Poor Law Amendment Act of 1834. Yet their extraordinarily extravagant spending on both Stafford House and Trentham coincided exactly with long years of severe national economic depression. The civil unrest of that period was exhibited in ways which touched the family's tenants and employees directly. In the early 1830s, for example, some of the Sutherlands' tenant farmers in Shropshire received anonymous letters threatening to burn their property, part of the 'Swing' riot movement; and in 1842 a Chartist meeting was held at Trentham with public speakers attacking members of the landowning aristocracy, including the Duke. For a few days the lanes around the hall were lined with striking miners. Both occasions placed extra burdens on estate employees in terms of concern about the security of property. Trentham was, after all, a fairly obvious target for such unrest.[16]

In the early 1830s especially, many of the Sutherlands' Midland tenants in both counties found themselves in the direst of poverty, losing work, deep in debt and unable to pay their rents. Despite a long-term policy of consolidation of farms on the estate – part of an adherence to agricultural improvement during the later eighteenth and early nineteenth centuries – there were still large numbers of smallholders and cottagers. These were particularly badly hit during the 1830s, which had a profound effect on the clerks whose job it was to collect rent arrears.[17] As we shall see, this resulted in some cases of serious distress.

The 1830s were thus a critical time at both Lilleshall and Trentham. The old world of aristocratic patronage, personal 'influence' and ancestral deference was still present. There were still families who could count their service to the Leveson-Gowers in generations, even perhaps centuries. The refurbished house at Trentham was a monument to this system, and yet on its very doorstep there grew a new world, the world of industry, new employment opportunities, collieries, potteries, roads and railways. In Shropshire, similarly, the family estates encompassed Ketley, an area of mining and ironworking. The Sutherlands did not ignore such developments; indeed, they played an important role in their planning and financing, and earned income from them. Their investment in the developing railway network in the 1830s was to some extent an attempt to replace the income lost from the Bridgewater Trust.[18] Yet they seem to have been blind to the full impact which all this would eventually have on the old way of life. Did they not see the long-term implications of the contrast between these two worlds, so clearly manifested in the extraordinary juxtaposition of the ethereal beauty of Charles Barry's new house, its surroundings 'gay with hanging woods mirrored in its still lake', and the 'muddy and miserable, squalid and unclean' streets of the Potteries a few miles down the road?[19] In the correspondence between Loch and his employees in the 1830s we can see small indications of the emergent new world. Loch, for example, had a huge network of powerful contacts which he was happy to use in recommending for employment people he respected, but his efforts were increasingly aimed at finding opportunities in industry, commerce and banking rather than traditional estate service. Nevertheless, it seems the servant world of Trentham carried on largely unchanged by such considerations.

PART ONE

1

The Servants of Trentham

Agents and clerks

The various households and estates of the Sutherlands formed a complex community which required a clear structure and an able management. From 1812 to 1855 the head of that management was James Loch, called at the time 'commissioner' of the Leveson-Gower estates, one of a small number of elite agents who were trained barristers/auditors working for the largest aristocratic estates.[1] Loch was based in London. From 1834 his large family – he had nine children in all – lived at 12 Albemarle Street, Mayfair, along with seven female servants and two menservants, where he also kept an office serviced by several clerks.[2]

Although Loch visited the estates in both Scotland and England on a regular basis, contact with his sub-agents by letter was critical, hence the surviving archive of correspondence. In addition to day-to-day letters he instituted a system of regular departmental reports, which covered every section of the Trentham household and estate, collecting statistics of income from sales or rent, of expenditure on purchases from outside, whether by cash or on account, as well as records of internal supplies from the gardens and estates – everything from pineapples for the dining table to hay for the horses. These were collated weekly, each departmental head then sending them off as part of their monthly report to London. From there Loch controlled the whole of the Sutherlands' administration, all the estates, the domestic management and personal financial affairs.

The man who was Loch's deputy as far as the estate based at Trentham was concerned was William Lewis. Between 1817 and

1834 he was land agent for all the English estates and their offices –
at Trentham in Staffordshire including Wolverhampton; Lilleshall
in Shropshire; and at Snitterton in Yorkshire. He supervised
everything to do with the economy and local politics of these
estates – park and woodlands, farms, cottages, roads, tenants,
rents, even who was voting in elections. Until 1833 Lewis also ran
the Trentham home farm. To cope with all this, he usually had a
part-time assistant in Shropshire and was supported by four office
clerks divided between the two houses. The junior of each pair of
clerks acted as cashier.

In 1834, at Lewis's request, a separate professional land agent,
William Smith, was appointed at Lilleshall, working directly to
Loch so that at that date the day-to-day administration of Lilleshall
and Trentham separated.

Outdoor staff

The number of staff employed in running the outdoor enterprises
under Lewis at Trentham is difficult to ascertain as these varied
widely over time and no specific wages list survives. We have to
rely on other records such as the lodge porters' books, Lewis's
own job description and various lists of people to whom issues of
beer were made.[3] These tell us there were seventeen gardeners in
1820, including Mr Woolley the head gardener. There was also a
head park-keeper who lived in a lodge on the estate, who himself
supervised at least two full-time assistants and a variable number
of casuals. There was a shepherd, poultryman, and a gamekeeper
in charge of five other keepers and a rabbit man. The surveyor
of buildings supervised bricklayers, quarrymen and stonemasons,
carpenters, two full-time blacksmiths, usually a painter with a
variable number of assistants and part-timers, in all totalling twelve
permanent workmen. There were also two daytime lodge porters
and a pool of night watchmen. These numbers tended to increase
over time but varied according to the state of the house.

House steward and travelling staff

On paper, everything to do with the management of the English
indoor domestic households (two households in London, plus
Trentham and Lilleshall) was separate from Lewis, under the
control of the house steward. From 1833 this was an Italian
called Zenon Vantini; he was replaced in 1841 by Richard Walker.

According to the staff structure, the house steward worked directly for Loch, though in practice of course he took his orders from the Duke and Duchess. He travelled with the family, part of the largest group of domestic servants, the travelling servants. These numbered twenty men and twenty women according to a list in 1839–40 (see Appendix II). Most of these were those servants who came into close personal contact with the family – the steward was supported by three grooms of the chambers (in less elaborate households the posts of steward and grooms of the chambers were later replaced by butlers), two under-butlers, three footmen and a variable number of valets. The family also took with them to their various houses the head chef and the confectioner, and the Duchess had her own personal maid with an accompanying personal laundry maid and a needlewoman. Also amongst the travellers were those servants dealing primarily with the mechanics of travel (two or three coachmen, postillions and grooms) and a small number of junior women servants (kitchen, house and laundry maids) who acted as supplements to the permanent indoor servants of whichever house they happened to be travelling to.

Housekeepers and resident staff

Whenever the family was away from a house it was left in the charge of a female housekeeper, who reported on routine matters by letter to the absent house steward but also enlisted the aid of the resident land agent when problems arose. At Trentham according to the 1839 wage list a temporary housekeeper, Mrs Henney, headed a resident staff of eight women (two housemaids, a still-room maid, two dairy maids plus one each in the laundry and kitchen); also five men (a carpenter in the house, plus two porters, a brewer and an usher in charge of the servants' hall).[4] At least one resident groom was needed to look after the stables and the horses used by the Trentham servants. For a large part of the year the housekeeper was in effect head of the domestic household.

The resident household of Stafford House in London was slightly smaller than Trentham (six men and six women) whilst the Lilleshall household was slightly smaller still (three men and seven women).

Part-timers

For an aristocratic household which moved frequently from house to house flexibility of labour was achieved not only by the insistence on a travelling household but also by the employment of casual part-timers from each locality. Some of these were regulars, others casually employed to help on special occasions – anything from a grand ball to the harvest – or covering for a full-timer in an emergency. In a society where a large proportion of women had experience of domestic service before marriage, local wives needing an extra injection of cash into their household budgets provided a valuable pool of experienced labour. In 1861 for example, the Trentham sewing women included the wives of a police sergeant, a cabinet-maker and a house-painter; the permanent laundresses were occasionally supplemented by two brickmakers' wives.[5]

Casual male labour was used for building maintenance, cleaning, vermin control and a whole host of small-scale but essential jobs. Using hourly-paid workers was more economical for the household, and for the workers it could be a valuable source of extra income, especially if the work was regular.

Trentham was thus home to five communities of servants all interacting with each other: the agent and his clerical staff; the outdoor staff; the travelling domestic staff; the resident domestic staff;

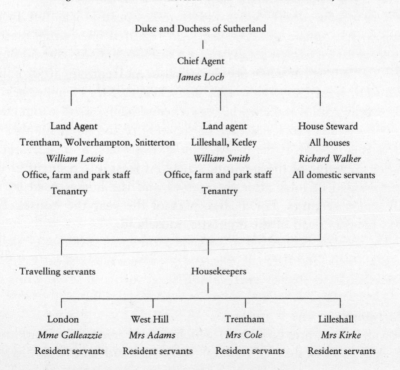

Management structure of the Leveson-Gower households and estates, 1841

Duke and Duchess of Sutherland

Chief Agent
James Loch

Land Agent	Land agent	House Steward
Trentham, Wolverhampton, Snitterton	Lilleshall, Ketley	All houses
William Lewis	*William Smith*	*Richard Walker*
Office, farm and park staff	Office, farm and park staff	All domestic servants
Tenantry	Tenantry	

Travelling servants   Housekeepers

London	West Hill	Trentham	Lilleshall
Mme Galleazzie	*Mrs Adams*	*Mrs Cole*	*Mrs Kirke*
Resident servants	Resident servants	Resident servants	Resident servants

and the part-timers and casuals. On a day-to-day basis the whole working community of Trentham seemed to depend upon the agent and the housekeeper. For much of the year the latter had a fairly settled, if busy, lifestyle, interrupted periodically by a flood of family and guests together with a variable number of travelling servants.

The structure was further complicated by the fact that within each house and within the group of travelling servants, women supervised women and men supervised men wherever possible. This theoretical structure broke down in some instances – for example, in practice kitchen maids worked for the chef on a day-to-day basis, not the housekeeper. This sometimes produced some unfortunate results.

Communications
Despite his being deeply committed to many other projects, James Loch kept in touch with his Trentham agent to a remarkable extent. The only communication system available in the 1830s and '40s was the letter. Many hours each day must have been spent on this, especially as the correspondence was backed up by a system of office copying and logging of correspondence. Both Loch and Lewis often wrote letters in their own hand but sometimes their rough drafts were rewritten by the office clerk before sending out. The clerks also made office copies, usually on very thin paper bound into books. This means that for most letters between Loch and Lewis there are two versions – the letter sent out and received by the other end and the office copy filed in the originating office. The two are not always identical. Unusually for collections of correspondence it is possible to tie letters to the replies.

Before the 1840s, the pages of the letters were usually folded into three and addressed on the outside – with no envelope. The edge of the overlapping page was fixed with a heavy wax seal bearing the family crest. The seal was usually red, but in the case of a family bereavement the seal was black. After delivery and after any required action had been taken, the receiving clerk carefully wrote on the outside fold the name of the sender, the date and usually a very short summary of the main topic. They were then filed according to name of sender and date.

Letters were exchanged between the two agents very frequently, often several times a week, occasionally twice a day – even on a Sunday when the post was carried by the mail coaches. In this way Loch in London was able to keep in touch with what was going on in Trentham, Lilleshall and elsewhere. This of course depended on the honesty and judgement of the staff on the ground. William Lewis was very quick to report incidents to his superior, sometimes rather too quick. Loch's reputation and authority frankly scared many of his staff, with the result that sometimes he was subjected to nitpicking details which must have irritated him. Only a few months after the death of the 1st Duke, for example, when the new household of the dowager (now called Duchess Countess) was being set up, Loch was in Scotland and crucially involved in pressing business in the highlands. Did he really need to receive letters such as this from John Smith, his London clerk?

John Smith to Loch
November 8, 1833

Dear Sir,

Mrs Bursby before she left Town wished me to separate the Linen which was at West Hill belonging to Her Grace from that which belongs, <u>strictly speaking</u> to the Duke – we went over the inventory together – she was satisfied that only <u>Big House</u> of right belongs to Her Grace – there never being but one set – when the family went down to Westhill, linen was taken with them.

There however was of necessity some always there, such as there is now for the servants – being dusters and coarse sheets, together of small value – We thought that these few things, distinct in the inventory, might if mentioned to you be allowed to remain, and be considered as the Duchess Countess's – value I suppose about £20. At a proper opportunity you will perhaps let me know how they are to be considered.[6]

The agents made full use of the fastest form of communication available to them, the Royal Mail. The uniform penny post was introduced in 1840, which simplified matters considerably. No longer was the cost of sending a letter calculated by distance, which required individual assessments to be made by postal staff and payment to be made at the end of the journey by the recipient. The new system required that a standard stamp acknowledging that payment had already been made by the sender to be fixed to the outside, thus simplifying the delivery method. In addition, the cost of a stamp was to be calculated by weight instead of the cumbersome and intrusive system which operated previously, by which letters consisting of two sheets of paper were charged double. In order to check this, heavy letters had been 'candled' by the postal staff, meaning the wax seal was softened by a candle and the letter opened.[7]

Even better, the new system provided for an outer wrapper by which the letter was to be 'enveloped', itself sealed with wax. The old system of folding the letter and sealing the pages with a wax seal was abolished. This is a tremendous advantage to the modern historian as breaking the wax seal present on the page of the physical letter often tore a hole in the paper right in the middle of the text, thus obliterating what always seems to be a crucial part of a sentence (see Illus. 9).

The new system, however, was not without its problems. Where possible it depended on the new railways, and in 1840 the railway did not go to the Potteries or Newcastle-under-Lyme, though it did go through Stone. (The railway never went through Newcastle, though it reached Stoke in 1848.) For some reason, however, the official postal delivery service to Trentham was via Newcastle not Stone and the nearest train station to Newcastle was in the small rural village of Whitmore. The Newcastle postman had to drive the horse-drawn mail box to Whitmore to collect the letters and newspapers, some five miles away. He did this each morning, collecting and sending off the London mail. He also went to meet the quarter past one train in the afternoon but this was a northern train only. He did not go to meet the teatime mail train from the south. This meant there was only one daily delivery and collection of the London mail to Trentham, which irritated Loch enormously. He could arrange for a delivery service from Stone where there were two deliveries from London, but the family would have to pay for it. This was a worse service than before the railway came, when the mail road coaches delivered and collected mail at the Trentham Inn on the A34 twice a day.[8] For a time the Sunday deliveries reverted to the mail coach, so the Sunday service was better than in the weekday.

Wages, board wages and day rates

Of the domestic household, the travelling servants were the more senior servants and therefore the most expensive. In 1839–40 the average annual wage for a traveller was around £30; for a resident servant at Stafford House and Trentham around £23; and at West Hill and Lilleshall slightly less, around £22.[9] Within these averages, of course, there was a wide variation of wages, according to responsibility, skill, experience and gender.

The most highly paid servant of all was a Frenchman, Napolion Binney, the cook on the travellers' list, who was paid £115 p.a. This reflected the market price of a top-class chef at the time and was £10 more than the house steward, then Vantini, soon to be Walker, the management head of all the domestic establishments. At the bottom of the hierarchy of indoor servants were the lower house and dairy maids at Trentham and Lilleshall and the nursery maids and kitchen maids in London, each paid an annual wage of 10 guineas.

Until the 1850s most of the servants were paid twice yearly, in June and December, six months in hand – a long wait for the first wage. In the eighteenth century and before it would have been even longer – an annual payment at Christmas. After the 1850s it changed to quarterly payment.

The annual wage rates are notoriously misleading, for they were calculated assuming bed and board (i.e. all meals) were provided by the house. When the family left Trentham, the cooks and most of the kitchen staff would go with them, the kitchen would largely close down and the remaining resident staff were expected to provide their own food, if necessary using the still-room which acted as the housekeeper's kitchen. To compensate for this, they would be given a set rate of 'board wages', a cash sum calculated on a weekly rate and paid by the housekeeper either weekly or monthly.

For resident servants, board wages often totalled more than the annual wage, though for travellers they would amount to very little. For the junior maids in one of the Sutherlands' country houses, board wages might well accrue to over £30 a year, three times their salary. In cash terms this would bring them up on a par with the lowest paid of the outdoor labourers, most of whom at Trentham, such as the woodmen, hedgers and labourers, received no board wages as they lived in separate cottages on the estate. The exception to this was the head gamekeeper at Trentham who, for some reason, received board wages every week even though he lived in his own cottage with his family.

There was a clear gender bias in the wage structure. Indoor menservants were more expensive to employ than women. This was partly because men occupied the most responsible posts, but even where it is reasonable to assume comparable duties there is a gender discrepancy: for example, in 1839–40 the Duke's valet was paid £52 10s in wages whilst the Duchess's lady's maid was paid £26 5s. This distinction was usual at the time and generally accepted by society – a woman was not expected to be the main breadwinner of her family and usually received roughly half the wage of a man for similar-type work. In addition, the government regarded the employment of an indoor manservant as a luxury which they eagerly taxed, whereas women servants were considered to be more essential and were not taxable.

Servant tax

Servant tax was first levied in England, Wales and Scotland in the budget of 1777 to help raise finance for the American War of Independence. The rate was 1 guinea a year for each servant. It applied only to indoor menservants, who were considered to be luxuries. Women servants were exempt, as were all servants of the royal family, foreign ambassadors, farm, shop and pub servants, and university colleges.

In 1785, the tax was extended to help finance the Peninsular War. Women servants were now included, as were many other categories such as clerks, bookkeepers, land stewards, bailiffs, porters, cellarmen, coachmen, grooms, stable men and even some farm workers. A sliding scale was also introduced. The tax on women servants was repealed in 1792. The tax rate for men was increased in 1798 and again in 1808, when the rate for one manservant was £2 4s per annum; for two servants it was £2 16s for each; for 3 it rose to £3 7s each; for 11 servants or more the rate was £7 1s each.

Servant tax was reduced at various times later in the nineteenth century and largely repealed in 1889, but not entirely so until 1937.

(Pamela Horn, *The Rise and Fall of the Victorian Servant*, Alan Sutton, 1986, pp. 9, 26)

The Marquess of Stafford's tax bill for Trentham for one year, 3 April 1824 to 5 April 1825
One four-wheeled carriage; eleven riding horses; one riding horse under thirteen hands; five draught horses not used in husbandry; seventeen dogs.

Male Servants no. 1 list

Andrew Chapman	Gardener
Thomas Elliott	Gamekeeper
John Penson	Park Keeper
James Wood	Groom
Thomas Beardmore	Brewer & Waiter
James Dix	Usher, Servants' Hall
Thomas Johnson	Helper in Stables
John Penson jun.	Helper in Stables
Charles and James Kirkby	Day and Night Porters
Samuel Hemmings	2nd Gamekeeper

List No. 3 list

James Loch Esq	Auditor
William Lewis	Steward
William Oakley	Bailiff at Lichfield
R. W. Kirkby	Office Clerk
Thomas Emery	Office clerk
William Sorton	Bailiff at Newcastle
John Hunt	Bailiff at Trentham

In London, the Marquess kept a further 16 taxable menservants. He was also liable for tax on: twelve men liable for hair tax; four four-wheeled, one two-wheeled carriage; eight coach horses; armorial bearings.
Total tax bill for London and Trentham £386

As one might expect, there was also a gender difference in the board wages, allowing for a larger amount of food and beer taken by men. In 1832 these varied from over £45 p.a. for senior men to over £31 for junior women.[10] This system was intended to be simple but in practice all sorts of complexities developed. Later on, when a new house steward, Walker, took up his post in 1841 he was scandalised when the London housekeeper Mrs Galleazie suddenly started to claim 17/6d a week board wages instead of the 15s she had been allowed previously. When challenged, she said she had found out that the other housekeepers at Trentham and Lilleshall were allowed free vegetables when on board wages; she did not get this 'perk' as she was in the town house, so the extra 2/6d was to make up for this.[11]

In summary, Trentham Hall around 1840 offered employment for a total of thirteen permanent domestic staff, excluding gardeners, park staff and estate clerks, at a wage bill of just under £300 p.a., plus roughly the same again for board wages. At specific periods of the year, notably later summer/autumn and Christmas when the family arrived, the Hall would see the appearance of up to forty additional London servants.

This pattern of servant distribution seems to have been very different from the servant household of a few decades earlier. A wage list which is undated but must come from around 1816 shows fewer travelling servants based in London – only twenty-three travellers in all, compared to forty in 1840. To compensate, there were more resident at Trentham.[12] The change reflects the growing extent of travelling by the family in the later period – longer stays in London, trips to Scotland and more prolonged stays on the continent, with consequently less time spent at Trentham. This no doubt was partly due to the lengthy rebuilding programme at Trentham, the increasing ease of long-distance travel by rail and also to the increased status of the family – the rise to dukedom and its associated activities, especially perhaps the fact that the Duchess was a favourite lady-in-waiting to the Queen.

Much later in the nineteenth century, many aristocratic families in London realised it was cheaper to pay board wages all the time than supply food within the household. It became common, especially for footmen, to go on permanent board wages, though often not without some major disputes.

The Sutherlands seem to have paid good wages to part-timers and casual workers, and their rates of pay were often better than agricultural levels. For example, the rabbit catcher and other assistants to the gamekeeper were paid between 2/6d and 3/- a day in the mid-nineteenth century and even a man helping out with heavy lifting in the laundry was paid 1s 6d to 2s a day.[13]

Helping Robert Wright the brewer was also a lucrative job, as at least one person had to nurse the brew through the night. In 1841 three men received payments for watching the brew and cleaning the brewhouse vessels. One of them, Phillips, also received payments for making faggots for oven fuel for the kitchen and bakehouse.[14] One of the brewhouse assistants was George Hemmings, a member of a family who, like several others, provided labour of various sorts to the Sutherland estate over many generations. The Hemmings and their like are difficult to track down as they were paid hourly and therefore not included in the wages lists. Though they appear in the censuses in the villages, their employment on the estate or in the house can only be inferred. Such servants, however, provided a stability and a familiarity with both estate and family often lacking in low-level indoor servants.[15]

Towards the top end of the Trentham hierarchy, Lewis's right-hand man for many years, the chief clerk Randal William Kirkby, was paid a salary of £120 plus various extras – more than any of the domestic staff including the house steward or the chef. In some ways Kirkby acted as a bailiff to the Trentham estate, collecting rents and assessing tenants. He was also clerk to the Trentham Savings Bank, parish clerk and overseer of the poor of the parish, all positions regularly invested in the senior clerk at Trentham. He thus enjoyed a good deal of status and control within the local community as well as earning extra income. He was probably decently rewarded when compared with a similar senior employee in a sizeable commercial enterprise. A full-time junior clerk's salary with the Sutherlands was around £50–60.

Family mobility

Whether or not the Sutherland family was in residence at Trentham made an enormous difference to the staff at the hall. We know from various records that the family spent little time at Trentham during the period of 1834 to 1840 when the house was being rebuilt by Sir Charles Barry. For comparison, it is worth having a quick look at the pattern of absences later on, when the household was functioning more normally. Fortunately, from the 1850s onwards, the comings and goings of family members and their guests were recorded in the 'meal books', large pre-printed volumes recording the number and dining place of all persons served each day: family, guests, servants, the occasional tradesman and sometimes 'half persons' (people who were presented with only a bread and cheese snack) and often even the numbers of dogs fed.[16]

It seems that in later decades there was a general pattern to the family's presences at Trentham but the details were variable, unlike, for example, the annual set routine of the Earls of Stamford who for decades split their year between Enville and Dunham, spending six months at each house.[17] In a busy year such as 1871, the Sutherlands made twenty-two journeys between their houses. Their longest stays were in London (137 days) mostly during spring and early summer, the period of the London season. Not surprisingly the visits to the two houses in Scotland (102 days) were during the hunting and shooting season. Lilleshall (64 days) seemed to have performed the function of a quiet retreat with some fox hunting and shooting fitted in. Stays at Trentham (62 days) were either short stopovers or during Christmas and the New Year. This last item, spending Christmas at Trentham, seems to have been one of the few events which was fixed over the years. The amount of travelling was prodigious, especially as the Duke's personal trips for various short-term meetings is not included in this summary. By the 1870s, of course, the longer journeys would have all been by rail.

Servant mobility

There was a tradition of long service to the Leveson-Gowers on the part of both individuals and families from Staffordshire and Shropshire. This was encouraged when appropriate; for example the agent in Shropshire entered Clifford, the Lilleshall carpenter, in a competition for a cash prize run by *The Shropshire Practical Farmer* for male servants who have stayed the longest in one place.[18] Even more, staying with the Sutherlands was encouraged by the possibility of help in retirement, and, as we shall see later, there are at least half a dozen families – of which the Pensons were the most extreme – which stayed for the long term.

The tradition of staying was balanced by the employment mobility of many of the junior members of the indoor staff – just those people whose wage rates were perhaps lower than in some other comparable households. Women filling junior posts at Trentham rarely served more than three years, and some posts such as the second housemaid and the still-room maid showed a continuous turnover. This was not unusual in country-house service, for according to long tradition women had to leave their employment when they married, whereas menservants above the level of footmen were allowed to stay in post after marriage and even liveried menservants were allowed to marry if their employers consented.[19] Many of the men on the list in the appendix show the stability of employment typical of the long-service families, for most of these were married with dependent families living in nearby Ash Green.

The staff on the London list were even more mobile in their employment record, perhaps because there were so many opportunities in the capital. This includes footmen, usually young men in their twenties, as well as the lower female maids.

The origins of servants

The 1851 census data for birthplaces (the first census which asked for such data) gives some idea of the extent to which the Trentham household offered employment to local people. Of the twenty-one servants actually living in the Hall during the census, eight were born in Trentham or other parts of Staffordshire. The rest came from other English counties, except for the piper who not surprisingly came from Scotland via London. The same census for the Sutherlands' main London residence (Stafford House) shows that six were born in Staffordshire, twenty from other English counties (mostly from the south), two from Scotland and Wales, plus eight from the Continent. In short, well over one in three of the Trentham list were Staffordshire in origin compared to one in six of the London list. The periodic arrival of the London household therefore brought to Trentham a cosmopolitan group of men and women.

The recruitment of foreign servants was a trend which increased during the years following the elevation of the Marquess to Duke and carried on well into the later nineteenth century. Due to the unfortunate juxtaposition of that elevation and the 1st Duke's death, a whole new household was needed at Stafford House. The dowager took many of the old servants with her to her own household, and others retired, so there was a temptation to rise to the occasion as far as household servants were concerned, particularly with respect to Vantini, the house steward then recruited. The wage list of 1839 thus includes five Europeans in Stafford House:

Zenon Vantini	House steward
Napolion Binney	Cook
Mme Galleazie	Housekeeper (of Italian family, born in Middlesex)
Mme Rousseau	Duchess's laundry maid
Mme Lemise	Duchess's needlewoman

During the following decades many more Europeans were employed, including a young man, then unknown, called Alexis Soyer, a French immigrant who went on to become the most famous chef in nineteenth-century England.

The extent to which servants married and settled down in Trentham with their families could give an indication of the impact of the household on the village. Of the staff actually living in Trentham Hall itself during the 1851 census, only the upholsterer and a carpenter were married. There were, however, other married servants living in adjacent properties at Trentham, some of whom were not local in origin. The man cook appears on the London wage list for 1851 as Peter Cripin, who often travelled with the Sutherlands but who must have spent most of his time in London.[20] Yet according to the 1851 census his wife, Caroline Cripen (born in London and described as wife of a man cook), was living in a Sutherland house at Trentham with one son and a daughter aged six (both born at Trentham), plus a local fourteen-year-old girl as nurse girl. In the same census for Stafford House her husband gave his name as Pierre Crepie, born in Paris – one of the exotic foreigners choosing to settle his family in Trentham rather than London, possibly because it was cheaper. The couple had been married in 1844 in the capital. Pierre was the son of Pierre Crepin, head cook to George IV, who died in Bond Street in 1836.[21]

The stud groom, Richard Topping, likewise lived with his wife on the estate – he was an incomer from Suffolk who married a local girl. The lodge porter, Charles Kirkby, born in Northumberland, had married a girl from Trentham and settled there. Unlike these, the poulterer, Joseph Machin, was born at Trentham and lived in the poultry house with his wife and family, which included a twenty-two-year-old son who worked as assistant poulterer. Like the chef, the poulterer could afford to employ a local girl as servant.

In some cases family connections can be inferred by combining the data in wages books and censuses for Trentham. The period 1840 to 1854 gives a total of 293 surnames of indoor servants living in Trentham Hall during the fourteen-year period. Within this group many names appear more than once: ninety individuals shared thirty-seven family names.[22] Many individuals were thus related, perhaps recruited by word of mouth through existing satisfactory servants. These would belong to a number of families with a long history of service to the Sutherland family: wages books, correspondence and censuses show that the Pensons, Hemmings, Wrights, Machins, Attwoods and several others provided porters, park-keepers, grooms, gardeners, ladies' maids and housemaids, as well as being tenants. Most of these families inter-married, usually several times and over several generations. Both the Sutherlands and their agents valued such families and often resorted to them first when recruiting staff – not always with happy results, as we shall see later from a study of the Pensons.

Comparisons with other households

Where did Trentham stand expenditure-wise in the league of great country houses? 1844 seems to have been something of a year of reckoning, for Loch and his staff carried out a survey of comparative households, mainly of those families related to the Sutherlands, itemising the number of staff employed and their wage rates.[23] The results were meticulously recorded in a table showing a breakdown of staff wages. They must have given Loch much food for thought:

Total wage bill of all domestic households, excluding expenditure of the family:

Duke of Sutherland – London, Trentham, Dunrobin, etc.	£2,685
Lord Francis Egerton – Tatton Park and other houses	£1,095
Earl of Carlisle (the Howards) – Castle Howard	£828
Duke of Norfolk (the Howards) – Arundel Castle	£1,118
Duke of Bedford (the Russells) – Woburn Abbey	£1,542

Generally speaking the Sutherlands' individual wage rates were higher than the other households, in some senior posts considerably so. The house steward and the chef were paid more than twice the rate of the equivalent post with the Carlisles and the Bedfords. On the other hand the footmen and the housekeeper were paid the same as at Tatton but less than at the other houses. The Sutherlands' steward's room boy did worse than in the other houses, as did the lower-level kitchen maids. Very noticeable, however, were the wages paid to coachmen, grooms and stable helpers, which were much better with the Sutherlands than with other families.

The difference in the total wage bill arose not just from higher wage rates paid to some individuals, however, but also because there were more servants – more footmen, more kitchen maids, many more staff connected with travel. In addition most of the other households had none of the very high-status servants which the Sutherlands employed, such as the Duchess' personal laundry maid and her personal confectioner, and none of the families listed above had a household piper. Here we can perhaps see part of the justification for Queen Victoria's supposed comment on visiting Stafford House: 'My dear, I have come from my house to your palace.'

2

The Benefits of Serving the Sutherlands

Where servants lived

There were clear rules about where servants lived which varied according to status, workplace and marital state. The domestic servants of Trentham lived in the hall if they were unmarried, which was the case with almost all the full-time women. The nature of accommodation was fairly good compared to that of servants working for employers further down the social scale, in single rooms if they were senior servants such as the housekeeper or if lower down the employment scale in dormitories for two, three or even more people, in the attics or the service yard, or in some cases adjacent to their workplace.

Servants' Bedrooms

In 1826, even junior maids' bedrooms were fitted with four-poster beds or tent beds with curtains for privacy, a mattress (probably straw) with a feather bed on top, three blankets each, a quilt and simple, standardised furniture, probably made by the estate carpenter. Many of them shared rooms – the number of blankets tell us how many slept there. More senior servants had more varied furniture, sometimes with a writing desk.

(D593/R/7/10b Inventory of the Household Furniture at Trentham Hall, 1826)

A senior manservant's accommodation – the house steward's bedroom

1 four-post oak bedstead and white furniture
2 mattresses – 1 feather bed
1 bolster – 2 pillows – 3 blankets
1 counterpane – 2 spring blinds
2 window curtains to draw up
1 carpet close fitted
1 hearth rug – 1 piece of oil cloth
1 green fender – 1 set of fire irons
1 footman – 1 hearth brush
1 sliding papered fire screen – mahogany stand
1 green folding stuff fire screen
2 mahogany armed chairs and covers
2 black rush-bottomed chairs
1 armed chair with black leather cushions
1 small deal clothes horse – 1 deal stool
1 round mahogany pillar and claw table
2 oak dressing tables
1 walnut wardrobe
1 painted writing desk with nest of drawers and green cloth on ditto
1 black writing desk with black leather top
1 black earthenware inkstand
1 swing glass
1 boot jack
1 bidet – 1 foot pan
1 basin and jug
1 water bottle
1 oval hand looking glass
1 night stand

Junior menservants – the footmen's room

4 oak four-post bedsteads
4 mattresses – 4 feather beds
4 bolsters – 4 coloured quilts – 12 blankets
5 deal presses – 2 oval tables
4 rush bottomed chairs

1 towel roller
1 lead sink
1 looking glass
1 old wooden coal box
4 small pieces of carpet
1 green fender and fire irons, 1 hearth brush

A senior women servant – the housekeeper's bedroom
1 mahogany four-post bedstead – striped furniture
2 mattresses – 1 feather bed – 1 bolster
2 pillows – 3 blankets – 1 counterpane
2 window curtains – 2 spring blinds
1 carpet close fitted
1 mahogany armed chair and cover
4 stuffed chairs and covers
1 cane armed chair rush-bottomed and cushion
1 low rush-bottomed chair
1 square mahogany table on claws
2 oak chests of drawers
1 folding mahogany fire screen (papered)
1 yellow painted dressing table
1 swing glass – 1 green fender
1 set of fire irons – 1 hearth brush
1 foot pan
1 sofa and white cover

Junior women servants – the laundrymaids' bedroom
1 four-post bedstead and curtains
1 tent bedstead and ditto check
2 feather beds – 2 mattresses – 2 bolsters – 3 pillows – 6 blankets
2 coloured quilts – 2 sets of window curtains
2 oak chests of drawers – 1 deal painted table – 1 swing glass
3 painted rush bottom chairs – 4 small pieces of carpet
1 green fender and fire irons
1 wood coal box – 1 japanned ditto
1 warming pan

Most unmarried indoor servants were inside the secure area controlled by the porter's lodge in the service yard. Married indoor staff (mostly men) lived in estate cottages beyond the lodges, in the villages of Ash Green, Hanford and Hanchurch, which were owned and controlled by the Sutherlands – examples of what historians have aptly called 'closed villages'.

Of the outdoor servants, those coachmen, grooms and stablemen who were single lived in dormitories within the perimeter of the hall site, mostly in the stable yard. This was probably reasonable accommodation for the period, for they at least had single beds, each curtained to give privacy. The London stablemen were much worse off, as many of them had to sleep two in a bed.[1] If they were married, like indoor staff they occupied their own household in a nearby estate cottage.

Workers involved in the park and the wider estate, such as poulterers, park and gamekeepers, porters, clerks and agents, also lived in tied cottages if married, but if single usually lodged with another member of staff in their cottage.

The head gardener and most of the garden labourers were married and lived with their families, but before 1841 the young apprentice gardeners lived together in a shed which was very rudimentary in its amenities.

Of the employees who were allocated cottages, those lower down in the hierarchy, the porters for example, were given a cottage near to the hall, usually in Ash Green, and had to pay rent, between £1 and £5 a year. Where possible they had a garden. The clerks were allowed larger cottages, usually valued at around £6 a year, but they were rent free as part of their remuneration (see Illus. 11).

In the early years of his career, the Trentham agent, William Lewis, supervised the home farm himself and lived in the steward's house near to the brewhouse and farm complex. Later he moved further afield to Groundslow Farm.

The casual part-timers lived in local households, mostly normal tenanted cottages.

Condition of tenancies
Routine jobs of maintenance of the cottages such as painting were the responsibility of the tenant or servant, though at the change of occupier the estate inspected the premises and carried out essential

repairs. A record book was kept and brought up to date at an annual inspection by the agent's clerks, recording the condition of each cottage, the number of children, the number of lodgers and usually a short comment about its occupier. Typically, this might be 'steady, clean and neat' (one of the grooms) or 'of weak intellect' (an elderly spinster).[2]

Smoking chimneys and grates seem to have presented a particular problem. Chimneys were the responsibility of the landlord, but grates varied. Theoretically the system was that the upstairs grates belonged to the estate and they therefore would undertake repairs to these, though this was rarely needed. The downstairs grates and boilers which took a lot of wear belonged to the occupier who was thus responsible for maintenance and repair. At the change of occupier, the estate legally took possession of all the tenant's fixtures, including the grates, and transferred ownership of them to the incoming occupier.[3] In the rare case of an enforced eviction, the estate was entitled physically to take out the fixtures because the tenancy was at an end and the old occupier had no further ownership of them. Thus the traditional method of a forced eviction included the removal of the main cooking fireplace and, in theory at least, the staircase.

In practice, of course, it was rarely as straightforward as this. Most houses had their history of tenants' alterations over the years which resulted in varying ownerships. These were logged into a record of fixtures which itemised the grates upstairs, grate below stairs, locks on doors and even fixed chairs, shelves or cupboards which belonged to the estate and therefore could be removed in the case of eviction.[4] In the case of farms or small holdings changing tenants, the estate usually bought the manure and straw outside, all of which would be owned by the outgoing tenant.

Allocation of cottages

Of those who were entitled to their own cottage, few had any choice as to which house they were given. In reality, when staff changed there was often a degree of shifting around – for example, one person might have to move to make room for someone else with a larger family. Finding suitable accommodation for a new member of staff could create real difficulties, causing both Loch and Lewis to rack their brains for a solution. Even a senior man could be stuck in fairly meagre lodgings for some time if he were single. The complications could be endless, enough to make an agent dread the very idea of setting on someone new, as a somewhat involved story about gardeners will show.

George Fleming, the head gardener at Trentham from late 1841, caused a good deal of disturbance to a whole string of people when he was first appointed, albeit no doubt unintentionally. Before moving to Trentham he had been head gardener at Lilleshall, where on his original appointment he had displaced the previous Lilleshall head gardener, Beckie, who was sacked. Unlike the situation faced earlier by the Lilleshall agent William Smith who had to make do with lodging in the Old Hall, there was an established house which went with the position of head gardener, sited near to Lilleshall Abbey. Losing both job and home at the time of his sacking, Beckie was of course in great distress, but Loch agreed that he could be leased some land and eventually a cottage to go with it, so that he could open his own market garden business.[5]

Fleming was in post at Lilleshall for only three years before being promoted to head gardener at Trentham, again replacing an established head gardener, John Woolley, who had been in that post since 1826.[6] By August 1841 Woolley had been told that, like Beckie, his services would no longer be needed and his house was required for his successor. Like Beckie, too, some thought had been given to his future but without, it appears, any consultation with Woolley himself. Loch wrote to him: 'The Duke has been kind enough to offer you a small farm in Shropshire which would afford you a comfortable retirement.' Unfortunately, Loch went on, Fleming needed the gardener's house before the farm could be got ready for Woolley, so in the meantime would Woolley mind living with one of the undergardeners?[7]

This arrangement, however, did not appeal to Woolley, who was getting on in years but still had a wife and family. In August of 1841 he went to see William Lewis at Trentham, 'in great trouble', saying the farm in Shropshire would not suit him as he was no longer capable of hard labour and moreover had a wife in very delicate health.[8] He had worked for the family for forty years and hoped for an annual pension, expecting to be able to retire to a small cottage with a little land where he could keep a couple of cows. (If he had worked for the family for forty years, this meant he had started as a garden boy aged eight or nine, which was perfectly possible.) Lewis thought all this reasonable and suggested to Loch that Woolley be given a pension of one guinea a week. Moreover, one of the older retired garden labourers, George Fernyhough, had died the previous week; his cottage at Rough Close would soon become vacant and his pension of 10 shillings a week was of course no longer a charge on the estate.

Such a simple solution was not to be. When Henney, the Trentham clerk, called to inspect Fernyhough's cottage, he found to his surprise not an empty house but one filled not only by Fernyhough's brother-in-law but also one of his daughters, together with a family of five or six children.[9] He also found that she had already applied to Lewis for approval to carry on the tenancy – this Henney was not aware of, as Lewis had recently had a stroke and was still confined to his bed.

Fortunately there was another tenant who was leaving soon and Woolley asked to be allocated his cottage instead. The tenant was not yet ready to go but was happy for Woolley to leave some of his goods in storage with him. Woolley still had not been given a formal date for his leaving, but because Fleming had now arrived to take over, he and his family had to vacate their home in a rush. They packed up the rest of their belongings and went to lodge temporarily with the Trentham schoolmaster.[10]

Woolley's problems were not yet over, however. Nothing formal seems to have been agreed with Loch about a pension for him, for towards the end of November he wrote to Loch, refusing the kind offer of the farm because he was too old for manual work and again asking for a pension, pointing out his long service and that of his ancestors and the fact that he had been removed from his job for no reason of his own fault. He had done nothing wrong, and 'my anxiety now is for my family'. The reply in Loch's hand is drafted on the bottom of his letter: he had been replaced because he was too old for manual work and he, Loch, was not prepared to approach the Duke again on his behalf. Around that time Lewis had visited him and described him as being in 'sad trouble'.[11]

Woolley was unfortunate in the timing of his retirement. William Lewis, who had promoted him to head gardener back in 1826, would probably have tried to fight his case for him but for the fact that he was himself forced by ill health into retirement in 1841.[12]

Although Woolley eventually got his cottage and some land in Rough Close which enabled him to continue work as a gardener, his pension seems to have been half forgotten, so that as late as February 1853 the Duke's secretary Jackson reported that he had called on the Woolleys to give them a payment of £5 pounds with a promise of the same on Lady Day, six months later – hardly a full pension for a man who had been head gardener. Jackson reported that Woolley was 'very changed in appearance ... he really cannot live very long unless he gets some speedy relief', which was unlikely since they were 'in very narrow circumstances'.[13] John Woolley's burial is recorded in January 1856 at Trentham.

Meanwhile, Fleming himself still had problems – the gardener's house at Trentham had been newly built under the Barry project and, unlike at Lilleshall, had no furniture to go with it (see Illus. 12). Fleming had no furniture of his own. Loch asked William Smith to take an inventory of the contents of the gardener's house at Lilleshall and then send it all to Trentham. Unfortunately, the new incoming head gardener at Lilleshall took this very hard as he had been promised a furnished house. In any case, the furniture was not suitable for Trentham since the head gardener's house was much larger and grander than at Lilleshall. In the end Fleming was told he had to find his own furniture.[14]

Fleming quickly found another problem. The Trentham gardens had four single apprentice gardeners who were living in very poor conditions in one of the garden sheds; Fleming was appalled at their accommodation. He insisted that an empty cottage which had been intended for another undergardener should be used for the apprentices. He also needed beds and a few pieces of furniture for them as the apprentices had been sleeping on the floor – apparently Woolley had loaned them beds in the shed and he had taken them away when he left.[15] Both house and furniture costs were approved by the Duke, but Fleming had to make all the arrangements himself including organising the apprentices' laundry.[16] Later the apprentices were accommodated in an elegant purpose-built bothy.

The status of head gardeners at Trentham was fairly low before the appointment of Fleming in 1841. Not only was John Woolley treated somewhat shabbily, but this was also true of Chapman, his predecessor, who was finished in 1826 and who retired seemingly into poverty. In addition the numbers of undergardeners increased greatly under Fleming. In the 1840s and '50s there were around fifty, approximately fifteen of whom were journeymen gardeners, four were apprentices, the remaining were labourers and boys.[17]

Pensions

We have already seen that there was sometimes an issue with pensions, though the possibility of being given one on retirement must have been a great incentive for servants to stay, for it was only long-serving employees who were so rewarded. This was entirely a matter of grace and favour; there was no entitlement. The amount was fixed the by the Duke or Duchess with guidance from the main agent.

In 1876, George Loch (James Loch's son who had succeeded his father as chief agent) felt guilty about not giving proper attention to the retiring housekeeper, Mrs Ingram:

> I have to reproach myself for having so long omitted to write to Your Grace about Mrs Ingram's pension, and I fear the good old lady may have been put to some inconvenience – when you spoke to me about it at Trentham, a week or two ago, you asked me to send you a memorandum of pensions that had been granted to serve as some guide in the present case.[18]

He then went on to list pensions which had been awarded previously, amongst them:

Wm Bursby (dowager duchess's steward)	£400
Mrs Lilly (widow of previous house steward)	£120
Elizabeth Wright (duchess's chambermaid)	£65
Dr Broomhall (Trentham's doctor)	£200
Mr Fleming (Trentham's head gardener)	£200
John Wright (groom of the chamber and valet)	£50
Robert Chandler (first footman)	£110
B. Bantock (gamekeeper at Dunrobin)	£65

In the event Mrs Ingram was given a pension of £50 p.a., plus a rent-free cottage at Hanchurch.

At the other end of the servant hierarchy, an elderly laundry maid at Trentham earned herself a pension of 6s a week and a place on the waiting list for the Sutherlands' almshouses in Newcastle.[19] Mrs Galleazie, the housekeeper at Stafford House, raised the matter of another laundry maid who was 'in a very bad state of health, an outdoor patient at Charing Cross Hospital'. She was one of those servants who after seven years' service with the Marquess continued to serve his widow for a further four years. She had eventually retired and the Duchess Countess had given her a box mangle, which enabled her to continue to earn a living as an independent laundress. (This was a very common form of 'pension' for country-house laundresses.) This proved to be of little profit to her, however, as her long years of hard laundry work now made it impossible to stand and she was no needlewoman, a skill to which elderly laundresses often resorted. She was in great anxiety for her future; it seems likely that Loch arranged for some small sum to be paid her.[20]

In February of 1853 the Duchess concerned herself at some length with two problems of servants in retirement.[21] The house steward Walker was elderly and in failing health, wishing to retire, but somewhat embarrassed to announce his engagement to the widowed housekeeper Mrs Marsh. The Duchess, however, was already aware of his 'attachment' and speculated to Loch on the nature of the pension which should be given:

> In what shape do you think the mark of regard to Walker should be? As a present of plate or money? Or as a pension? I consider it strictly as a mark of regard during well performed 13 yrs of service. I believe them both to be amply provided for, Walker having had beyond the usual rate of wages – £200 a year – and a well-off friend left him money. Mrs Marsh is said to be also well off from her late husband.

Loch's reply was to the point as usual:

> £40 with a piece of plate would be a fit allowance, or £50 without any present. An inkstand might be a good present, it would be always seen and a teapot or any article of this sort requires some accompaniment ... I don't think Mrs Walker's means should be taken into consideration in estimating what he should have.

In the same letters early in 1853 the Duchess worried about another long-serving employee, John Wright, who was brother of the Trentham brewer and baker Robert Wright. John Wright illustrates the classic promotional route of the male personal servant. Various wages and logbooks tell us that he had worked at Trentham as a young boy, probably helping in the servants' hall. At the age of sixteen he had been appointed as the steward's room boy, keeping the steward's room clean and serving the senior servants' meals. In 1821 he became a footman to the Marquess's family and in 1833 joined the 2nd Duke's household in Stafford House as groom of the chambers (in effect the senior footman and assistant to the house steward). Six years later he became valet to the 2nd Duke. Duchess Anne treated him very kindly on one occasion when he was ill:

> Mr Wright is still very suffering at times and we wish him to have more cheerful rooms till he is better. He may sit in the little dining room for the present and the Duke wishes it prepared for him this morning by the time he is up. Would you hand his writing table, chair etc round to it ... He is to move into Francis' room which he may keep this winter in his absence.[22]

He had, however, a personal problem which he must have managed to keep in check most of the time, but which became the cause of his retirement. Again the Duchess wrote to Loch:

> Wright was found in an insensible state yesterday morning ... a continuation of his old failing. I believe it would be right and best for him that the Duke should pension him – and that his brother the Baker should take care of him – and prevent the acquisition of spirits ... I think it might be better before the change [i.e. a new steward was shortly to be appointed] – as it would be hard for him to be found fault with by a stranger. How much should the Duke allow him? It should be enough and not too much with this foul failing – he was with the Duke before I married.

Again Loch was clear: the pension should be assessed according to the salary not current failings and so should be £40 p.a. (In fact he was given £50.) John Wright died five years later, aged fifty-eight.

On the whole Trentham took care of its long-standing servants, but this was never assured or to be taken for granted. Although Loch tried to standardise the level of pension, it does seem that the more personal servants, valets and lady's maids did better than others and that long service and individual behaviour counted. Personal maids to the duchesses fared better than most other women servants. The £65 p.a. pension of Elizabeth Wright listed above was partly made up by an annuity left on the Duchess's death which brought her £24 a year. Many others received a one-off bequest from their master or mistress.[23]

Some people seem to have been treated unfairly, as shown by the treatment of Woolley. Perhaps he was not a very capable or honest head gardener – we cannot truly speculate. The family did keep him for many years, yet it seems they did the absolute minimum for him on retirement. This contrasts with the Duchess's attitude towards an elderly garden labourer, Fernyhough. In 1833 when the Duke instructed Lewis to finish four of the staff in the gardens as part of a cost-cutting exercise during the rebuilding of the house, the Duchess gave a counter instruction that on no account should Fernyhough be 'put away' – 'poor old Fernyhough must be taken care of' – even if he could do no useful work. Like Mrs Tungate he was highly favoured. Of the four other gardeners finished at the same time, two were 'nearly worn out and not capable of full work'; both had worked at Trentham for thirty or so years and so were given a 'superannuation'. The other two had both got new jobs. Ironically the cutbacks in the garden staff did not achieve much financial saving. As part of the exercise most of the flower gardens and other grounds were put down to grass, but within two years several new men and boys were needed to mow them 'to keep them looking respectable'.[24]

Medical care

One of the most valuable advantages of working for a family such as the Sutherlands was the payment of medical expenses – attendance by a doctor and the cost of medicines as well as access to hospital treatment (see Illus. 19). The estate used regular local doctors for their employees. One, Dr Broomhall, became a tenant of the estate in Tittensor and earned himself a generous pension.

It was an area of expenditure, however, which came under Loch's scrutiny, a fact which had not escaped the attention of the head clerk at Trentham, Randal William Kirkby, when he sent in some doctors' bills for approval by Loch in 1832. Kirkby himself had gone through the costs, which appeared large but were, he thought, legitimate.[25] He had discussed the matter with Dr White, the doctor used by the estate at Trentham, and reported to Loch: 'You must be well aware of the delicate situation in which a medical Gentleman is placed when attending the domestics of a Nobleman like the Marquess' establishment – the fear of giving offence in either quarter when a servant is ill.' Dr White, said Kirkby, had been made anxious by Loch's interest and had suggested that some formal guidance be given to him. It was probably a difficult area fraught with problems, for no further comment from Loch seems to have been forthcoming.

There were always lines to be drawn and issues to resolve about the extent of payments for medical assistance, however. The main problem was whether servants' families were entitled. In principle the answer was that they were not, but the issue was not always so clear-cut. A letter from Mrs Kirke, the housekeeper at Lilleshall, explained the problem.[26] Was the porter's wife entitled to have her medical expenses paid by the estate? Mrs Kirke had been told that at Trentham the porter's wife was not entitled, but at Lilleshall the previous porter's wife had been. The new porter was set on by the steward, Vantini, on exactly the same conditions of service as the previous one, so what should she tell them? She was wary of setting a precedent as there were so many married servants. The point was that the old porter's wife had also worked for the estate as a casual day-worker, cleaning the men's accommodation over the stables, and this brought her the entitlement. What would be the position for a servant's wife who lived in a lodge and controlled the gates when her husband was out at work? Again the answer from Loch has not survived.

Another problem was how long the medical expenses of retired employees were to be paid. There seems to have been no set rule for this, and certainly the doctors themselves were uncertain, as shown by an enquiry from Messrs Dudley and Tate asking whether they were to continue sending to Loch their account regarding Mrs Marsh, the retired housekeeper from Trentham now living in Newcastle.[27]

As well as paying doctors' or apothecaries' bills the Sutherlands were subscribers to two local hospitals, which entitled them to make nominations for both out and in patients – £20 a year to the North Staffordshire Infirmary gave them entitlement to name ten inpatients and two long-term outpatients a year; £23 3s to

Stafford Hospital earned an entitlement of 22 inpatients and 44 outpatients.[28] This must have been seen as a great benefit for those connected to the estate, covering as it did both staff and tenants. Strangely enough the record shows it was little used. In 1836, for example, only nine people were nominated.

Various people's state of health was a constant subject of report and concern in all the staff letters, possibly because this impinged on the workload of others but also because of a general fear of infectious disease. In August 1838, for example, before the family set out for Trentham, one of the clerks pointedly reassured Vantini that there were no infections amongst the people there.[29] Perhaps here the unspoken word at that time was cholera.

Funeral expenses

It seems to have been only in exceptional cases that a long-serving employee's funeral costs were paid by the estate. This was usually a matter of the death occurring whilst the person was actually at work on the estate, as would have been the case with two of the young Penson men who had fatal accidents at work. This was not really the case with Richard Wright, the baker at Stafford House, London, who was thrown from his horse whilst on holiday visiting his wife's family near Rugeley in Staffordshire. It was the Duchess's personal wish that his funeral expenses be paid by his Grace. William Lewis, however, took care to pay the bills as a one-off occurrence out of his agent's account, since if it went out of the house steward's accounts it might set a precedent for the future.[30]

When any member of the family died, naturally the cost of putting the household into mourning was borne by the family. For little Lady Blanche's funeral in February 1832, for example, black scarves, hoods and gloves were bought for all the women, and hatbands and gloves for the men. As a footman at West Hill noted in his diary: 'Mrs Galleazzie gave me 4 pairs of black worsted stockings & 2 pair of black silk & 2 pair of black gloves.'[31]

Servants' clothes

One of the advantages of service for menservants, though not usually for women, was the supply of work clothing. The men who wore livery – footmen, porters, and gamekeepers for example – had their work uniforms found for them. The cost of livery itself varied with the status of the job concerned. The price of a set of footman's state livery could be astronomical, whilst the cost of a gamekeeper's everyday working suit was obviously less, though even this mounted up – green jacket, waistcoat and coat, boots, leather breeches, gaiters and a morning suit for best.[32]

The point about livery, however, was that it did not belong to the individual. When they left or retired it was handed back. When a new footman was appointed, he would be allocated an already-used set of clothes for a few months until he had proved himself worthy of permanent employment, at which point the house steward would arrange for him to be measured by the livery tailor for his own set, usually two suits a year.

Women servants had no such luck and usually had to supply all their own clothing except for aprons.

Allowances

There was a complex system of allowances or 'perquisites' of various sorts, especially for those who lived in their own households in cottages. Whenever a senior post became vacant during the 1830s Loch questioned both salary and perquisites. The answer to one such enquiry provides a useful picture of the true extent of servants' rewards at Trentham:

Mr Elliot, the gamekeeper, annual wages and allowances, July 1836:

Salary	£42 p.a.
Board wages at 11/6d per week	
Annual total	£71 8s p.a.

Allowances p.a.:	
Horses and saddler	£30
Ale and beer	£5 5s
Spirits	£2
Coals	£5 10s
Milk	3
Candles and soap	5
Potatoes, etc.	2 5s
House and garden rent-free	£6
Total allowances	£59

Plus two complete sets of clothing.[33]

If Loch was intent on keeping a check on these expenses, he was not successful, for by 1841 they had certainly not lessened. Elliot had retired and the new gamekeeper, James Pearson, was paid an increased salary of £72 a year plus almost £30 board wages, bringing the total up to £102 18s. He was also allowed two quarts of new milk a day, free coal, candles, soap, mops, brushes, plus two bushels of potatoes a month, the keep of a horse and ale and beer.[34] Even if a member of staff had no formal allowance of vegetables and potatoes, they were given deliveries from the garden and farm whenever they wanted; in the early 1830s there were twenty-two such people, from Lewis himself and his chief clerk to the kitchen and housemaids.[35]

One of the payments which Loch tried unsuccessfully to eliminate immediately after the 1st Duke's death was the standard travel allowances for coachmen, grooms and footmen. This was a traditional payment of 1/6d per head per journey to cover their expenses en route – typically food and accommodation. It was paid for every journey, long or short, the short compensating for the long.[36] Yet Loch must have eventually succeeded in getting rid of this allowance, probably as each member of staff changed, for in 1841 Walker, the new steward, reported that the Duke's footman had resigned because his wages were too small and he had not been given any journey money. Walker thought this ridiculous – they should never have been given anything except perhaps on the rare occasions when they had to wait for their passengers in inns.[37]

Another allowance which was not usually given by the Sutherlands was washing allowance, a cash sum to cover the cost of the servant's personal laundry in those households which sent their laundry out. The arrangement adopted at both Stafford House and Trentham seems to have been the usual one in larger households, that servants were responsible for their own washing but could use the house laundry facilities at specified times when it was not busy. The only regular exception to this refusal to pay washing money was to her Grace's chamber maid, who sometimes laundered delicate items for the Duchess herself and therefore received small sums of cash, presumably to pay for soap and starch.[38]

Opportunities for earning extra cash

It was generally accepted that some servants had opportunities for earning payments over and above their wages. A private unpublished diary kept by a footman in service with the Sutherlands in London, James Lewis, explained how some evenings his Grace would go out to attend a public banquet, taking with him one or more of his own footmen to help serve the meal. One such occasion in 1838 was a dinner at the Guildhall held in honour of a number of foreign ambassadors. The Sutherlands' coachman and two footmen set down the Duke and his brother Lord Francis Egerton in good time at the ceremonial entrance to the Guildhall, but the carriage then had to queue round the back for an hour in order to get the footmen themselves into the hall. When James eventually arrived at the dining room he found his Grace had already finished the fish and was eating some beef. For this he was paid 4*s*.[39]

Trentham's head gardener too had opportunities for legitimately earning a bit extra. It was usual practice for a head gardener to charge the young gardeners an apprenticeship fee which went to him personally. The fees amounted to an extra £20 a year. At first the head gardener Fleming decided he did not want to do this, but later changed his mind after the negotiations for his salary. His predecessor had been paid £100 a year wages and the Duke had offered Fleming £115; Fleming felt that he could not accept the increase as the estate already paid an allowance to his elderly mother who had worked for the estate up in Scotland. (Fleming's sister Margaret was also a scullery maid at Stafford House.)[40] He finally agreed to accept the extra in return for taking on the apprenticeship training, the fees to go to the estate not himself.[41]

Another form of perquisites which were no doubt commonly received but rarely admitted to were 'vials' – tips given to servants by visitors. With a family like the Sutherlands these must have accumulated very nicely. The footman James's diary, referred to above, records the occasion at Trentham when he was asked to valet Charles Barry who was visiting in September 1838:

Charles says to me you must valet him I says not I, I have got sufficient to do already. O but you must says he, presently I meet Mr Vantini [the house steward] O you must attend upon Mr Barry very well sir because Charles has got Mr Gilpin says he. I got to bed about 11 … Got up this morning ½ past 6 … set about my work & got it done by 12 I then cleaned myself and then had orders to prepare Mr Barry's things … directly I went into his room and found his things all ready to come down I brought them down and then the chaise was at the door I carried his bags etc & put them in & when he was got in he put 5/- into my hand.[42]

One perquisite common elsewhere but which was absolutely forbidden in the Sutherland household was the giving of tips or 'percentages' by tradesmen to servants such as housekeepers, house stewards and footmen who were in a position to select suppliers of goods. This was specifically prohibited by the Duke in 1840 when a new house steward was appointed.[43]

There was a background story to this which explains the Duke's attitude. In March 1835 his agent Loch had received a letter from a Mr J. W. Farrer complaining about the behaviour of the Duke's servants in London. Farrer had been a grocer in Jermyn Street who relied heavily on a small number of local aristocratic households for his trade. The Sutherland servants had badgered him for presents, in effect bribes for giving him the Duke's trade, to such an extent that he could no longer continue the practice, and he had told them so. At this they threatened to take the Duke's custom away from him. He persisted, they carried out their threat, and the man's trade was ruined. He had written several letters to the Duke but they had been intercepted by the servants involved and never reached him, which was why he decided to write to Loch instead.[44]

Loch investigated, thinking that one of the servants in question might have been the house steward, Vantini. He wrote round to a number of regular suppliers in London but found his suspicions totally unjustified, as a letter from the brewer they used in London made clear: Mr Mantell, of Castle Brewhouse, Bloomsbury, had never given any percentage payments to his Grace's servants, indeed had never been asked by any of them including Vantini. Yet the suspicion may have persisted.[45]

Opportunities for travel

One of the attractions of service in a great household was the opportunity for travel, especially long distance. The footman James Lewis was bitterly disappointed when he was not chosen to go with the Duke and Duchess and their older children on their tour of the Continent in 1838. It made such an impression on him that he decided to pay for lessons to learn French, so that never again would they leave him behind at West Hill, helping to look after the younger children. He was given some consolation when he was ordered to accompany his Grace on a nine-day trip north to Glasgow to attend a meeting of a cattle show.[46]

A more frequent journey for the Sutherland travelling servants was to and from Dunrobin, undertaken several times a year. Today, according to the AA, the journey from Dunrobin to London by modern roads would cover over 600 miles and take just over eleven hours non-stop. Using only horse-drawn carriages and the posting system, the journey in the 1820s took an exhausting eight, nine or even ten days.[47] Four years later in 1838 a new day was dawning, however, as the railways connected London to Birmingham (in June 1838) and on up to Lancashire. This shortened the southern end of the journey considerably. By the following year, 1839, the railway had reached Preston, but even so it was still a long, hard and expensive journey, which is worth following in some detail.

For the journey south from Dunrobin in February 1839, the Duke and Duchess had two companions inside the heavy long-distance travelling carriage, probably a valet and lady's maid; outside were a footman, groom/postilion and coachman. They used hired post horses which were changed at prearranged stages – posting inns en route – all of which had to be pre-booked by letter. In addition to the hire of the horses, therefore, payment had to be made for post boys, whose job was to return each string of tired horses back to their home inn, and for accommodation at the overnight inn and for the tips to waiter, chamber maid and bootboy. According to the coachman's posting book, each day's travel covered several stages: the shortest but most difficult day was the second day, covering four stages between Aviemore and Dalnacarroch over the dreadful Drummochter Pass, which was deep in snow and which meant the cost of extra horses and an extra postilion, as well the purchase of a fair amount of whisky for the additional helpers. The next day was easier and saw them safely over the ferry to Edinburgh, where they paid for extra fires and candles in their lodgings and where the carriage had to be washed and greased. Then followed a long day over the Southern Uplands to an inn just north of Shap, which needed ten changes of horses. The next day began with the climb over Shap Fell itself, difficult enough to warrant the laconic coachman's comment of 'bad', but this day saw them into Preston. Here they no doubt thankfully loaded themselves and their carriage onto the railroad to Newton-le-Willows. The next day they boarded the train to Birmingham and straight on to London. The coachman's record shows a total expense of £108 4s 6d for travel, accommodation and food.

Despite the railways, this must have been a stressful journey. Apart from the long, dark February days, the snow and the biting winds, heavy travelling coaches were well-sprung and therefore many people suffered from travel-sickness in them. For the coachman and servants it must have been a nightmare, but one which tested their skill and perhaps gave an exciting change from negotiating the crowded streets of London or the twisting lanes of Staffordshire.

It is not surprising to find that in July 1840 James Loch arranged a different solution to the problem of getting to and from Dunrobin. He accepted a quote for conveyance by the North Star Steamer for the whole of the household (eight family and eleven servants), plus luggage and horses, between London and Littleferry – a village at the mouth of Loch Fleet a few miles south of Golspie. The total sum was £220. Since the coachman did not need to keep his posting book there is no record of how this journey went.[48]

In the 1850s the family could have taken the railway for a much longer part of the journey, as far as Inverness, but even so in June 1850 Lord and Lady Stafford took seven days to travel between Lilleshall and Tarbet. The journey to Dunrobin was considerably easier after 1870, however. The Sutherland Railway was extended to Golspie in 1868, after which the Duke, no doubt partly thinking of the numerous guests to be invited to his castle, paid for a further extension to Brora and on to Helmsdale, with a station at Dunrobin.

For normal day-to-day travel, the agents and some of the other senior staff had horses bought for them, while the other servants used one of the household horses when needed. This must have been a useful additional facility, the equivalent of the use of a company car, and the purchase and care of horses figured fairly frequently in the correspondence between agents.

Accidents either with riding horses or horses harnessed in gigs seem to have been fairly common. Lewis suffered several times and there were two fatal falls from horseback by menservants. Loch himself once broke his shoulder. Advice about the quality of horses, especially riding horses for Lewis and Loch, and the relative merits of grooms and which of them should be promoted to coachman were all subjects of discussion and sometimes disagreement.

For this reason, in the 1840s the 2nd Duke contracted out the supervision of his horses and stables in London to a true professional, George Lewis (no relation to William Lewis), who inspected all the family's carriage and riding horses, advised on sales, purchases, training and veterinary care. Unfortunately, he was head-hunted to a more prestigious establishment around the corner from Stafford House, nowhere less than the Royal Mews, though for a while he did carry on his service with the Sutherlands on a private contract basis, later recommending his brother for the position.

3

Food and Drink

Where and when did servants eat?

In a status-based community, where people eat their meals is a telling point. When Loch was reviewing the household expenditure in 1840 he wanted to reduce the number of tables at which servants ate their meals, on the premise that this might save time and serving staff. Why, he asked the new house steward, Richard Walker, could not the kitchen maids eat their meals with the other servants in the servants' hall rather than in the kitchen?

Walker's answer explains the complex lunchtime arrangements when the family and travelling servants were present at Trentham.[1] The complexity was made worse by the fact that some people, namely the servants and children, ate their dinners at lunchtime, whereas the main family dined in the evening:

At one o'clock the stewards' room (senior staff such as house steward, housekeeper, butler, and lady's maids) and the nursery room dinners were served. The remains were taken back to the kitchen at half past one.

At half past one dinner was taken to servants' hall for the main body of servants (including living-in outdoor servants such as grooms) and also up to Lord Frederick (aged eight) and the governess.

At two o'clock the luncheons (as large as a dinner) were taken up to the family.

Therefore, between one and two o'clock was the busiest time for the kitchen maids – 'all hands are needed' to give 'the most strict attention' to loading meals onto the hotplate and clearing them on return.

At a quarter past two the kitchen maids sat down in the kitchen to 'something left from the dinners' and the still-room maid was served separately in her room with 'a plate of meat' – she was equally busy beforehand supplying bread, butter and tea.

This routine gave five different tables to be served, plus two workplace servings. As Walker explained, he had gone through all this in detail with the head kitchen maid and he could not suggest improvements to the system that had developed over time. In 1840, of course, the kitchens, sculleries and still room, along with many of the domestic offices, were brand new.

When the family and travelling servants were absent the situation was very different, for then the beer records show that servants seemed to have taken their meals in gender-divided groups. Those indoor manservants who remained at Trentham continued to eat in the servants' hall, whilst the women split up – the seniors went to the housekeeper's room and the others ate in their workplace – in the laundry or housemaids' workroom. This was because servants were entitled to board wages with which to buy food, and so working teams made their own arrangements to suit their timetable.

Outdoor and clerical staff that lived locally ate all their meals at home. In the 1840s Trentham was still filled with craftsmen and tradesmen working on Barry's alterations, and these ate and drank in two clearly different groups – the few on long-term contracts tended to eat in the servants' hall when the family were present but separately when they were absent. Shorter-term tradesmen ate separately all the time, as did the low-status day labourers in the house, people such as washerwomen and chars. Here we begin to get a glimpse of how complicated were the overlapping systems of status and community.

Measuring the meat
Unfortunately, menu and recipe books used in country houses were usually the personal possessions of the individual cook, so

have rarely survived in archives. We have to look at other types of records to assess what we can about the food provided. Both the 2nd Duke and Duchess were aware of the extravagance of the Sutherland households, especially when 'at housekeeping', that is when the family and travelling servants were present. The Duchess instructed Loch to take steps to try to curb the spending. The usual way of doing this was to keep a record of the amount of meat consumed by the household, and in 1841 she asked Loch for regular reports from Richard Walker.

According to Walker's report for Lilleshall for the four weeks ending 4 December 1841, the total number of main meals provided was just over 2,000, providing an average per head consumption each day of 3 lbs (with a total value for the month of £173 16s 3d.) Half of the meat came from their own estate at Lilleshall, the other half from Trentham. The per capita rate in reality was slightly less than on paper because of the practice of using the breast and scrag ends of the racks of mutton for broth for the poor.[2]

Walker thought this 'economical', and indeed the record for 1839 shows the meat consumption was even higher at 3¾ lbs each per day at an average weekly cost of £60 (the cost per lb was 6d).[3] Enquiries made to various chefs by Loch in 1840 endorsed Walker's opinion. A letter from the Duke of Northumberland's cook agreed that '3lbs of meat per person is scarcely sufficient for a house like Trentham', bearing in mind the need to make broth for the poor and that the elaborate soups, sauces and jellies made for the family table took up a very large proportion of the meat.[4] Advice from a man who had been the Duke of Newcastle's chef also said that 3 lbs per head was not extravagant, whilst Mr Ude, the famous chef at Crockford's, said a country establishment could not be run on less, though a town house would be more economical as there were fewer meals given to messengers, strangers and poor people.[5] The meat consumption at Castle Howard, the Duchess's family home, appeared at first glance to be slightly more abstemious, but the figure of 2 lbs excluded venison, game and poultry.[6]

In 1843, however, the Duchess was still not happy and expressed herself to Loch as being a 'little disappointed to find that we are living more expensively than other houses'. Looking for a new chef after they had reluctantly sacked the previous one for immoral behaviour with a kitchen maid, she had taken the opportunity presented by interviews of candidates to ask them about per capita meat allowances.[7] The Duke of Bedford's chef 'would not do' for the Sutherlands for some reason but had told her that he had allowed 1 lb 13 oz of meat per head per day at Woburn, but that this was thought too extravagant. Sounding somewhat mortified she wrote, 'I find that ours is 2¾ in the country and in London 2½.'

She had asked Walker about this, to which he replied that the reason their 'consumption is greater is that there are so many dinners which cannot be brought into use as the servants will not always eat hash – such pieces are used for the poor's soup'. In other words, the Sutherlands' servants were not content to be fed on the cheapest cuts of meat and were not afraid to say so. Walker tried to justify the amounts but the Duchess was disappointed, for she had thought that the new steward was more careful in his expenditure than his predecessor and she had persuaded herself that 'we were living more economically than other houses'. Things would have to change with a new cook.

She again asked Loch to find out what the real meat allowance was in her father's house at Castle Howard. Eventually this was established as being 1lb 9 oz per head, which for 12,730 people fed during nine months of housekeeping came to 19,883 lbs of meat.[8] Well into 1844 Loch was still sending slightly embarrassed questions to other households. By May 1844 Walker was able to report to Loch that the amount of meat allowed per head at Trentham over the last two weeks had been reduced to 1 lb 9½ oz and that he would continue to send notes about this to Loch on a weekly basis.[9]

The problem with all this careful recording was that the figures were based on the carcase weight of the meat brought into the house. In a room near the stable yard lodge at Trentham there was a balance weighing machine for checking all the goods brought in. Despite this, there was no accurate way of telling how much meat actually found its way to the various tables and how this was divided between people of differing status. Perhaps a more meaningful way of recording expenditure was by cost. There survives a record from 1873 giving target figures for the per capita cost of daily meals according to the place of eating.[10]

More than any other record this illustrates the hierarchy within the household:

Per head daily cost of meals

Parlour	16s
Secretary	8s
Governess	8s
Nursery	4s
Steward's room	2s
Servants' hall	1s 6d males, 1s 4¼d females
Kitchen	1s 6d males, 1s 4¼d females
Dogs	3d

Inevitably some food would go astray, and there are several records of incidents when this was discovered. Zenon Vantini, the house steward before Richard Walker, kept a logbook of the servants' details, which records the sacking of chef Hipolith Belangen in 1834 because he had regularly sent dinners from the hall at Trentham to his wife who lived in the village.[11] Another unfortunate incidence was the affair of Phillips' wife, as reported to Loch by the Duke's secretary.[12]

Thomas Phillips had been a farm labourer on the estate who also did odd jobs around the hall. Lewis however had never trusted him and was glad when Walker sacked him in May 1841.[13] He was still paid a few shillings, though, to make soup for the poor, in a small building near the gas house. The poorer cuts of meat and trimmings were taken there by the kitchen man. One night in October 1841 a policeman who had been secretly tipped off was waiting under the trees opposite. He saw Phillips' wife come out of the soup building carrying a large basket. He stopped her and found some pieces of meat, 'of no great value', wrapped in a cloth. She said she had bought the meat in Newcastle. He let her go but appeared at the hall the next morning. The Duke said he should speak to his house steward rather than himself, but unfortunately the steward was out for the day; he asked him to return later.

At noon the same day a senior policeman presented himself first to the Duke's secretary, then to the Duke. He was extremely angry, saying the woman should have been arrested last night and 'would hear of nothing short of taking her before a magistrate'. This was his duty, he said, as the matter had been reported in the officer's notebook. The police, not the Duke, prosecuted the case, and witnesses were found – the Newcastle butcher denied all knowledge of Mrs Phillips and the kitchenman recognised one of the pieces of meat. Mrs Phillips was committed to be tried at the Quarter Sessions in Stafford despite the Duke's remonstrations, both verbal and in writing, to the effect that the whole thing should not have gone to trial, as it was far too rigorous a measure. Evidence was found that this was not Mrs Phillips' first offence.

The figures for meat consumption did not include the gardeners or outdoor labourers who ate in the gardeners' bothy or at home. All the outdoor men were, however, given a special Christmas allowance of beef, along with the poor of the parish. In 1844, the distribution of this sounds slightly chaotic. Two men had the job of distributing tickets for 'various portions' to the parishioners. Everyone – including the estate labourers and those working under the land agent – collected in the parish church for the distribution of the meat; by 10 a.m. the church was completely full. The clergy then distributed the allowances. Loch thought this was unseemly – the distribution should be done by the land steward in his office.[14]

There was another rather unusual allowance which, according to Loch, was a 'mistaken custom' that had crept into the system, and which he asked Walker accordingly to put an end to. This was the tradition that 'fresh meat has been given to sick persons on the simple certificate of the medical gentlemen ... and amounting in the whole to a very large quantity'. Somehow Walker was to find a way of telling the doctors they were to cease this practice without upsetting them. Only exceptional cases were to be approved for such relief and then only with the consent of the Duchess.[15]

Self-sufficiency

Self-sufficiency of food supply was a fundamental philosophical ideal of the country house, an ideal which goes back to the writings of Socrates, Plato and Aristotle, through to the desire of Christian monasticism to embrace withdrawal from the world, and thence to the country houses after the Dissolution. By the sixteenth and seventeenth centuries writers such as Sir John Oglander and Daniel Defoe described the virtues of the self-sufficient household.[16] The desire to achieve these virtues was responsible for many of the subsidiary buildings we see around our country house estates – the deer parks, fish and duck ponds, dovecotes, rabbit warrens, poultry yards, corn mills, dairies, ice houses and brewhouses.

The theoretical advantages of self-sufficient food supply were numerous. It gave the household security over the supply and delivery of food as well as its quality; it enabled the selection of favourite varieties; it gave the country house family both status and pleasure. It also presented certain problems: issues of storage and preservation; the agricultural challenges of inconvenient seasonality; and for large-scale enterprises, such as Trentham or Lilleshall, it created the need for a bureaucracy to control a large labour force with all its issues of wages, accomodation and transport. It was also something of a myth. There were many foodstuffs which Trentham, Lilleshall or Stafford House could not supply themselves, including such items as tea, coffee, cocoa, rice, sago, currants, vermicelli, macaroni, treacle, oils, exotic nuts and a multitude of spices, to say nothing of the sea fish, shellfish and extra beef, veal, ox tail and calves' feet which appear in bills and receipts from grocers, butchers, and fishmongers.[17]

One of the functions of a house in the country was to supply meat, fruit and vegetables for the family throughout the year in whichever of their houses they were staying; thus Trentham and Lilleshall were expected to send regular consignments of garden produce to Stafford House, which had no garden to speak of. Each week large baskets of carefully packed fruit, vegetables and even flowers were sent by road carriers and later the railway, and any servant sent to London might be burdened with baskets of produce. In addition, all the Lilleshall and Trentham servants, whether they lived in hall or cottage, were given vegetables, including potatoes, all the year round – in effect whatever was not eaten by the family.[18]

Therefore, the house steward's accounts show a clear difference in the degree of self-provisioning between town and country. Vantini's accounts during the 1830s show that whilst staying at Trentham or Lilleshall the family did indeed live off their own farm produce, even when entertaining lavishly. This is shown clearly in the record for the first week of January 1834 when Trentham worked its way through 500 lbs of beef, 40 lbs of mutton, 150 lbs of veal, 40 lbs of pork and 25 head of game, plus almost £40 worth of vegetables, fruit, ale and beer, butter, cheese and eggs.[19] The total value placed on this was almost £60, all from the estate, none of it bought in.

Each productive enterprise kept its own accounts in terms of both quantity and value (in modern terms it was its own cost centre). The estate farm and its yards near the house played an important part in the enterprise, as well as the kitchen gardens (see Illus. 15).

In contrast, the same record shows that Stafford House lived almost entirely off bought produce, except for fruit and vegetables which came from Trentham. For the rest, the household kept accounts with a butcher, baker, brewer, confectioner, oilman, poulterer, butterman, milkman, green grocer and fishmonger, all of whom were paid weekly. Monthly accounts were kept with more specialist provisioners such as the grocer, tea dealer, brewer, plus a host of general household service suppliers – a picture cleaner, coach maker, blind maker, carpet man, wig and dress maker, china shop, rat catcher. In addition, there were the regular half-yearly bills paid for essentials: the stationery man, coal merchant, wine merchant, wax chandler, tallow chandler (for servant candles), ironmonger, and apothecaries.[20]

The kitchen gardens

The aim of self-sufficiency was at the heart of the kitchen gardens. Stafford House had no kitchen garden, but the Sutherlands' other London house in the 1830s, West Hill, had both farm and gardens. The Duke, possibly influenced by Vantini, the house steward, who was an enthusiastic self-provisioner, determined to try an experiment in forcing fruit, especially grapes, in the kitchen garden at West Hill. This was unsuccessful but the Duke was reluctant to give up entirely. He had Loch write to Woolley, the Trentham gardener, to ask for a report on the times when he could supply grapes, pineapples, peaches and nectarines, and on how this would affect his supply of autumn and winter vegetables and fruit. This was so that his gardener at West Hill could plan to make up any deficiency – a more modest aim rather than supplying the whole requirement at Stafford House.[21]

The kitchen garden at Trentham seemed fairly successful in its supplies. In the annual statement for 1838, for example, the clerk Henney reported that fruit worth over £662 and vegetables worth over £127 had been delivered to Stafford House during the year.[22] There was also a long tradition of Trentham supplying garden produce to Lilleshall, according to Lady Granville who stayed at Lilleshall in 1817, who was fed on vegetables and fruit from the Trentham hot-houses.[23]

The Trentham poultry yard was also reasonably productive at this time. The agent Lewis, however, was never an enthusiast of either the poultry yard or the kitchen garden, complaining many times of the cost of growing exotic fruit like pineapples, the fashion for which he clearly thought idiotic: 'If this Department of the Garden Establishment was done away with the expense would be much reduced ...'[24]

Lewis was also in a dilemma over the production of mutton and beef at Trentham, for there was always a competition between self-sufficiency and earning income. As he explained, now that the Barry alterations were nearing completion family and guests would be staying at Trentham more than in the past, the farm would struggle to supply them. It therefore needed more land, but Lewis was reluctant to increase the farm's acreage, indeed he thought more land should be put out to let to earn more income.[25]

At Lilleshall there was a more pressing problem. While the home farm and the poultry yard were reasonably successful, (the latter provided well over 300 chickens over a six-month period, plus smaller numbers of turkeys, ducks, pigeons and a large number of eggs), the kitchen garden was definitely not up to standard.[26] Early in 1837, the Duke and Duchess had gone to Ireland while the rest of the family stayed at Lilleshall for several weeks. During that time supplies of fruit and vegetables had to be sent over from Trentham two or three times a week, as the Lilleshall head gardener Beckie had nothing to offer. Later he started to supply vegetables and potatoes supposedly from the kitchen garden but it turned out he had bought almost all of them out of his own pocket, not apparently for the first time. Moreover, he had no accounts to show for several years because in 1836 Loch had changed the accounting system and Beckie had burnt all his records.[27]

In September of 1838 when the Duke and Duchess left Trentham to go to Lilleshall, as they took their leave of Lewis in the hall they raised the issue of Beckie, whom the Duke was thinking of transferring from the garden to the woodlands. Lewis's opinion of the gardener was not high, as shown later that evening when he wrote to Loch: 'Put him where you will he will be a pest in any establishment ... I have not seen the place lately, but I believe it is in its usual state of dirt and weeds and without a vegetable.'[28]

This was not new on Lewis's behalf. As early as 1832, Lewis was scathing about Beckie, who had put in a claim for increased allowances including candles, soap, bedding and linen. Lewis thought this outrageous but did admit that Lady Gower had more than once said his wages were not high, 'but in my opinion a great deal more than he is worth'.[29]

In 1839 Beckie was given notice to leave. As applicants for his job were sending in their letters, Loch again took the opportunity of writing to other houses – including Alton Towers – this time to ask for comparable figures of costs of running a kitchen garden.[30] By January of that year, Lewis had told Beckie he was being replaced by George Fleming.

As we have seen, Fleming was a Scotsman recruited from Sutherland, in fact the son of a gardener at Dunrobin. As a young man he had worked for a short time at the gardens at Trentham, and then gone to train at a London nursery, before going to work for a Mr Rankin at Dulwich, who gave him an excellent reference.[31] Once in post at Lilleshall, Fleming very quickly reported his detailed findings to Loch: he would have to start completely afresh, nothing could be worse than the state of the kitchen garden at Lilleshall, as left by Beckie.[32]

Fleming was so successful at Lilleshall that within three years he had been promoted to replace John Woolley at Trentham. By March 1841 Loch and Lewis were discussing delaying the gravelling of the new garden paths at Trentham until Fleming had arrived.[33] He started work at Trentham during September and by mid-October had submitted a report on the repairs and alterations needed in the gardens.[34] As at Lilleshall, it seems the kitchen gardens at Trentham had been rundown during the period of the rebuilding of the 1830s; certainly much of the flower garden had been grassed over and the number of staff cut. It is clear that a brand new start on the gardens was made in 1841 with the appointment of Fleming, who indeed went on to make Trentham a garden famous for innovation.[35]

As far as the food supply was concerned, Fleming wanted to replace the existing hot flues running through the heated walls of the kitchen garden with the more up-to-date system of hot water pipes to his own design, which would be more efficient in ripening fruit and save money in the long run. The garden also needed substantial repairs to the vinery and two completely new peaches houses. All the framing needed repair and painting and an extra horse was required for the cart. His annual estimate for 1842 envisaged a round expenditure of £2,400 – a considerable increase over the previous annual expenditure of around £1,300:

Salaries and wages	£1,142 for 34 gardeners, boys, a carter, etc.
Building materials	£442
Contract work – smith, etc.	£279
Coal for stoves	£250
Seeds and plants	£200
Gravel and other materials	£84

All this was hardly cheap, but growing one's own food at this level was a matter of prestige and status rather than economics. The house steward Walker pointed out this problem when he reported to Loch that buying in poultry feed rather than growing their own grain and milling it themselves would save about ten shillings a week.[36] Despite this, the kitchen garden at Trentham flourished, continuing to supply fruit and vegetables for the various houses of the Sutherlands throughout the nineteenth century, so successfully, in fact, that by the 1880s nearly half of the produce was sold for profit.[37]

Beer at Trentham

One of the food allowances which the country house was obliged to give its servants was an agreed amount of beer and ale, to be drunk usually with meals. This was a right, not a favour, part of the wage agreement, and was based on the idea that beer was a food, a source of energy rather than mere enjoyment. Many of the features of beer allowancing can be traced back directly to the great noble houses of the medieval world, when wages were paid partly in kind rather than cash. The tradition flourished right up until the end of the nineteenth century and even survived into the twentieth century. It was one of those extraordinary survivals, the very tail end of a medieval tradition.

The Trentham brewhouse

The old brewhouse at Trentham was situated on the east side of the house (what became later the clock tower side). The building of this is recorded in the seventeenth century and it remained in use until around 1815. This original brewhouse was old-fashioned and too near the house. Correspondence dated 1815 included some discussion as to a new site. His Lordship had suggested a site within the main house area, but further back near the church. Loch thought this would be too confined, allowing no free circulation of air; the trees of the churchyard and the house would tower above it and would force the smoke and vapours downward. So a site in the outer yard beyond the porter's lodge seemed preferable. According to Loch, the new site involved the conversion of an existing building housing a large barn and coach house which were little used.

A letter dated July of the same year shows the brewer had commenced business in these new premises. The brewhouse remained on this site even during the remodelling of the house in the 1840s, though Barry modernised the interior plant and reworked the outside elevations, building new ventilation louvres in the roof (see Illus. 18).

Few houses have better brewing records than Trentham, and this is particularly true of the 1840s, when the house steward Richard Walker required the brewer, Robert Wright, to fill in a printed monthly form listing the quantity of malt and hops used, the gallonage brewed and the amount issued to members of the household. The entries name groups and individuals, and as both beer and ale was usually drunk at meals, they enable us to identify who ate together.[38]

In the seventeenth century a household made three or four different strengths of malt liquor, for different purposes, ranging from strong ale, ale, table beer and small beer. A good-quality table beer would have been about the strength of a modern light ale; a strong ale would be the equivalent of a barley wine or stronger; a mixed small beer would be like a bitter shandy in strength, though 'entire' small beer could be much stronger.[39]

In addition to this variety, the household would add flavourings, fruit, spices and herbs to the drink immediately before serving. In winter it would be heated. Different strengths were happily mixed to arrive at whatever drink was needed – be it a drink for a man sweating at a hard day's work in the fields or an invalid, a child, a nursing mother or a weaning baby. This level of flexibility is typical of a staple food, but by the nineteenth century both ale and beer were drunk usually only by the servant household rather than the family and variety was declining. By 1848 the Trentham brewer made only two strengths, ale and beer; and by 1879 he made only one beer. By 1897 it seems no beer was brewed at Trentham, but as there was still a demand for it from some of the servants, they formed themselves into a club to purchase and distribute beer.[40]

Scale of production and distribution of beer
How much beer did this complicated household brew and how was it distributed? In many country houses brewing was a large-scale activity, institutional in character rather than what we would think of today as 'domestic'. In the late eighteenth century, a large household would brew anything between 10,000 and 15,000 gallons of ale and beer a year, a similar production to that of a good-sized public house or inn of the same period.

Because there were no artificial means of controlling the temperature in an old brewhouse, there was a strong seasonal pattern to brewing, usually falling off during summer, so the spring brews were larger than in other months. On a daily basis, the issues of ale and beer were made by the brewer at twelve o'clock midday. The stronger ale was subject to stricter control than the weaker table or small beer. While the family was in residence, the brewer Robert Wright gave out an average of 445 gallons of ale a month to the servants' hall. This allowance was then distributed by the usher of the hall, Edward Herrington, at the dinner table. In 1832, for men this was usually three pints of beer a day and one pint of ale on Sundays; for the women it was two pints of beer and one pint of ale on Sundays.[41]

The weaker beer was distributed much more freely. Wright was allowed to make direct issues to individuals such as outdoor staff, craftsmen and tradesmen, as well as a bulk issue to the servants' hall. The latter received on average over 600 gallons a month.

Whilst the household was on board wages Trentham continued both beer and ale allowances to its servants, though many smaller country houses had ceased this tradition at these times of the year. By 1848 many women chose to drink tea rather than beer, but two sets of casuals who often came to work in the hall when the family were absent seem to have preferred the old traditions: day-work washerwomen did not eat in the servants' hall and brought their own food with them, but they were allowed as much beer as needed to be taken to the laundry for them; and the same applied to the chimney sweeps – a regular but casually paid man and boy who were allowed four pints of beer a day between them and two pints of ale a day for the sweep.

Other exceptions to the centralised system of ale distribution were made for special jobs, to compensate for cold or extreme exertion. Some were regular: the housemaids who were scrubbing floors and laundry maids when they were mangling were all allowed extra; and the gamekeepers and their assistants were given ale and beer on shoots.[42] Other 'ale jobs' were annual, such as cleaning the fish stews and filling of the ice house.

Even during the 1840s Trentham was hardly ever without some contract craftsmen. The brewer's forms are a useful record of their attendance. As late as 1848 women were working on the upholstery, and there were locksmiths throughout the house. For the first four months there were bookbinders busy in the library; in May bell-hangers came to repair the domestic pull system; and in the autumn painters, tailors and carpet-beaters arrived. All of them were given suitable allowances.[43] By 1848, of course, the world outside was largely turning to tea-drinking except for farm work and heavy labouring, so for these visiting workers, stepping into the world of the fashionable servant must also have been like stepping back in time.

Special issues of ale were also made at particular times such as birthdays – over 400 pints were given out to servants and workmen on Queen Victoria's birthday in May 1848, and on the Marquess of Stafford's birthday in August the workmen alone were given 416 pints of ale and 124 pints of beer.

The brewer

By the nineteenth century, commercial brewers were providing more and more of the beer consumed in domestic households. Of those who persisted in the declining tradition of brewing their own beer in their own brewhouse, most employed only casual, part-time brewers when needed, for brewing was highly seasonal. Even the wealthiest households usually combined brewing with baking, thus making up a full-time post. The common link was, of course, a technical one, relying on an understanding of the peculiar properties of yeast.

Robert Wright, the brewer-cum-baker at Trentham throughout several decades, came from a family with a long association with country-house service. He was born at Swancote Hall, near Bradeley, Staffordshire, in 1799. In 1819 he was engaged at Trentham as under-baker, and from 1827 he was also the Trentham parish clerk. In 1831 he was keen to be trained in brewing to help fill the gap left at Lilleshall by Mrs Tungate's semi-retirement.[44] By 1833 he was advising Lewis on the equipment needed for the completion of the new brewhouse at Trentham and also travelling over to Lilleshall with him to do the spring brew. Lewis thought highly of him and sang his praises to Loch: 'A practical man is worth 20 fine fancy schemes.'[45]

After the death in 1839 of the London baker and brewer Richard Wright (a cousin of the Trentham brewer) Robert became the only brewer employed by the Sutherlands.

Richard Wright and his death

In 1838 Richard Wright was the baker at Stafford House, but his family came from Standon in Staffordshire. In April 1838 he had taken a few days off from London and one afternoon decided to pay a visit to his wife's father who lived near Rugeley. His brother-in-law, who was working in a nearby field, saw him leave the house and ride down the lane 'rather swift'. He then heard a 'heavy fall'. He ran to the lane and found Richard 'on the ground, with his head bent quite under him, much fractured … he never spoke after the fall', and died during that night in his father-in-law's house. It seemed he had been 'riding too fast for his experience and that the horse shyed'. The horse had a history of accidents.

News of Richard's death was sent to Mrs Kirke, then acting housekeeper at Trentham, who sent off letters first thing the following day to Loch and to the Duchess, and also to Mme Galleazie, the housekeeper at Stafford House, asking her to go to see Richard's wife who was living in lodgings near West Hill. The Duchess herself broke the news to her maid, Richard's sister Mary Penson.

Richard was taken to Standon to be buried alongside members of his family. John Penson, licensee of the Tittensor Arms and ex-groom to the Duke, arranged the transport and funeral.

Although Richard had not been at work when he fell from the horse, the Duchess agreed to pay the funeral costs, including the tombstone.

Richard's wife had accompanied him to London and worked as a seamstress whose services were used by some of the servants to mend their clothes. She went back to Staffordshire on her husband's death but kept in touch with the household, for four years later the Duchess wrote to Loch that she had been searching for a suitable woman to look after the almshouses in Newcastle which the family had founded. At last she had succeeded: 'I have found a very lively person in the widow of our former baker, Mrs Penson's brother Richard Wright, sister of the wife of the workhouse master at Stone.'

In such ways did the system of aristocratic patronage work.

Besides Richard and Robert this one generation of the Wrights provided John, the groom of the chambers and valet, and the Duchess' personal maid, Mary Penson *née* Wright. The extended family provided also an under bailiff at Trentham, two labourers, a joiner and several tenants.

Robert appeared in the wages books for Trentham in 1840 as baker and brewer, and it was he who filled in the brewing records in the 1840s. He must have been a more than competent brewer, for he was lent out to brew for several other households including the Sneyds at Keele Hall. In 1851 he was living in a cottage in the village with his wife Sarah, two daughters and a son, all born at Trentham. He was still working as brewer in 1861 and died in 1875, when his family subscribed towards the cost of the encaustic tile still on the wall of the church at Trentham.

Cutting down

Within the Sutherlands' various houses, the consumption of food and drink was almost institutional, an important element in the communal structure. William Lewis, the agent, thought all this excessive, and the regime he tried to inaugurate was tough compared to many other estates at the time. He did not approve of giving beer to any tradesmen in the house and had also cut down on the home farm allowances. Thus beer and ale were given at the farm only during the harvests and then only by the order of the farm bailiff, depending on the amount of work done and the weather. At these times a man was allowed two quarts a day, a woman three pints, and more could be given for men carrying or ricking. The mowing of the meadows was let out at 5/- per acre with no allowances.[46]

On one unusual occasion, tradition was challenged by a servant, Thomas Thurgood. In April 1844 James Loch received a remarkable letter from Thurgood, the baker at Stafford House. In it Thurgood condemned both the quantity and the strength of the ale issued to the servants of the aristocracy in general. He suggested that the ale provided by the Sutherlands be halved in strength and that allowances of quantity be cut, and none at all be issued before dinner (i.e. in the morning). Such restraint would improve the health, character and morals of the servants.[47] Thurgood's letter certainly implied that ale was distributed more frequently than indicated in 1832, and it must have hit a nerve, for later that year Loch gave instructions to reduce the strength of the ale and beer. Thurgood replied:

> I duly received your kind note which conveyed to me the information that you had given to have the strength of the beer reduced, allow me to say that no circumstance in the whole course of my life has afforded to me such a degree of unqualified joy as the knowledge of that fact and I sincerely trust that with an <u>unrelaxing</u> hand you will carry out that determination to the utmost extent of your influence.[48]

But the teetotal Thurgood was nursing a number of other grievances. He wished to go onto permanent board wages, to be given cash instead of taking his meals in the servants' hall:

> The reason for my asking for board wages is, my duties very often require my attention at meal times and one or the other must be neglected and it has not infrequently occurred that things in the oven ... have been both burned and spoiled thro' going to breakfast and dinner at the time required. Now the laundry maids are allowed board wages on similar considerations. Another reason is, that refusing to conform to the drinking usages I have been, and still am, the butt of insult, and the object of scorn. But if I had my meals in my own apartment I could better attend to my duties and escape their insult.

He also wished to forgo the provision of livery uniform, which he thought unnecessarily extravagant, and to be given the cash saved, the reason being that he was getting married and was worried about supporting his wife financially. Loch consulted the Duchess, who refused the brewer's requests about board wages and livery, wondering instead whether he was a Roman Catholic as he did not attend the family church. About the strength of the beer she agreed, however: 'Fair enough about the strength of the ale and beer – you can give him support in this as it will be very unpopular with the servants.'

The senior servants, however, approved. Shortly after Thurgood's letter, Walker, the house steward, had reported that the ale brewed at Trentham was considerably stronger than at a previous house he had worked in. He had taken it upon himself to reduce the strength of the ale drunk in the steward's room, but this would not do generally as it would not keep well. Loch's investigations showed that in 1844 the allowances had crept up well beyond those issued in 1832 – they had now increased to two pints of ale each day for men and one pint of ale for women, with unlimited small beer 'whenever they wish it'. Nevertheless, wrote Walker, the Trentham household on the whole was 'a steady and moral set of servants'.[49]

In the later 1840s the household succeeded in cutting both strengths and quantities and the introduction of the pre-printed monthly forms previously mentioned for the Trentham brewer were obviously the mechanism of its control. Also in the late 1840s the household introduced at Stafford House a servants' library, organised by Thomas Jackson, the Duke's secretary, as a means of provided an alternative leisure activity to the supping of beer.[50]

Wine and Spirits

Did servants drink wine or spirits? There is evidence of the consumption of fortified wine. The cellar book for Trentham records two separate columns for the steward's room, one for port and one for sherry. According to this record, during a couple of weeks in December 1857, the nursery staff had one bottle of port and one of sherry, the housekeeper and the kitchen one bottle of sherry each – both these last may have been used in cooking, as the housekeeper's still room made the desserts for the family dinner. The only item which might indicate personal consumption in some quantity was the sending of four bottles of sherry to the governess. Later, in July of that same year, the family children came to Trentham, and the same issue occurs – four bottles of sherry for the governess over a period of fifteen days.[51]

The problem of drunkenness was probably more prevalent amongst the male staff. In 1862, for example, two 'helpers' (i.e. stable hands) were disciplined for drunkenness. The Duke's secretary Henry Wright gave orders that they were to be dismissed: 'Ford must go – I think he is the worst of the two and he was left in charge and therefore had the greater responsibility.'[52]

That alcohol consumption could cause trouble is clear from a record from the Leveson-Gowers' household at West Hill in London. This small estate south of the Thames near Wandsworth, in the 1830s was used primarily as a nursery for the Duke's younger children. When the Duke and Duchess and their older children were at Stafford House or abroad on the Continent, the younger children were left in the peace and quiet of West Hill, staffed by a small permanent team of maids and two footmen, all in the charge of a housekeeper and gardener.

We have a detailed account of the behaviour of these servants at West Hill from 1838. One of the servants was a young footman called James Lewis. In 1838 he was twenty-three years old and employed at Stafford House as second footman. From July 1838 to July '39 he kept a diary, which has survived incomplete, now held in Staffordshire Record Office.[53] Although this manuscript was for some reason attributed in the title simply to 'Thomas', careful family history research combined with wages lists make it clear that the writer was in fact James Lewis, a country-bred boy from a family of small farmers in Norley near Frodsham, Cheshire. After a career as footman in a number of prestigious households in Cheshire and London – after the Sutherlands he went as footman to Earl Grey at 13 Carlton Terrace – he married and spent the rest of his life as a small-scale farmer in Rainhill, Lancashire. James died in 1899, and his diary must have been inherited by his son Willie.[54]

James' life with the Leveson-Gowers was structured into phases which changed with the demands of the social season. The most glamorous part of his work was definitely at Stafford House. The Duchess of Sutherland was mistress of the robes to the young Queen Victoria and James was involved in waiting on the family in a hectic round of socialising at the very highest level. Some of his diary is taken up with this, but then followed a period taken up with a round of journeys to Lilleshall, Trentham and further afield to Glasgow. This was followed by a longer stay of several months at West Hill, where James was clearly under-occupied. His diary contains details of the servants' social activities and we get a glimpse of the importance of alcohol – not just beer and ale – when James describes the Christmas celebrations in 1838. These began on 20 December with a formal servants' dance held to celebrate Lord Stafford's birthday. James helped organise the lights, the decorations and the drink – the arrangements for the latter occupied a good deal of his diary. The household provided two sittings of a supper in the servants' hall, accompanied by unlimited ale. In addition, the steward sent him the official allowance for such occasions, two bottles of brandy and two of rum. No wine was allowed, so James made a collection, putting 5s in himself and collecting 1s each from the rest of the servants and outdoor men. Of this he gave 16s to a band of violin players and with the rest bought wine and other extra drink. James recorded in his diary that the dancing carried on till early morning when they had tea. He went straight to work 'as well as I could'.

The day-to-day running of the West Hill servants was in the hands of the housekeeper, Mrs Adams, and her job was unenviable, managing a houseful of bored young men and women with time on their hands. On Christmas Day, after their traditional Christmas dinner and tea, they entertained the gardeners, playing cards and drinking until well after one o'clock at night, after which they all grew so noisy and quarrelsome that Mrs Adams had to come down in her dressing gown to speak to them. The problem seemed to be caused by the house and laundry maids who were jealous of the attention paid by the gardeners to the nursery maids.

At New Year's Eve, the gardeners organised a party and collected two pounds to spend on drink. James the footman took control of it and made a 'grog' from gin and water, brandy and rum, sherry and port. The dancing went on till four o'clock, and, since someone else had got into his bed, James went into the servants' hall and fell asleep in front of the fire. Since there were five bottles of rum and gin left he planned to have another party, but this so dismayed the housekeeper that she threatened the gardeners with dismissal if they came up to the servants' hall.

At the beginning of his diary James claims that he drank nothing stronger than ale and not much of that. Later he records with relish the many occasions when he took whisky or brandy; he developed a habit of buying the odd glass of brandy for himself and friends when out in London. One cannot help but feel that James was at the top of a slippery slope, even though there was no shortage of dire examples. James' friend, the porter at Stafford House, was consistently the worse for drink, or, as the household jargon had it 'going for a jury', meaning he was absent with a hangover; James often had to fill in for him.

By continuing the tradition of household brewing and the allowancing system which went with it the Duke of Sutherland could be seen to be exercising paternalistic power over his extended household, defining his domestic space and showing to the outside world the wealth and extravagance of the Sutherland dynasty. To some extent, h e was controlling the members of his household – if servants drank at home, they at least were not drinking in public houses. Yet under this there is a glimpse of a counter-culture. On many occasions servants from other high-status households called in or were invited, and the alcoholic drinking, the parties, dancing and music, the frequent visiting of servants by servants, all this is a sort of parallel of the social etiquette of the employing elite families. You could see this as a rather pathetic aping of one's betters, but you could also see it as an indication of a vigorous social life amongst servants which the family tried to direct and control – not always successfully. The parties were opportunities for genteel networking between households at the servant level, oiling the mechanisms of sexual contact and job mobility. Junior servants in the nineteenth-century country-house world were notoriously fickle in their employment, moving from house to house, job to job within weeks. Socialising amongst themselves – both internally and between households – was one of the means of keeping up to date in work methods, finding out about new jobs or the merits of different employers and, perhaps most importantly, assessing new marriage prospects.

PART TWO

4

No Pressure ... ?

'It will all shake up right' – Three Housekeepers

An efficient, honest housekeeper was the most essential ingredient to the successful management of any country house, but especially one where the family was often absent. Her role was to run the house on a day-to-day basis and throughout its seasonal routines, whether or not any member of the family was present. For much of the year, therefore, the Trentham household was under female supervision, the housekeeper working with a handful of women servants, the only male support being the porter, carpenter and brewer. Of all the servant posts hers was probably the most highly pressurised. There were, however, different forms of pressure.

Part of the general housekeeper's job involved the control of the cleaning and routine maintenance of the house contents, including the care of furniture, laundering and textile repairs. The arrival of guests required close liaison with her ladyship to ensure the right bedrooms for family or visitors were prepared. She would receive instructions by letter when the family was away and in person at a daily meeting with her ladyship when she was in residence. A good part of her day would have been taken up with ordering and receiving a wide variety of foodstuffs and general consumables, in fact most of the goods coming into the house, checking and issuing them out to the staff at a set ritual every morning. She would interview, check references and discipline all resident female staff in the house, including casual labour required for extra cleaning, washing, spring cleaning and needlework. She paid their wages and kept her own household accounts and vouchers, sending monthly reports to the house steward. The housekeeper usually kept an annual inventory of all the furniture, fittings and linen for which she was responsible, as well as routine stores lists of consumables. The still-room maid was her personal assistant, responsible for all the assemblage of afternoon tea and much of the ingredients of breakfast – hot drinks, toast, sandwiches, cakes, jams and preserves – as well as many of the desserts for dinner. Through the still-room maid she had care of the sets of china.

Housekeepers had to make a home for themselves out of their workplace, where they were on call twenty-four hours a day. Marriage and a family of their own did not fit easily into this scenario and this was especially so when housekeepers were expected to move from one house to another, perhaps filling in temporarily in someone's absence. Sutherlands' housekeepers illustrate well the networking between their various houses: of the ten housekeepers recorded during the 1820s and '30s, five worked in more than one house, and two of these worked in three.

The three housekeepers featured here were entirely conventional in their circumstances insofar as they illustrate the three most common marital states of housekeepers: one never married, one married late in life after retirement, and one was widowed when young. All three experienced the high pressure of working for one of the richest families in the country. Two looked after Trentham during an unusual period when the rebuilding was at its height. Many books have been written about the refurbishing of country houses from the architectural or design viewpoint, but here we pose the question: what was it like to be *living* in such a building at such a time? The third housekeeper ran the house in the manner for which it was designed – as a centre for aristocratic hospitality.

Martha Cleaver

With the death of the 1st Duke in the summer of 1833, his son set about a substantial redesign of several of the family's houses. The completion of Stafford House was already underway, followed by major alterations to Trentham, Dunrobin and later Cliveden, all the work of Charles Barry. From 1834 until 1840 Trentham was literally torn apart, and for much of this time the house was in the tender care of Martha Cleaver.

Martha Cleaver had been housekeeper at the Leveson-Gower's house at West Hill in London since at least 1822.[1] There is no record of how she came to be at West Hill or what her work experience had been before that time, but we know she was born in 1790 in Hanslope, in Buckinghamshire, of the sort of family traditionally associated with the supply of high-class country-house servants – respectable, middle-sized farmers, described in her father's will as 'gentleman'. It was a large family; in 1831 when her father William died his estate was divided between twelve surviving children. She was a beneficiary of both of her father's will and that of Elizabeth, an unmarried sister, so she must have had a few savings to turn to.[2] At the time she was moved to Trentham in 1832 her title of Mrs was purely conventional, for at forty-two she had never married.

Martha arrived at Trentham in a hurry, sent there by the Duchess to hold the fort in the difficult situation left by the previous housekeeper Dorothy Doar, a character whose story will be told later. As Martha made her way northwards into a strange county, she must have had misgivings about her new, if perhaps temporary, post. She was an experienced housekeeper, however, and after a few months she had helped to manage the aftermath of the affair of Mrs Doar as well as could be expected, and had further coped with the stresses of that situation with credit all round. She must have taken to Trentham, so very different from South London, for she agreed to stay on as permanent housekeeper. Little did she really know of the poisoned chalice she was accepting.

After a couple of years Martha became lone caretaker of a complex builders' site. This may partially explain what seems to have been a series of one illness or misfortune after another, though always we have to allow for a degree of exaggeration in William Lewis's reporting.

It began a mere couple of months after her arrival in 1832. Martha was standing on a chair, probably reaching for a picture or curtain; the chair slipped beneath her and she fell heavily, breaking two ribs and suffering extensive bruising. The doctor who was called by Lewis thought she'd damaged her spine. By the beginning of September, she was still 'in a very precarious state' and 'not yet out of danger'. Lewis had contacted her family in Hanslope and a niece had come up to Staffordshire to care for her in her room in the house. Lewis himself was injured at the time, still lame from a collision between his trap and a gig which had come too fast round a corner in a lane.[3]

Martha recovered, but over the next few years there are intermittent but frequently repeated reports of unspecified illnesses or 'indispositions'. In January 1836 one of these sounded quite serious, an 'inflammatory attack', perhaps a septic infection in an injured thumb, during which she was 'much reduced'. Lewis thought she neglected herself – perhaps not surprising for by this time no family were visiting the hall because of the building work and the house staff must have been greatly depleted, so that for much of the time she was virtually on her own, though Lewis seems to have developed a habit of calling into the house to see her. He was convinced that the condition of the building was damaging her health: 'Her anxiety about the trades people being in the House is great and I think does her injury.'[4] Again he contacted her family, and this time her brother Thomas, who had inherited the family farm at Bullington End, Hanslope, came over to stay with her, to be replaced after a few days by her niece.[5]

In the last week of January, Lewis returned to Trentham from a trip to Shrewsbury to be met off the coach by a very worried Dr Mackenzie, who said Martha was much worse and that he had 'little hopes of her recovery'. A week later however, she was much better, having started to sleep properly. All this time her niece looked after her, with instruction from the Duchess to 'let her want for nothing'. By April she was strong enough to set off on a coach journey home, but at the point where she changed coaches in Birmingham she felt so unwell she decided to turn back to Trentham.[6]

She seems to have recovered over the next few weeks, and it is not until two years later in 1838 when we hear of another crisis. She was again confined to her bedroom for some days, looking 'very thin and delicate'. Her room was isolated in its situation and with only a couple of young housemaids in the house she had trouble calling for help, so Lewis moved the 'girls' into bedrooms nearer to her and installed a temporary bell.[7] Her niece arrived shortly afterwards.

This time, things had come to a head. In May 1838 Martha decided that she had had enough of Trentham and through Lewis informed the Duchess that she wanted to retire, though she would not 'think of moving from Trentham until <u>quite</u> agreeable to her Grace'. She herself wrote to the Duchess thanking her for her kindness (i.e. the promise of a pension) and apologising that she would not be able to leave things in the house as satisfactorily as she wished. Her final comment via Lewis was telling: 'She is only afraid to encounter another winter in the present state of the House.'[8]

Later that summer she was overlapping with the housekeeper who was to succeed her, Mrs Kirke; shortly afterwards Martha went home, probably to live with her brother. But we are far from finished with Martha Cleaver – nor has she done with Trentham, as we shall see later on, in the story of William Lewis.

Mrs Kirke

At this point it is interesting to imagine what a great country house was like when it was being completely renovated. In fact, we have no shortage of descriptions. The building work under Charles Barry and the clerk of works was proceeding very slowly, and one person after another was dispatched to report on progress or lack thereof – Vantini the house steward, Jackson the Duke's secretary, as well as Loch himself. Of course someone had to act as caretaker on the ground, and the unfortunate individual who was chosen to succeed Martha Cleaver was Mrs Kirke, the housekeeper at Lilleshall who was asked to split her time between the two houses (she had only recently returned from filling in at Stafford House). To her fell the unenviable task of finding somewhere suitable to stay for the visitors who had been asked to report back, for the house was in an appalling state of upheaval. To Loch she wrote that the only room he could use was the large library, though it was mainly filled with furniture from elsewhere. All the rooms in the attics and on the first floor were full of workmen.

To cap it all, around this time, January 1839, the West Midlands experienced a full-scale hurricane, which caused serious damage to Lilleshall and other problems at Trentham. In February Mrs Kirke reported another very frightening incident when some 'undesirable people' got into the house during the night – and could she have a night watchman please? That the Duke was planning to pay a visit when he returned from the Continent appalled her; she would make arrangements for him to stay at Lilleshall, instead, for the confusion at Trentham 'is daily increasing and the House is insufferably cold'.[9] Though she urged Loch to visit Trentham to see the state of the house at first hand, she was pleased when he decided to book accommodation for Charles Barry and himself at the Trentham Arms rather than put her to the trouble of finding rooms for them in the house.[10]

Part of the problem was a strike for higher rates of pay by Barry's stonemasons working at the house; later the carpenters also went on strike. More worryingly, according to Jackson, the organisation of the work was such a disaster that Mrs Kirke was 'in despair'. Everything was covered in dirt and dust, and most rooms had no fire grates in them though the paper-hanging and painting had already been done. In the Duke's own sitting room the plaster friezes had got so dirty they had to be cleaned, but in doing so the workmen had damaged the new paintwork below. The dining room was still full of scaffolding and this had damaged the new plaster ceiling, which had to be remade. In the library the mahogany shelves were covered in paint splashes, and the books had been stacked into boxes by the workmen with no attention to their order so the catalogue was useless; the chimney piece was discoloured and looked 'frightful'. In the new clerical offices the walls were still damp to the touch, far too damp for the office to receive valuable deeds. The usual method used to dry out new buildings was to light charcoal stoves, which had the disadvantage of depositing a fine dust over everything.[11]

Vantini's report dated from a few months later, when the bedrooms, library, breakfast room, dining room and the servants' rooms under the conservatory were all finished and in use. Much of the service block and the domestic offices were due to be finished within the month, viz. coal and ale cellars, lamp room, servants' hall passage, kitchen, larder, pastry, vegetable room, confectioner's room, brushing room and salting room. A long list of rooms remained unfinished, however: the main passages still had to be paved and polished, and progress was slow on the conservatory, terraces, state rooms, main entrances, staircases, steward's room, lodge, servants' hall, housekeeper's room, six servants' bedrooms, entrance yard and the stable yard. The first floor of the house was also progressing only slowly. Generally, work had been desultory whilst the family had been away on the Continent but progress had improved over the last three months whilst senior servants had been present. The gasworks were on a fixed contract and therefore almost finished, and Vantini planned to light the gaslight around 19 December.[12] This was unduly optimistic, because it soon emerged that one set of workmen had installed the retort in the gas house and another had worked on the mains. The apparatus had been so badly fitted that inspection by the firm's head engineers in Edinburgh was needed and alterations made. The Duke was furious.[13]

All in all, it is not perhaps surprising that some of the permanent occupants of Trentham developed health problems. In addition to coping with all this, Mrs Kirke was expected to provide the usual housekeeper's accounts for both Lilleshall and Trentham and to supervise some of the tradespeople working on the interiors at Trentham. In 1838 Loch had been worried about the beer allowances given to these, and Mrs Kirke's report to him gives us details of their presence: two new upholsterers (man and woman) had been employed right at the beginning of the project, as soon as the family left, to start removing furniture and paintings from the house, and these were engaged as if they were servants, with full allowances of board wages, milk and beer. Two more male upholsterers who came to help later were treated as contractors and therefore given three pints of ale a day. An extra woman to help towards the end of the project was paid 1/6d a day wages and two pints of beer a day. Many more day workers would be needed before the house was put back to rights: a large number of beds and stuffed furniture needed to be cleaned and re-covered, and for this Mrs Kirke proposed to pay 1/6d a day plus beer. Painters of furniture were allowed two pints of ale a day. They were shut up in a closed room all day breathing in noxious fumes so Mrs Kirke gave them this extra for health reasons.[14]

By March 1839 Mrs Kirke felt it was all too much. She told Loch her position was untenable and that the two houses, Trentham and Lilleshall, needed their own permanent housekeepers. He had passed this on to the Duchess, who agreed, giving Mrs Kirke the choice of which house to stay with. Although she preferred being at Lilleshall, she bravely offered to stay on full-time at Trentham for a while, as this was where she was most needed, especially since the family would be returning from the Continent soon.[15]

This arrangement did not last for long, however, for in January 1840 Loch was anxiously writing around his contacts for suggestions for a new housekeeper for Trentham (see Illus. 20).[16] These requests seem to have borne little fruit, for a wage list dated April 1840 records Mrs Kirke back at Lilleshall and the Trentham housekeeper's post occupied temporarily by Agnes Henney, the wife of the office clerk at Trentham, who nobly stepped into the breach. Another wage list from later the same year records a Mrs Cole at Trentham.[17] By the census of 1841, however, the Trentham housekeeper was Mrs Marsh, a thirty-five-year-old widow from Watford, who stayed in post at Trentham until 1854 when she became housekeeper at Stafford House.

By 1841, most of the builders and painters had left the main house at Trentham, except for one man painting the sash windows. There were still twelve carpenters in the house moving and repairing furniture, putting down carpets and making washstands and tables, which caused Walker, the new house steward, to enquire somewhat brusquely why these were under the superintendence only of the housekeeper. Work was still needed on the fire grates and on the pavements in the conservatory and entrances and on all the outside walks and borders. By the following year builders were still on site, finishing off the church and entrance lodges and pulling down the old office block, the old blacksmith's shop and the old poultry yard.[18]

It seems that the experience at Trentham may have unsettled Mrs Kirke, for after returning to Lilleshall she remained there only a few months, replaced by a new housekeeper in December 1841.

Jane Ingram

Though the records of the 1830s give an interesting picture of the practicalities of living at Trentham during Barry's rebuilding, they give no idea of how the house eventually functioned. It would be good to think that it was finally to perform its true role, a house in which to entertain family and guests, a fitting backcloth for the Duke's enormous wealth. Instead of the dusty, paint-bespattered, half-plastered rooms and a job which was like nursing a sick child, could we imagine a housekeeper delighting in the soft glow of gas and candlelight, the smell of beeswax on wood, the glimmer of silver polished the true way, with gnarled bare fingers? The story of Jane Ingram takes us a leap forward into the 1850s and beyond, to a time when the house had come into its own. In it we see Trentham at its finest, working as Charles Barry and the Duke and Duchess no doubt planned.

Mrs Ingram was a successful servant. Though she experienced bereavement in her private life and no doubt a good deal of stress in her working life, she was not afflicted like some of the other servants. Her story here is mainly about her work, which is entirely fitting, for her life was mainly work, and sometimes highly pressurised work at that.

Unlike so many of the senior servants at Trentham, Jane Finney was a Staffordshire woman, born in 1803 at Farley near the small town of Alton in the Staffordshire moorlands. She came from a respectable servant family, possibly attached to the household of the Earl of Shrewsbury at Alton Towers, just down the road from where she was born. She probably became a nursemaid and she certainly moved to London as a young woman, for when she was twenty-two she married James Ingram at St George's, Hanover Square, London. In 1832 she gave birth to her daughter Jane, but shortly after it seems her husband died and like many in her situation, she went back into service, presumably putting her daughter out to the care of a relative, possibly her sister Hannah.

She became nursemaid to the children of the second Baron Wharncliffe in Hanover Square, Westminster, who was related by marriage to the Sutherlands. She was still there in 1841 but by 1847 was at Stafford House as first nurse, replacing another young widow, Mary Penson, who had been promoted to the position of the Duchess of Sutherland's personal maid and who became Mrs Ingram's long-term friend.[19] Ten years later Mrs Ingram was still at Stafford House as nurse and she was still there in 1853.

By 1861, her charges had all grown up and she had moved on to become housekeeper at Trentham with her daughter Jane as assistant housekeeper, though the latter never appeared on a wages list and there is a slight puzzle over Mrs Ingram's salary. Her annual wage when she was first nurse in 1847 was £31 10s; when she finally retired in 1876 as housekeeper, her wage was exactly the same. Her replacement in 1876 was set on at £50 p.a., and even Janet Macdonald, the head laundry maid, earned only £5 less than Mrs Ingram. It may be that the arrangement which was agreed in 1861, when she was already in her late fifties, was that her daughter Jane would live with her as her personal maid and assistant, bed and board provided, and that Mrs Ingram's salary should take account of this. A letter from Sarah, Mrs Ingram's sister's daughter, would seem to support this. Referring to Mrs Ingram's daughter Jane, in 1861 Sarah wrote:

I have waited so anxiously every day to hear how you were getting on, I was so glad to find from Jane's letter she was content and getting along nicely with the exception of a cold and cough. I do hope she will be of great use to you and save you running about so much ... Mother is quite pleased with the idea of coming to see you ...[20]

There is little information about Mrs Ingram's career as a nursemaid and nanny, though some of her charges kept in touch. There are personal letters, carefully kept by her, from two earls who both addressed her affectionately as 'My dear old nanny'. One, signed simply 'Drogheda', described excitedly the birth of a 'fine boy', and the other was from Edward Montagu-Stuart-Wortley Mackenzie, the third Baron Wharncliffe, in reply to her letter of congratulation on his advancement to the earldom of Wharncliffe.[21]

A letter from a nasty dirty little boy
Wharncliffe House, Curzon St., W

Dec. 31, 1875

My dear old Nanny,

I am going to stick to the old name and be Earl of Wharncliffe – also Viscount Carlton. It is ages since I have seen your dear old face, and I could fall on your neck and kiss you now with as much tenderness as when I was a nasty, dirty little boy. God bless you, my affectionate old Nanny, your letter was a real pleasure to

Your loving old child

Wharncliffe

This last letter especially is a touching reminder of the bond, strong enough to last a lifetime on both sides, which could develop between child and nanny. Perhaps this was one of the reasons why so many nannies seem to have been widows. Not only might they have experience of bearing their own children but if they still had their own offspring in later life, the breaking of the bond with their charges became more bearable when inevitably the time came to move on.

By contrast with her career as nanny, there are many records and letters regarding Mrs Ingram's work as housekeeper at Trentham between 1861 and 1872. The collection of 'vouchers' or receipted bills kept by the housekeeper give an idea of the scope of her job.[22] The most regular item was the purchase, delivered by a two-horse cart, of kindling for the family rooms, kitchen fires and bakehouse ovens. Also regular were monthly bills from two railway companies – the North Staffordshire Railway bringing ceramics from Burslem and other packages from the Potteries, and the London and North-Western Railway bringing a wide variety of goods from London, Liverpool and Birmingham – boxes of tumblers and glassware, candles, tea, coffee, starch, cases of wine, boxes of sugar, lemons and even eating apples. Mrs Ingram bought salt by the ton direct from the salt works at Northwich, oatmeal by the hundredweight from Glasgow and whiskey by the gallon from Brora. Many other goods were from suppliers in nearby Newcastle-under-Lyme: ribbons, linen, braid, laces, barrels and corks, new baskets and basketwork repairs to chairs and hampers. She also paid bills for stationery, stamps, liniments and pills, and she bought from the village sixteen quarts of cowslips and ten quarts of bilberries.

She had to receipt weekly bills, even from suppliers from within the Trentham household, because James Loch had followed an old system adopted by many country houses whereby productive departments had to keep a record of the quantity of food produced for internal consumption. In some cases, Loch added records of value as well as quantity, and so each department became its own accounting centre. It was a paper transfer and no cash changed hands.

One bill may give a picture of Mrs Ingram herself, as she might have been dressed in her best outfit, probably of dark red silk. It was from a local dressmaker, dated 1871:

Making silk dress	9s 6d
Lining	4s
Braid, whalebone & buttons	1s 9d
Black velvet bonnet	£1 5s 0d
White blond cap	12s 6d
Total	£2 11s 9d
For red elast boots, 2 pairs	6s 6d and 12s 12d

In addition to this routine work, one of Mrs Ingram's most important jobs was to prepare the house to receive family and guests. The meals books record visits from family and friends, often accompanied by their servants.[23] On other occasions the presence of 'extras' indicated meals for keepers and beaters for a day's shooting, or bread and cheese for men getting ice into the ice house.

The Rich Man's Table
A meal for two visitors at Trentham – Lord Granville Leveson-Gower (2nd son of the 1st Marquess of Stafford) and his wife Lady Granville, from a letter written to Lady Granville's sister, 1810:

Our reception was really ridiculous, but you shall judge. The dinner for us two was soup, fricassee of chicken, cutlets, venison, veal, hare, vegetables of all kinds, tart, melon, pineapple, grapes, peaches, nectarines, with wine in proportion. Six servants to wait upon us, whom we did not dare dispense with, a gentleman-in-waiting and a fat old housekeeper hovering behind the door to listen, I suppose, if we should chance to express a wish. Before this sumptuous repast was well digested, about four hours later, the doors opened, and in was pushed a supper in the same proportion,

in itself enough to have fed me for a week. I did not know whether to laugh or cry. Either would have been better than I did, which was to begin again, with the prospect of a pill to-night, and redoubled abstemiousness for a week to come.
(Leveson-Gower, F., *Letters of the Countess Granville*, vol. 1 (London, 1894), pp. 8–9)

The meals books also pinpoint occasions when Trentham really came into its own, affording a glimpse of the high-pressure living with which its staff had to cope. The last full week in July 1872 seems to have begun quietly enough. Tuesday saw a 'normal' family household: two members of the family, six guests and the usual full-time servants totalling around forty staff. Saturday, Sunday and Monday following saw more guests arriving at the house – on Saturday alone there were seventy-seven sitting down to luncheon. These were members of the landed aristocracy, most of them related to the Sutherlands by marriage: the Egertons from Tatton, the Cavendishes from Chatsworth, the Cokes from Holkham, the Westminsters and the Fitzgeralds. They stayed over the weekend, with the Prince and Princess of Wales joining them on the Monday; on that night the first of three balls were held. On the Monday there was a 'ball supper' for 300, on Tuesday for 400 and Wednesday for 421. Two bands had to be fed for three days – twenty-two members of the Rifle Band and fifteen of the Volunteers Band, plus an extra 100-odd helpings of bread and cheese suppers for other volunteers. All in all, it amounted to over 1,300 extra meals for the three balls.

The correspondence for that period takes us closer to the practicalities.[24] Most of the arrangements fell on the shoulders of the Duke's secretary, Henry Wright, and, of course, Mrs Ingram, with help from the house steward, Henry Prentice. All the cooked meals were provided by the London chef who travelled up from Stafford House with an augmented kitchen staff. The baker Robert Wright made all the bread with the help of an extra baker, and Mrs Ingram's staff in the still room, supplemented by some extra women, prepared all the sandwiches, bread and cheese suppers and all the hot drinks. Her enlarged staff of housemaids did all the normal house cleaning, bed-making and laundry.

Even more stressful must have been the preparations in the days before the great event, when Mrs Ingram was the only senior servant at the hall, the family being away in Scotland. She was kept in touch with their requirements by Henry Wright, whose letters, though to the point, show him to have been good-humoured and considerate towards her. Well beforehand he warned her:

Dear Mrs Ingram   Stafford House, May 30, 1872

We will have a swell band from London in July, 25 men and the Bandmaster.

 You will have to hire beds for them and I think the best place to put them is in the long gallery in the Farm Yard where the people have suppers sometimes. Will you consult Mr Menzies [the agent] about it? They will be wanted 2 nights.

A week later he wrote again on the subject of beds and other needs:

I enclose you a cheque, also a list of extra beds required ... Please write at once your suggestions in the matter.

 There will be a Ball for 400 for two nights, there will be plenty of Hands needed for washing china etc. It would be as well to be prepared with the necessary women for the Dance. I hope to get down a week before the time. We would then settle how many would be wanted, till I see the place I cannot form any idea of the numbers but at a rough guess I should say 20 women would be wanted. In your letter in answer to this tell me how many beds provided for the Band. I think you said 25, but there were 40 here the other night ...

He then went on to list the other extra beds required: thirty-one for visitors staying over; seven for extra kitchen staff; four for illuminators, in charge of gaslights and candles; one china and glass man; and twenty-five waiters. A couple of days later he wrote to ask if beds could be put up in the stables and whether there were any beds to let in the village. Even the family guests would have to make do with temporary accommodation, and several of the men would have to sleep in dressing rooms (by modern standards, a dressing room would be a substantial bedroom).

The Sutherland Livery
A bill from Barber and Calvert, livery tailor, 123, Pall Mall, 1848.
As might be expected, the Duke of Sutherland's footmen's livery uniform was rich but, by the standards of the day, not too gaudy. Each footman's set comprised:

Light drab [i.e. light brown] cloth dress livery coat, laced with silver and silver lace and crest buttons £5 – 1 – 6	
Pair of rich silver and scarlet bullion epaulettes with gold embossed crests and coronets £4 – 18 – 0	
Pair of scarlet cloth dress breeches	£2 – 8 – 0
Pair of silver lace garters with bullion tassels	£1 – 2 – 0
Striped jean jacket and morning trousers	£2 – 2 – 0
2 pairs of stout calico drawers	11 – 0
Pair of drab milled long gaiters	18 – 0
Drab milled cloth great coat with cape £4 – 14 – 6	

A single bill included five such sets for different footmen, plus sets of dress trousers, fustian work jackets, waistcoats, frock coats, great coats and drawers for the baker, porter. Steward's room man, watchman and lampman.

Total bill
£278 – 15s
Less 5% discount
£264 – 16s

Though this was an exceptional occasion summer balls were fairly regular occurrences, and the Prince of Wales had visited several times before, so it is reasonable to assume that Mrs Ingram coped with all these arrangements. Aged seventy, she was however no longer a young woman, and perhaps Henry Wright was a little concerned about her. Towards the end of June he dashed up to Trentham to check the arrangements. There seems to have been some issue with a hired piano which had to be sent back to Broadwoods, and inevitably there was a problem with the supply of hot water:

> I am convinced there is a defect somewhere. I have however done all I can so far in the matter – There will be someone down to look at it. I cannot run risks on such occasions if I am to be held responsible.

He was in such a rush to get back to London and then on to Dunrobin that he left his travelling bag under the bed at Trentham by mistake, and he asked for it to be sent on via the fast coach. For some reason he had also borrowed some face powder from Mrs Ingram: 'I see I've brought away your violet Powder box which you lent me. I did not know you used powder or paint Oh! Fie!'

As the time of the ball approached, the house steward back at Stafford House, Henry Prentice, began to deluge Mrs Ingram with warnings: some table linen and a dessert service would be sent down to Trentham, also some copper saucepans would arrive with a kitchen maid – this because the chef said the coppers at Trentham had not been re-tinned properly and were not safe to use, and in any case did not have an engraved crest on them. An assistant baker would arrive by train at Whitmore – could she send the van to meet him? A great many packages would also arrive the same way, including a seltzer and soda water, crates of cider, ginger beer, an extra twenty-four dozen bottles of champagne, and livery uniforms for some of the extra servants. Prentice also sent a box containing some preserved meat, which he asked Mrs Ingram to see was given to 'the poor people also that preserved milk etc in the store room next my office'. He himself had hoped to come down on Monday to help but now found they had royalty to dine that day.

The week before the family were due to arrive, Henry Wright sent further letters: the Stafford House upholsterer would arrive shortly to help, the numbers in the band had increased from 25 to 32, and he was going to find dress livery for the man on the gate. If Mrs Ingram needed any special stores she was to write him a list and he would get the Co-operative to send them down. As far as the accommodation for the guests were concerned, the Duchess would set aside a whole day, the Friday before the event, to settle where everyone would sleep. Henry Wright signed off:

I dare say you are as busy as you can be 'and so say all of us'
Take it easy – it will all shake up right,
Yours very truly,
Henry Wright

It did indeed 'all shake up right' as shown by the report of the Prince's visit in the *Staffordshire Advertiser* for 22 July 1872, which reported the ball in glowing terms, explaining it was held in honour of the coming of age of the Duke's eldest son and heir.

Mrs Ingram's daughter Jane was still at Trentham in July 1872, so she must have helped out with all this. She would also have assisted with the aftermath, not the least of which was coordinating all the bills from suppliers and carriers and arranging for their payment, through cheques sent from the London clerks which Mrs Ingram had to cash. The house steward Henry Prentice also sent cheques for the extra wages.

Dealing with more normal routine visits of the family, the Duchess Anne herself wrote regularly to Mrs Ingram telling her to arrange for visitors to be picked up at the railway station at Stone or Whitmore. Very grand guests might bring a good many servants who would arrive by train separately; on one occasion she had to arrange for twenty native servants to be met. The Duchess herself frequently travelled with only her maid Mrs Penson and her particular friend Lady Barker, and she always gave notice of this.

Often, instead of speaking directly to Mrs Ingram, the Duchess seems to have preferred to write short notes to her – even when at Trentham, and especially if she was dissatisfied with the food which the still room supplied for breakfast. In particular, the toast seems to have caused problems: it was sometimes soft and saturated with butter; at other times the butter had been put on whilst lumpy.[25] Whether or not the housekeeper appreciated written instructions in this manner is uncertain as Duchess Anne had virtually indecipherable handwriting.

Mrs Ingram did not have the right to hire and fire her staff without reference to the Duchess, though usually her suggestions were approved. On one occasion, Mrs Ingram must have complained about her still-room maid: 'Let the stillroom maid leave immediately, it is too bad of her to be rude to you.' There seems to be one area of the household, however, over which the Duchess had strong feelings:

> I am afraid I shall not get back to Trentham at present. The Duke goes to Egypt on the 1st.
>
> I have been rather vexed and surprised to find that both laundry maids are Roman Catholics – a thing I very much dislike as a rule, in the Establishment – I cannot understand the last one at least, having been engaged without my knowing it.
>
> I have now seen a very nice looking young woman who would make a very good head one – if the present one now temporarily at the head (who was second) objects to this one being put over her, I think she had better leave.
>
> I cannot go on with two Roman Catholics, for one because it was the cause of the last one leaving – and I would rather have none.
> Yours truly,
> A Sutherland

Mrs Ingram must have soothed her ladyship, at least to some extent, for the next letter was in a calmer tone:

> Of course from what you say, Janet Macdonald must remain as the head, and this new young woman is willing to be the second. The other I am sorry to say must have warning, however good, as I cannot have two Roman Catholics. You must tell her that I was not told she was one – and that I only retain Janet Macdonald because of her long service.[26]

Another of Mrs Ingram's correspondents from Stafford House was John Whittaker, who was the house steward after Prentice. The tone of his letters to the Trentham housekeeper was very different from that of Henry Wright or Prentice, especially on the subject, once again, of laundry maids:

Stafford House
St. James's
London
April 26th 1876

Dear Madam,

I cannot understand what you mean about the new Laundry maid. All I can say about her is, that she had a most excellent character as a good strong hardworking and willing young person. If she had not been so I would not have engaged her.

In the meantime I shall be glad if you will not listen to what Janet McDonald or anyone else says against her for the short people often work better than the taller ones. After I had engaged this young person one of Janet's friends applied for the situation: but if I had not been settled I should not have engaged her as she talked too much.

So Janet must make herself comfortable as I shall not think of discharging the girl without just cause.[27]

On receipt of this letter Mrs Ingram would have had good reason to be annoyed, and so too had the head laundry maid, because the point about height was a valid one. It is perhaps worth an explanation. The amount of large-scale household linen going through the Trentham laundry was huge – great quantities of tablecloths, towels and sheets, many of which would still have been made of linen. This required skilled pressing whilst damp – pressing heavily downwards with both hands on the iron, rather than lightly passing the iron across in a wide sweeping motion, which was only possible once the fabric was dried and 'set'. Pressing was especially important for the seams, the heat killing any bedbugs which might live there. Given the amount of pressing to be done, the only way to avoid causing repetitive stress to the arms or shoulders was by bending over slightly, using the upper body weight to provide downward pressure. Thus the relationship between the height of the laundry maid and the height of the work surface was critical. The ironing boards in the Trentham laundry would have been wide, sturdy, fixed pine tables, so a shorter maid would have to stand on a specially made box, in itself a dangerous position if she moved sideways. One can almost see the harassed housekeeper rolling her eyes on receiving Whittaker's letter; obviously one could not have expected a mere male to have the practical experience to understand.

The laundry seemed to have been a bone of contention for Mrs Ingram in several ways, or perhaps it is sheer chance that letters about it have survived. On one occasion Mrs Ingram received a very sharp letter indeed from the Trentham farm manager Mr Reid:

Trentham Farm, Aug.11, 1875

Dear Mrs Ingram,

I am in receipt of your note and the contents has rather astonished me – now will you be good enough to say who is in the habit of carrying off the Laundry coals at the same time I hope you will kindly give me your authority for saying so – The last Coals carted to the Laundry was put into the Cellar the next day after their arrival consequently they could not be carried away – we have had plenty of Coals in the Farm yard and had no need to take the Laundry Coals – if you will allow me to give you an advice don't be too ready to believe the Laundry people in the matter if they chance to burn too many Coals tis very easy to transfer the blame to others. You threaten to complain to Mr. Menzies. You can do so if you see proper and I will be prepared to explain matters to him when he speaks to me on the subject – tis very easy to write scolding letters but you should be quite sure of the right party before you do so.

Madam, I am yours etc John Reid.[28]

There is also a short undated letter sent by the house steward, which at a quick glance seems of little interest but is one that marks a first step into a modern world, and the cessation of a practice hundreds of years old:

I have this morning made arrangements respecting the Washing being sent to a Laundry in London and shall begin this week. You will therefore be kind enough to make your necessary arrangements at Trentham with your Women and let me know at some future time how many can be dispensed with.[29]

It had long been a belief that washing dried in country air was much healthier than in the town. Partly because of this, and partly for reasons of efficiencies of scale, great London households had for centuries sent their dirty laundry to their country houses, which were equipped with spacious wash houses, ironing rooms and secluded drying greens. The clean, starched linen was returned in neatly folded canvas bags, carefully packed into large hampers. Before the nineteenth century this would take place perhaps once a month, the hampers being loaded onto horse-drawn carrier wagons. Once the railways appeared, the exchange took place on a station platform every week, usually on a Friday. The Sutherlands had obviously been in the habit of doing this, and the implication of the change to a commercial laundry service for the London house was that the Trentham laundresses would be reduced in number. It may be that this did not last – many households found their own house laundries more effective and many changed back when the spread of various infections was associated with commercial laundries.[30]

The exchanges with Reid and Whittaker were towards the end of Mrs Ingram's career as housekeeper. She had lived with and worked for the Sutherlands for thirty years, half of that at Trentham, but she had also lived in other rich and famous households in London. As nursemaid and nanny she no doubt had travelled widely with 'her' children. Even as Trentham housekeeper she had been to Dunrobin several times. The time came, however, when the Duchess wrote to Mrs Ingram to say the new housekeeper would arrive at Trentham soon; she hoped Mrs Ingram would like her and would she please make her comfortable.

Mrs Ingram retired in 1876 with a pension and an estate cottage in the quiet village of Hanchurch. She still had the company of her daughter, then aged forty-four. Mrs Ingram died in 1880, aged seventy-seven.

Among the work letters kept by Mrs Ingram are some more chatty letters from other servants, mainly about the weather and various people's health, including Mary Penson, the Duchess's maid who was a great friend, the family's French governess who complained about how the new gas light dazzled her, and Margaret Stevens, an ex-servant of the Sutherlands who had got a job in the household of the Duke of Edinburgh. Unusually, before Mrs Ingram and her daughter finally left Trentham for the cottage in Hanchurch she must have filed away some of this private correspondence along with her work letters, and so they found their way in to the archive.

5

The Public Face of the Sutherlands

'Well educated, steady and trusty people' – The Porters

When a guest arrived at a country house, the first person to greet them was a lodge keeper. In many estates this was a retired or part-time worker on the park or farm, allowed to live rent free in a lodge at the entrance in return for opening and closing the gates. Whilst the man was out at work, his wife would take on this responsibility, so the position was ideal for an elderly but still active couple whose family had left home. This was true of the outlying lodges at Trentham, but those porters working in the entrance lodge to the main service yard were a different matter altogether. Perhaps because of the house's proximity to the growing industrial towns of the Potteries, their posts carried many serious responsibilities, including security, payment of wages, adherence to regulations by other staff and distribution of alms to the poor. They were the public face of the day-to-day estate – a combination of security guard and public relations officer. Their records give an insight into areas of the day-to-day running of the household which are otherwise closed to us.

Their work required a fair degree of skill in both writing and arithmetic, men of faultless honesty and politeness, of good appearance but with a natural toughness. As with his agents, Loch preferred young men whom he could mould to his own values. As Loch explained to the new house steward Vantini, who was the porters' line manager in the 1830s: 'Porters both here [Lilleshall] and at Trentham have always been obtained from the North of England – they are strangers – well-educated, steady and trusty people, all essential qualities for the proper discharge of the duties required of them.'[1] Because they were recruited from distant parts they could be relied upon to be impartial as far as local squabbles and pressures were concerned.

Loch here had in mind especially a time earlier in the nineteenth century, when Trentham was subject to a slow invasion from the north by the Kirkbys, four brothers from Northumberland. They came from a family of thirteen children in Kirkhaugh, an isolated village near to Alston, on the banks of the upper Tyne in a valley high up in the Pennine moorlands (see Illus. 21). Their father was the Revd Thomas Kirkby, rector of Kirkhaugh church. He had been married twice; four of the children were by his first wife, who died in 1777, and the remaining nine by his second wife, Hannah, who died in 1826. The four brothers were part of the second family, and were by no means poor; in fact they were well educated and from the sort of family which produced agents, bailiffs and gamekeepers. They were not in the first flush of youth when they came to Trentham, and at least one had experience in the same type of work, but they must have wanted to move away from home to a less isolated part of the world to find suitable employment with prospects.

It is not clear whether all four brothers came to Trentham at the same time. The eldest, Randal William Kirkby, had settled sufficiently into the parish to marry a local girl in 1813. His brother Charles had been appointed as porter at Trentham in 1810 and both were working as lodge porters by the end of 1816, when the lodge book included the list of the 'Porter's Rules' signed 'R & C Kirkby, Porters'.[2] It seems that a third brother, James, was also at Trentham by then, as he was married in the parish in 1817. The rent books show that he lived in an estate cottage for which he paid four guineas a year. He may well have been a night porter.

By 1818 Randal had been promoted to the post of clerk in the office (his story is told in a later chapter). His job as porter was taken by James and for fifteen or sixteen years the two brothers, Charles and James, ran the porters' lodge and controlled the entrance to the service yard. Their two stories, however, have very different outcomes.

Charles Kirkby

Charles was born in Kirkhaugh in 1786. He came to Trentham in 1810 and probably shared accommodation with his brothers since he does not appear in the rent records until ten years later when he got married, aged thirty-seven, to Elizabeth, one of a family named Peake, of Trentham. The couple lived with their three sons in an estate cottage in Ash Green, for which they paid rent of just over £5 a year. In the estate's 'Report on Cottages' in 1835 Charles was described as a 'steady' tenant who kept his house in good repair, though it only had two bedrooms, both of which were very small.[3] With three growing lads the house must have been cramped, but they had enough outdoor space to keep a cow for dairy supplies. In 1838 his rent increased so they probably moved into a bigger house, which fortunately allowed them to find space for Randal's widow in 1839. Charles himself died in 1854.

There are few personal records of Charles in the Sutherland archive, probably for the good reason that he was a successful, loyal, reliable servant, exactly as described by Loch, giving no reason for anxious letters to be written about him. He remained as lodge porter at Trentham for at least forty years, well into his sixties, an important kingpin in the daily routine of servants and family and, as far as we know, was a classic model of the long-serving faithful family retainer. As the first person to greet visitors he was of immense importance to the Sutherlands' reputation.

The porters, however, were not highly paid and not even entitled to a rent-free house (unlike their elder brother Randal who as clerk was given free living accommodation). Certainly Charles earned a good deal less than Randal (£40 compared to around £120), though he was given a good many allowances such as board wages of £12 p.a. and free coal, beer, milk and vegetables.[4] He did manage to make deposits into the savings bank and after his death in 1854 his widow told the 1861 census enumerator she was 'proprietress of railway shares'.

None of Charles' three children had any prolonged education, for according to the 1841 census only the youngest, James, then aged ten, was not working; Thomas, aged fifteen, was employed in the pottery industry as a china painter and Charles junior, aged fourteen, was a carpenter. There were no daughters. By the standards of the day they were not impoverished but they were hardly comfortably off. Yet Charles' family was a good example of upward social mobility, as all three sons created successful careers, two of them independent of employment at Trentham.

The eldest, Thomas, became a majolica painter in the pottery industry and was talented enough to become an artist in his own right. In the censuses up to 1881 he was still living in Ash Green with his wife and family. He deposited small amounts of savings into the Trentham Savings Bank throughout the 1850s and '60s. He was obviously a man of some cultivation as shown by a collection of his notebooks which have survived, one of which is a copy of an Italian instructional manual on ceramic colour grinding and mixing, dated 1548.[5] Kirkby's copy is in Italian on the left-hand page with a careful translation on the right. The same collection includes notebooks recording his attempts to run a singing class which he called the 'Mutual Improvement Class' at Trentham for the church choir (obviously not successful as the Duke gave instructions that the choir was not to sing anthems when he was present); lessons in instrumental music (which proved impossible as the class had a miscellaneous collection of instruments all tuned to different keys, so he had to buy a set of instruments himself and lend them to the boys); records of the time spent by his own children in practicing the violin; and notes on the use of artificial lighting in photography. In letters he was addressed as Curator, Minton China Works, Stoke-on-Trent. According to the national probate calendar, he left a personal estate of £438 and was there also described as Art Curator.[6]

Charles Kirkby junior, the young carpenter, moved to London as a young unmarried man and lodged in St Pancras. He went on to become an architect and surveyor and settled in Islington where he married his first wife, Helen. They had three children: Thomas, Helen and Charles Samuel. His wife Helen died in 1860, and the census taken in the following year found the family split up. The father remained working in Islington, but his children had gone back to Staffordshire to live temporarily with his extended family: Thomas (aged eight) and Helen (aged seven) with James Kirkby, their uncle; Charles Samuel went to live with his great uncle, Reuben Penson. No doubt wishing to keep his family together, Charles junior did the usual Kirkby thing and quickly remarried, to Elizabeth, the daughter of one of his mother's relations, Richard Peake, who had gone to work as a gardener at Apedale Hall. By her he had a further four children. He must have been successful professionally because, despite supporting such a large family, his personal estate at death was around £800.

The third son, James, became schoolmaster at the boys' school at Trentham and was still in post during the 1891 census. He lived in the schoolhouse at Trentham, providing a home for his widowed mother Elizabeth as well as the two of his widowed brother's children and another young boy boarder. All of them were probably being educated at school in Trentham – by this date there was a separate girls' school as well as boys'. He himself remained single until 1874 when he married another daughter of Richard Peake. He was sufficiently affluent throughout his career to be able to employ a young servant to help look after his family and to make regular if modest deposits in the savings bank. His personal effects at death were valued at £882.

Despite going in different directions the three boys kept in touch with each other, helping each other out in times of difficulty and visiting each other; according to the 1871 census the eldest Thomas was visiting Charles junior in London. In some ways their father could be said to have produced the most successful family of the northerners. In contrast to most of the others, and despite (or because of) his relatively low status and wage as porter, he had a small family of only three sons, all of whom made successful careers. James Loch, a convinced Malthusian, must have approved.

James Kirkby

The story of the other Kirkby brother who partnered Charles in the porter's lodge has a very different ending. James was born in Kirkhaugh in 1790. There, in his father's church, he was married in 1817 to a seventeen-year-old girl called Susan Walton from nearby Knaresdale, though by that time he had already started work at Trentham. Before moving to Trentham he had worked as gamekeeper on an estate near Alston. The couple had five children (one died in infancy in 1819), all born at Trentham, and all living in a small estate cottage for which he paid rent of four guineas a year.[7]

Life changed drastically for the worse for James and his family in 1835, when Lewis reported to Loch that James 'was in difficulties with his family and intends moving all to Cumberland, his own wife's native place'.[8] The reason for this was not explained but it later emerged that Susan was experiencing serious mental health problems, which meant James could not cope with looking after her and the children without the help of her family, especially her mother. James had to give up a secure, reasonably well-paid position to go back to the north.

Some eighteen months later, in 1836, Loch received a letter from the vicar of Castlecarrock, near Brampton in Cumbria, asking for help for James, who had been working as a thatcher on the estate of the Earl of Carlisle but had been discharged when jobs were cut. There were no suitable posts for him in the area. He was thus 'entirely dependent on the charity of his neighbours and in a very destitute condition. He has a wife labouring under insanity and four children.' He wished to find a job such as the one he had previously with the Duke of Sutherland. If Loch were to hear of any such position, would he be kind enough to recommend James. He was 'a quiet sober man', wrote the Revd Vaughan, and Lord Carlisle's steward would also 'speak to his character'.[9]

No doubt Loch replied to the Revd Vaughan, but he also sent the letter to James' brother, Randal William Kirkby, to ask how, exactly, he could help. In Randal's reply to Loch he thanked the people in Castlecarrock who were helping his brother and suggested that any work as either a porter or gamekeeper would suit James. He was honest, hard-working and wrote a good hand. If Loch could find a post for him, he, Randal, would undertake to support Susan in Stafford Lunatic Asylum; his children would remain in the care of their maternal grandmother in Cumberland, so there were no problems about supporting the family. He himself had not been unfeeling to a brother in such anxious distress and had already sent him twenty pounds, and on receipt of Loch's letter had sent him another ten.[10] Loch obviously made some suggestions as to possible jobs, for in another letter Randal told him that James was 'at least forty-five years old, far too old for entry into the Excise service', but he did not know if this was a problem for the railroad companies. James was thus not short of friends who were concerned for him, but there, in 1836, the correspondence about him ends. Unfortunately, Randal William, potentially his main prop, died three years later.

The census, however, tells a touching story about the later years of James and his wife. No clerical-type position came to fruition, but in 1841 the couple were living at Garthsfoot, Castlecarrock with two teenage sons. There James was working as a gardener. Ten years later the couple were in the same place, on their own, and this time both James and his wife were working as farm labourers – a tough life no doubt for one who had been used to wearing the livery of the Duke of Sutherland, but one in which at least the two were together, with Susan free of an asylum. James died in 1867 and was buried in the church at Castlecarrock. All their children had left home, but one at least must have kept his links with Trentham for in the 1861 census he was working as a farm labourer and living in Ash Green. No record of what happened to Susan can be found.

Henry Kirkby

Henry, the youngest of the four Kirkby brothers to move to Trentham, had a similarly troubled life. He was married at Trentham to a woman called Anne Middleton, at which time he was the school teacher at Trentham school, paying a small rent for the schoolhouse. His wife died only a year later and the last record of him in the rent book is dated 1819–20, when he moved away from the area.[11] Eventually he appeared, having remarried, in the census of 1851 as schoolmaster in Nether Denton, near Brampton in Northumberland, a few miles from his brother James at Castlecarrock and back near to his original home area. He too, however, must have met with some misfortune, for in the 1861 census he was an inmate of the Newcastle-on-Tyne workhouse, a fate which even the unfortunate James managed to avoid.

The Hemmings

After James Loch's death, the estate seemed to be more flexible in choosing porters. In 1864 a new porter was needed but a suitable candidate could not be found. The agent at that time, recently promoted from gardener, was Fleming, who suggested that the fifty-seven-year-old Thomas Hemmings, one of the night watchmen, be made lodge porter, but only on a temporary basis at least at first:

He knows the duties and every detail. He is perfectly steady and trustworthy. His appearance is portly and suitable to the occupation, while he is still active and enjoys good health. Hemmings can read and write and upon the whole I feel more satisfaction in placing him in the Lodge than anyone else here.

The only problem was his appearance. This had not mattered previously when he was on duty at night, but during the day he had to make a good impression. Fleming felt that he should be paid his present salary plus a few shillings extra to make himself more 'respectable'. Not unnaturally, Thomas expected to be paid the proper porter's remuneration: £40 p.a., plus 12/- board wages, three loads of coal a year, one quart of beer per day and a cottage and garden for which they paid £4 p.a. rent. In the event, as he was only temporary, he was paid 3/8*d* more per week than his previous wage, plus beer. There remained the problem of his appearance. Fleming considered he was 'very well' while the family were away, but 'I do not think he looks quite the thing ... he would look better than he does were he in livery'.

After his promotion, Hemmings' place as night watchman was taken by his nephew Samuel Hemmings, who had been employed as a labourer in the gardens. He had helped with the night watch before when his uncle had an accident, and Fleming had confidence in his 'good judgment and attention, having before observed that he is steady, attentive and sensible of how much the care of the place depends upon him during the night'.

Fleming was keen to have both men appointed permanently but was worried what the Duke would think when he saw them. Yet they were good at their job:

There is much in having men here who are proved to be steady, attentive and well acquainted with the place ... The Hemmings are short men, and not adapted for ordinary labour as digging and cultivating. But they are capital fellows for watching and any employment not requiring excessive exertion.[12]

The Hemmings were certainly well acquainted with Trentham. The family record of service, mainly in the outdoor jobs, spanned well over a century.

Duties of the porters

The records associated with the lodge porters are useful for illustrating the context of the life and work of Trentham which would otherwise be impenetrable. The porters' lodge books list their duties usually in the first two pages.[13] The lodge book was open for inspection only by the agent or the house steward; otherwise it was to be kept locked up. In essence the porter's duties were:

1. To keep the lodge-keeper's book and to write down the names of everyone who passed through lodge gates between eleven o'clock at night and working hours in the morning (see Illus. 23).
2. To enquire the business of strangers. No person was to be allowed through the gates without the knowledge of the porter.
3. To allow nobody to loiter or wait in the lodge.
4. To write down the names of everyone who should have spent the night inside the site but who did not and of those who did remain all night but did not belong to the establishment, unless the porter was certain that the house steward or housekeeper had authorised it.
5. To write down the names of anyone who appeared drunk or in any other way is guilty of 'irregular behaviour'.
6. To observe generally what was going on and report anything wrong, regardless of any reasons or excuses.
7. To keep a list of certain persons employed on site and once a fortnight to pay them the necessary wages.
8. To allow no person to smoke tobacco within the stable yard or its buildings and to report such infringements.
9. To lock the gates as soon as it was dark – winter and summer.
10. To unlock the letter box and take the letters to the Post Office at five o'clock each morning when the family was in residence.
11. To distribute bread and beer to the travelling poor, a pint of beer each and three-quarters of a pound of bread to adults, children by proportion. The travellers were to ring the lodge bell but not be allowed through the gates. No bread or beer was to be given to any travelling soldiers, people who lived locally or people who worked for the Duke and Duchess. An inventory of the lodge taken in 1826 included twenty-one quart cans and three smaller cans.[14]

12. To take part in the night watch rota. In 1810 the night patrol instructions were fairly general, listing the places to be checked but instructing the watchman to vary his times. In the yard and at the fronts of the hall and the farm house he was to call the hour: 'He must call it loud enough to be heard by those who are awake, but not to disturb those who are asleep.' In 1849 his duties were specified in greater detail: the first patrol was to start at 10 p.m., pass through the farm buildings, the estate yard, round the west front of the house, through the flower garden to the kitchen garden, going round the outside first and returning past those sheds with fires in them. The porter was to return by the dairy and again pass round the front of the house on the way back to his base which was the weighing house in the stable yard. This should take two hours. He could then rest in the weighing house for an hour, and start the same round at one o'clock, returning at three o'clock. He could take another hour's rest before going on a third round. By six o'clock the people would be arriving for work.[15]

What sort of incidents did the night watchmen report? Unfortunately, no night book has survived of the 1830s or '40s but there are records from a few decades later. Many of the incidents related to weather – high winds which blew down trees or smashed glass in the greenhouses. Once there was a false fire alarm which made them turn out the fire engine, and there were occasional incidents of petty theft – people's gardens were robbed of vegetables and bundles of firewood tied up ready for later collection. There were also routine problems: gates not shutting properly, doors to the smithy and saw mill left open, the stable yard clock stopping suddenly, and on one occasion in the farmyard a cow was calving but no one was sitting up with her. Sometimes the hall residents gave trouble: the porter caught a butler sneaking in late along the waterside; one stableman was a repeat offender in this respect. He also found a man asleep in 'the bread and beer place' and another trying to climb in over the bank near the lodge. Horses were left untied in the stable yard, lights were left burning in the hall where they should not be, the front door to the hall left unlocked at midnight. One night the porter found a foxhound which had escaped from the kennels 'caught on them spikes on the trent bridge'.[16]

The record of people coming through the gate to work each morning and leaving each evening was kept rigorously by the day porters. For example, in November to December 1816 the name, function, days and times were recorded for thirty-one people. Seventeen were gardeners or garden labourers, all arriving at 7 a.m. or a few minutes after and leaving around 4.45 p.m. Similar times were kept by the eight tradesmen working in the house and by one stableman, the second stableman staying on duty all night on a rota basis. Others worked longer hours: the kitchenman arrived for work at 4.30 a.m. and did not leave until 8 p.m., and the usher of the hall, whose job was to run the servants' hall, worked from 5.45 a.m. to 7.30 p.m.

Even so, perhaps the day porters were not always as careful as they might have been. One illustration of this took place in 1844 when Charles Kirkby was still head porter, with a new porter, George Penson, fairly new to his position as the second. The problem came to light through an anonymous letter that complained about the behaviour of Henry Kelly, one of two grooms who were permanently based at Trentham. He had developed a little illicit sideline for himself, breaking and training horses for other people in the neighbourhood, often taking them into the hall stables and feeding them on the hall's hay. In one case, alleged the anonymous 'Well Wisher', a colt belonging to one of the tenants stayed at the stables for about a fortnight and was regularly and severely beaten by a 'most outrageous and Brutish attack ... with whips, sticks, pikel stales which ... continued about 4 hours, after which it was left a complete mass of blood and being more dead than alive, also being the next day unable to move'.[17]

For Loch the real crime here seems to have been the besmirching of the family's reputation and the misuse of the Duke's premises, especially the fact that the strange horses 'must have deprived the Duke's horses of their fair allowance of food'.[18] The groom concerned was dismissed but Loch's anger did not stop there, extending to the porters and even Henney, the head clerk whose office overlooked the gates:

I cannot conceive either how such horses could pass and report by the Office windows and not be seen from them ... I have stated to his Grace what I repeat to you, that there seems to have been great laxity throughout the whole establishment. It could have been unknown to none, that no groom was entitled to misspend his time by breaking horses for another person. It is worse than nonsense to say that it was not known to the Porters that the grooms were not entitled to take strange horses into the Stables. They are much to blame ... The Porters must be again spoken to. The Duke is very much displeased at the whole transaction and reasonably so.[19]

Henney investigated and found that the porters knew that Kelly was in the habit of exercising and training neighbours' horses, though no one thought this wrong as it was in his own time. According to Henney, the real problem was that the two grooms did not have enough work to do. They had to attend to only one horse, an old mare used by the housekeeper and to fetch the doctor, and a pony for messages.[20] The fact that someone was under-employed, of course, was music to Loch's ears, and when Kelly was dismissed his post was not filled, leaving the remaining groom with the hardly arduous tasks of caring for the two horses, cleaning the family carriages and harness, and delivering household messages. One feels that Kirkby and Penson, the porters, were lucky to escape further wrath.

Another important job for the porters was the distribution of alms to the travelling poor. The giving of bread and beer took place only when the family was in residence, since the tradition dated back to much earlier times using the leftovers from the great hall. The Trentham porters recorded the giving of alms in a book, which thus forms a diary of the family's seasonal occupation of Trentham.[21] For example, in 1849 beer was distributed every day between January and April, then again in December.

During the months of residence thirty-two hogshead casks of beer were delivered to the lodge by the brewer, each cask containing fifty-four gallons. At the end of April fifteen gallons were left and returned to the cellar, so over 1,760 gallons were given away over the winter and early spring.

The bread issues show a similar system in that they were only given out when the family was at home. Bread was brought from the baker in the form of six-pound loaves, each divided between eight people. During a period of twenty-one days in 1848 over 4,000 people received bread relief, using 482 loaves. The majority of those receiving alms were men but some were women and children. 1848 seems to have been a high point for such relief around this time, as during the 1850s the numbers declined. Sometimes the porters wrote a few comments to provide an explanation of a particular pattern: 'very bad weather accounts for the small numbers of Travellers on 2 or 3 days' and 'chiefly ribbon weavers this month' (these from December 1860).

In line with the terms of an old, endowed family charity, alms of 'broken bread' were also distributed at the porter's gates to specified local poor people. The clerk keeping this record entitled them the 'crumbs that fall from the table'.[22] This took the form of leftovers from the still room given to two recipients each day, each person once a week only, every week of the year. In 1817 there were fifteen of these, mainly widows, at least two of them widows of men who had worked on the estate.[23] By the 1840s this dole seemed to have changed to issues of milk, with a pattern which relates to seasonal availability – more in spring, less in December. Most was new milk, rarely skimmed, issued at a rate of one or two quarts per day, every day. Again the recipients were named, local poor people, most of them widows.

The porter's lodge was also the point of sale of the estate milk to the public. In 1841, Thomas Jenkins, the clerk of works for Charles Barry, complained about the short measure of milk purchased on his behalf at the lodge from the porter's wife, Mrs Kirkby. He later realised his own maid servant had been in the habit of drinking some from the jug on the way home. He turned her out of the house immediately and apologised to Mrs Kirkby, who had never complained that the money he had sent for the milk was not enough.[24]

By the late 1870s the milk dole had again changed, this time to soup, given out to around thirty named people twice a week, on Tuesdays and Fridays at ten o'clock, in special cans, one quart per single person, two for small families and more for larger. Most recipients were from Hanford, a few from Hanchurch.[25]

One of the porters' duties which was not mentioned in the lodge books was the weighing of goods delivered at the gates. There was a large-scale weighing balance in the weight room near the stable-yard gate for this purpose. Intriguingly this was also used for humans: there survives a scruffy little notebook dated 1788–1804 which recorded the names and weights of some servants and visitors to the household, including several entries for children.[26] The keeper of the weight notebook, who only identified himself by the word 'self' but who must have been a porter, clearly had a problem. He started the record weighing fourteen stone but went up to well over seventeen and a half by 1803. One eighteen-stoner, only identified by the initials 'TH' (probably an ancestor of the Thomas Hemmings mentioned previously), earned an occasional note: 'less a little' or 'more than ever'. By contrast, Penson the park-keeper kept a very even weight of eleven stone, and the clerk George Henney, father of William Henney who was clerk in the 1830s, weighed a mere ten stone.

Some people were being weighed regularly, once a month, so clearly there was an awareness of the importance of one's weight. Was this because of worries about health, or rather about the appearances of liveried servants as with the later Hemmings? Perhaps one hint towards such a reasoning comes from a different source. The house steward's logbook of servants in the 1830s records the downgrading of Alexander Sutherland, who had been employed as a groom in 1833 but was reduced to helper (i.e. stable hand) because he was 'gating havy' (Vantini's spelling), perhaps too heavy for a smart turnout with the family. He did not last long, even then, for in 1835 he was discharged for getting tipsy and tumbling from a horse whilst taking it from Lilleshall to Trentham.[27] Appearances obviously counted.

6

A Woman's Place

'Who could guard against such a Devil?' – Another Housekeeper

Mrs Dorothy Doar seems to have been an efficient housekeeper, but her story brings us up against three issues relating to the responsibilities of her post.

Firstly, a housekeeper's life in the mid-nineteenth century was totally circumscribed by her job. Because the house was not only her permanent workplace but also her main and usually only home, she was almost always either single or widowed, with few family ties elsewhere – very different from the situation in the twentieth century when married couples became a popular choice for housekeeper and butler. The nineteenth century and earlier usually made no such concessions to the married state. In the 1820s and early '30s, however, the Leveson-Gowers employed a housekeeper who did not conform to this tradition and who created problems for both the management and herself, the end product of which was trauma and tragedy of the first order.

Secondly, the purchase of large quantities of household consumables required good but honourable relationships with local tradesmen and suppliers and a certain scrupulousness in the distribution of supplies. This was often a problem for employers: it was easy to see whether the house was being run properly but more difficult to detect whether a housekeeper was honest in her purchases. The Duchess Harriet for one was aware of the temptations when, in 1840, she was about to set on a new housekeeper; she wished Lewis to advise on the 'company that she should see, and the conduct that she ought to pursue towards the Newcastle [trades] people'.[1]

Thirdly, the housekeeper was expected to set a good example in terms of honesty, loyalty, personal morality and conduct to the younger, less experienced women servants in her charge, often mere teenagers, at Trentham usually referred to as 'the girls'.

Dorothy Doar seems to have started to work for the Sutherlands in 1818 or 1819. The then house steward Mr Lilley recorded payments to Dorothy Doar in his London and Trentham daybooks and accounts throughout the period 1819 to 1821.[2] She was part of the travelling group of personal servants moving with the family from the London house to the country, assisting in preparations for special family celebrations such as weddings and births. By 1823 she seems to have settled permanently at Trentham, taking over from the elderly housekeeper, Mrs Forrester, who was frail enough to need a woman to help her. After Mrs Forrester's salary was finally paid off when she died in August 1823, the housekeeper's petty cash receipts were all made out to Mrs Doar.[3] Thereafter the Trentham accounts record her salary payments at various times. Interestingly, in April 1830 she was absent from Trentham and the house was in the charge of a temporary housekeeper, awaiting her return.

Mrs Doar, however, was an unusual housekeeper. The normal practice over centuries was that female servants gave up full-time living-in service on marriage, and the title 'Mrs' was given to all senior women servants only as a courtesy. Yet Dorothy Parker had married Mark Doar, a footman, on 24 May 1818, in the parish of St Marylebone, Westminster. The couple had a child, a daughter Emma, who was born sometime in 1820, so when Dorothy was inscribed in the Trentham day book of that year she had only recently given birth to her first child, whom she must have put straight out to a wet nurse. This explains the intermittent nature of Lilley's early payments to her – she was part-time and casual.

Over the next few years she showed herself to be an efficient and loyal member of staff, though her husband often seems to have been unemployed and this was probably the reason she continued full-time work. In November of 1830 Lewis explained to Loch that Mrs Doar 'seemed in great trouble that her husband was again disappointed of a situation, Mrs Snead of Keel is at present to remain in London and does not require a House Steward'.

Mrs Doar was anxious 'to get him fixed under Lord Gower in some way', and Lewis went on to endorse him as a 'well behaved correct man'.[4]

For Mrs Doar, serious problems at work began early in January 1832 when Lewis reported that she had been unwell but was now much better, though Doar could 'hardly say what is her complaint'. This somewhat obscure comment was followed by another: 'The last conversation I had with Dr. White he said Mrs Doar was in a very precarious state.' In February, she was again reported to be 'very unwell', Lewis beginning 'to doubt of her recovery', and Loch was sending her advice about hot flannels. By April there was no hiding the state of affairs: the Trentham housekeeper was pregnant![5]

Today it is difficult to imagine the uproar that would have been provoked in this refined household, which was simply not geared up for such a situation either practically or morally. Women servants, however senior, were rarely married, and any pregnancy was scandalous, usually resulting in instant dismissal and disgrace. Mrs Doar had written to the Marchioness informing her of the pregnancy and she had received a letter in return, sympathising but telling her she must leave. Loch was regretful but clear in his instruction to Lewis: 'She cannot stay, it would be a bad example to others and a Housekeeper who has maids to look after should not be bearing children even to their husbands.' The Marchioness, reported Loch, 'laments the circumstances exceedingly' and had instructed that Mrs Doar be told she 'was a most excellent, zealous and faithful person, who did her duty amply and conscientiously'. Her ladyship also authorised Loch to pay her travel expenses to wherever she wished to go and moreover she was not to be 'hurried away by any means'.[6]

Lewis dutifully passed on the bad news that she had to leave her place, with the result that the next day Mrs Doar sat down and wrote a heartfelt letter to Loch himself:

Sir – You will excuse my troubling you but having experienced great feeling and kindness of hart from you on former occasions made me take the liberty. I sincerely hope you will intersede with Lady Stafford on my behalf. You have heard from her Ladyship of my situation, I was in hopes her Ladyship would have let me keep my situation as usual after my confinement which will take place early in June, I would put the child out to nurse so that it could not in any way interfere with my business. I hope ... Sir you will be my friend and prevail on my Lady to allow me to stay if it's only for a short time as God knows what will become of me – my poor husband for a long time has been so very unfortunate and the Education of my little girl has taken every shilling we had so that I have not the means of going in any way of Business that I could be getting a little to enable us to live. Doar has got a situation and I hope he will be able to make it answer but the sallery is low so that I must do what I can to enable us to live. If Lady Stafford will not allow me to stop, here is my situation – do you think Sir, my Lord and Lady would have any objection to my, if I could meet with a small shop in Newcastle, undertaking it, but God knows that cannot be done without the aid and assistance of some sincere friends ... I assure you at this time my heart is allmost broke, I have been upwards of 14 years in the Marquess of Stafford's family and it grieves me much, very much indeed to leave it – indeed Sir to describe to you the distress I am in would be impossible but I hope by leaving my case in your hand, who I have always considered my friend, that you will be able to prevail on Lord and Lady Stafford to do something for me.[7]

A series of letters from Lewis clarified that what Mrs Doar wanted was the lease, presumably on favourable terms, of an empty property owned by the Sutherland estate in Newcastle to set herself up selling groceries and confectioneries.[8] At this point she was clearly distraught, sending a servant running out into the yard to catch Lewis just as he was about to set off on a journey to Lilleshall and confessing to him that she had not managed to save a shilling. Lewis in turn was upset by her distress and, although he had instructions to tell her again she must leave the house, he thought she was not in a fit state to be moved. Moreover, he informed Loch he was happy to 'throw my little influence in her favour for I do consider she has been a very good and faithful servant', and he thought she had a good chance of setting up a successful little business. Loch obtained agreement to this plan from the Marquess and Marchioness who seemed to have felt guilty about turning out their pregnant housekeeper though they were still clear that she could not stay in post. As Loch said, 'It is quite impossible in such an establishment to admit of her breeding and rearing a family in the House and if she went away for a time who then would look after the girls – besides it would be an example for other upper servants – and it would be Castle Howard over again in its worst times.'[9] (What on earth happened at Castle Howard?)

A couple of days later Loch clarified: 'You may take steps to put Mrs Doar into her shop and give her a little assistance ... let it be known she has her Ladyship's support and that she goes on good terms.' The Sutherlands in fact were prepared to offer even more tangible support; the Marquess had agreed to help her start the shop, provided that the financial assistance given was 'secured from her husband's debts' – perhaps a reasonable consideration under the circumstances. Loch wrote directly to Mrs Doar:

> Mr Lewis will tell you that both the Marquess and Marchioness of Stafford are of the opinion that the best thing for you to do is to settle in a shop in N'castle where your experience and skill, will, with their countenance and appreciation, give you some little trade. Mr Lewis will give you some aid from His Lordship – and he, as will myself, will be most happy to do you all the good we can.[10]

Around this time the housekeeper at Lilleshall, Mrs Kirke, was taken ill, hence Loch's comment to Lewis: 'A Murrian appears to have got amongst our House Keepers.'[11] The two agents, in fact, were in something of a quandary regarding Mrs Doar. They wanted to remove her from the house, as, apart from the effect of her situation on the morale of the rest of the servants, she was clearly unwell and not able to do much work. Yet they needed her to hand over her work to a successor, the usual procedure for this being the taking of an inventory of the stores in her charge. Moreover, bearing in mind the Marchionesses's previous instructions, they did not want to appear cruel by simply turning her out. On the Marchioness's instructions, the housekeeper from West Hill, Martha Cleaver, arrived on 7 May to take temporary charge and to go through the inventory with Mrs Doar. The latter had arranged lodging for herself in Hanford and was preparing to leave. It seemed that various problems were beginning to resolve

themselves, despite just a tiny hint of worry in Lewis's mind that all
was not well – Mrs Doar, he thought, 'does not estimate properly
the great kindness shewn her by the family, still thinking she
ought to be continued'. His suspicions were fed by the news that
Mrs Doar had been packing up eight dozen bottles of sweet wine
(i.e. home-made wine) and sending them off in her name.[12]

Two days later, all was confounded. Mrs Doar was taken in
premature labour in the morning, and during that night, in her
room at Trentham, gave birth to a stillborn seven-month female
child.[13] Loch was appalled but ever practical:

> Mrs Doar, when she is <u>fully</u> able must go to her lodgings in
> Handford ... take care that directions are given that all her
> linen is kept separate from the rest of the household and ... that
> everything in her room be well scoured – let a temporary female
> wait upon her and let the house servants attend to their duty ...
> surely the sweet wine must be her own making, she never could
> think of partaking of his Lordship's.[14]

The sweet wine issue rumbled on for a few days, seemingly a
welcome diversion from the greater scandal of a servant, even a
married one, giving birth inside the servants' quarters. Eventually
Lady Stafford approved the allowance of the wine, much to Lewis's
chagrin.

According to instructions, Mrs Doar was allowed to recover
in her room which was thoroughly scrubbed; the other house
servants kept at a distance from her, as if pregnancy were
contagious. But she was granted a woman to care for her, and the
Trentham accounts for 31 May record a purchase of 'leeches for
Mrs Doar', which implies the presence of a medical attendant,
probably Dr White who was the usual doctor for the servants at
that time.[15]

Meanwhile Martha Cleaver took over the running of the
household, including the checking of the inventories.[16] The next
couple of days appear to have been a period of uneasy calm as
Mrs Doar recovered and to all appearances started to pack ready
for her departure to Hanford.

Then the rumours started, culminating in a letter to Lewis from
Randal William Kirkby, the estate clerk at Trentham:

I cannot refrain from reporting to you how much Mrs Doar's conduct with respect to the sending away of packages from the Hall has become a matter of great notoriety in the neighbourhood – in consequence of which Mr Woolley has sent back to the Hall 3 hampers and 2 boxes which Mrs Cleaver has locked up in the Stewards Room –you are also aware that three heavy boxes have been sent to Miss Wilmhurst's supposed to be near 3 cwt also a large box to Whitmore by Josh Chatterley of greater weight than clothing could make it – besides these Mrs Cleaver says that there are now in one of the rooms at the Hall a large trunk and box nailed and corded by Mrs Doar's own hand which to Mrs C appears much heavier than any clothing ... there appears to exist in the minds of the Hall servants a great suspicion that Mrs Doar has been sending away articles she ought not to have done and as the case has become so notorious permit me respectfully to suggest to you of your laying the same fully before Mr Loch, by doing of which you will fully exonerate yourself from all blame – I need hardly repeat how much I feel hurt by this affair having always formed the highest opinion of Mrs Doar's honesty and fidelity.[17]

Lewis sent this letter to Loch, his covering note sounding both enraged and reproachful. He now referred to Mrs Doar as 'the woman' and grumbled, 'I was not by any means reconciled to the sending off the sweet wine, it afforded great room for conveying away anything else if so disposed'.[18]

At this point, despite being closely interested in the political crisis then unfolding around the passing of the Reform Bill and the resignation of the Prime Minister, Loch proceeded with great circumspection regarding Mrs Doar, the more so since Lord and Lady Stafford had handed over the affair entirely to his judgement:

I confess that I am slow, most unwilling to believe anything against Mrs Doar – I have always considered her a good and faithful servant and being still of that opinion, I am quite sure that she will not hesitate to show you what has been conveyed away ... and thus put an end to all the stories ... and by doing so enable me to proceed in doing what I have authorised to do for her.[19]

Then followed a careful letter to Lewis on the art of domestic management:

> You will investigate carefully the stories regarding Mrs Doar and if after a calm and deliberate enquiry you think her conduct really liable to suspicion, you may and should give her the enclosed letter. But recollect two things, how easy a thing it is to whisper away a person's character and how serious a matter it is to do so, recollect also how ready the base and low people are apt to think that they can obtain favour by turning against those that are out of power and to whom they fawned while they possessed it. If her inventories are <u>correct</u>, why are you entitled to say that every thing besides are not her own – don't forget that her place entitled her to certain perquisites and that system being approved of by her Ladyship, it cannot be thrown up against Mrs Doar and I must caution you also at being led away entirely by Kirkby, he is as honest a man as breathes, but he is a man of strong passions and liable to be prejudiced and he never liked Mrs Doar, for she resisted his authority.
>
> The enclosed letter gives you full power to act, if upon full enquiry you think it proper to do so, which one on the spot alone can judge of, and recollect that your own character for justice and discernment in some measure is involved, on the result of the enquiry if made and if it should fail. On the other hand, if I was Mrs Doar, now that the reports are abroad, I would rather that they were sifted to the bottom as not.[20]

Mrs Doar, however, surprised and disappointed Loch by refusing to allow Lewis to search her boxes. Lewis thought her unwise: 'In my opinion, for a thorough justification of her conduct she should not hesitate to open every box, parcel she might have.' He went on: 'Her present weak state of health and the affair altogether so unlooked for, proves most distressing to my feelings.'[21]

Lewis's persevered in his examination of Mrs Doar's boxes and a few days later sent a long explanation of what must have been a most dramatic scene in her room:

> After the examination of Mrs Doar's boxes yesterday, which displayed a most disgraceful scene of robbery, I was so much

agitated and affected that I was really unwell all day. The Hampers were examined first and contained some dozens of home made wine such as gooseberry, ginger etc. The boxes contained nearly a collection of every article necessary for housekeeping, many of which she claims are her own property, which however is doubtful. Mrs Cleaver and I did not feel disposed to dispute with her except as far as the linen went. She has still a great quantity of it of every description, marked D, several of the hand towels are so marked, but she gave them up as Lady Stafford's property (the D appears recently put in). There is still a very great deficiency in the linen, we received from out of the boxes, 10 dinner damask napkins, 7 table covers, 35 chamber towels, 3 pillow cases, 8 waiting napkins, 1 damask tablecloth, 9 tablecloths for steward's and housekeeper's room, 2 glass cloths and 3 pair of sheets. She also exhibited from the boxes, quantities of tea, sugar, coffee, foreign wine, soap, candles, mops and many new brushes for shoes and cleaning house with all, which she acknowledged to be the property of Lord Stafford. It is dreadful to contemplate on such proceeding and to witness such depravity in one who had every confidence put in her and it was amazing how hardened she appeared. As for the linen, she said it was old and she was entitled to it but Mrs Cleaver told her she had taken the best and left the old. Mrs Cleaver is to be again among the linen today and will be able to give some account of what is deficient. I can assure you I am much pleased at the conduct of Mrs Cleaver in this affair and it is most desirable for her comfort and the peace of the establishment that Mrs Doar should be moved from the House instantly. She is quite well able to be moved, but of course, I await your decisive answer, the articles enumerated except the linen, remain in Mrs Doar's bedroom, please to say how I am to act with them and her. I was never so deceived in a character in my life and it is really enough to drive confidence from being placed in anyone, do let me hear from you as soon as you have seen Lady Stafford, for I feel so very uncomfortable.[22]

Loch's response was to sympathise with his troubled agent who was clearly way out of his depth. He instructed him to tell Mrs Doar that she had 'forfeited all the favour of Lord and Lady Stafford' who required her to remove herself from Trentham. Items which clearly belonged to the house should be retained but such things as the wine and anything due to Mrs Doar should not be interfered with. Mrs Cleaver was to make a new inventory which should also itemise any new items needed for the household. Did Lewis think Mrs Doar's guilty activities had been only recent, or of longer standing? Were Mrs Cleaver's wages enough? After all, 'to make people honest and above suspicion they should have enough'.[23] Finally, Loch passed on Lord and Lady Stafford's commendation of Lewis's conduct.

On 1 June Mrs Doar left Trentham, but not before Lewis had ridden to see her husband, who was lodging at Whitmore, to ask him to attend at Trentham where a further examination of her rooms in the house was to take place.[24] According to Lewis, Mr Doar 'went through the unpleasantness with me and behaved with much propriety'. Items claimed by the steward were packed in separate boxes and Mrs Doar's boxes repacked. As it was a wet day Lewis himself walked to the Trentham Inn to book a room for her. On his return he made another check of the items left in her room, only to find many of them missing. Convinced that one of the servants had helped Mrs Doar to steal them in his absence, he asked Mrs Cleaver to question the girls carefully, but all declared their innocence. Then

the woman who attended the wretch, for I can call her nothing else, was also examined and we found that she had been sent out of the room at times and on her return, found the room in an intolerable stench from burning, such as hair brushes, mops or flannel. Drops of burnt glass have been found in the ashes and the nail of a new mop. Not a doubt now remains in my mind, but that the vile wretch had communicated many articles to the flames, his Lordship may here say that I ought to have taken the Boxes away out of the room, but the whole was so blended up with her own apparel that I felt a delicacy in doing so and I thought had so arranged as to prevent any of the articles being conveyed away and all would be found again, but who could have dreamt of such depravity or who could guard against such a Devil.

Loch summed up his feelings in response:

> I assure you that I have read your letter of the 2nd with the most distressing feelings possible, the disposition that could have led to the destruction of the things you mention, must have been of the worst description. I only am thankful that it has led to nothing worse or more criminal, I say so most sincerely. As to yourself I only know I should have acted entirely as you have done, no one could have expected such depravity.

Lewis also was obviously extremely upset by the whole affair but was 'willing to think that Mrs Doar has not been long in her nefarious trade, but it is hard to judge after the display I have witnessed'. His final reply to Loch on the matter was that he thought Mrs Doar's wages were too small in relation to her duties, which was the reason he supported her in the first place.[25] Nevertheless, Lewis seems to have emerged with flying colours from the affair. Both Loch and Lord and Lady Stafford were at pains to endorse his behaviour and congratulate him on his handling of the difficult circumstances. The situation must have been way out of his experience.

A number of questions arise. Were Lewis's feelings correct about Mrs Doar's wages? How did they compare either to other Sutherland housekeepers' wages or to those of housekeepers elsewhere? Why did they employ a married housekeeper in the first place? What subsequently happened to the Doars? And what prompted Loch to say that a housekeeper having children, even to their husbands, set a bad example?

At first sight the salary structure of the Sutherlands' housekeepers seems strange, insofar as those in charge of the London houses were paid much less than those working in the country:

Housekeeper's wages in 1840

Mrs Adams (West Hill)	£31-10s
Harriet Galleazie (Stafford House)	£36-15s
Mrs Cole (Trentham)	£57-15s
Mrs Kirke (Lilleshall)	£63

For Mrs Cleaver, the move from West Hill to Trentham entailed a considerable rise in wages. In addition, board wages, paid in the absence of the family, accumulated to a much larger sum in the country than the town. There is logic here, however: the housekeepers were paid by responsibility, which was considerably greater in those houses where the family were absent longer. When the family was present, decision-making and staff control were shared with the family as well as other servants such as house stewards, butlers or secretaries who travelled around the country with the family. So at this date and at this level of society, a housekeeper's role was considerably curtailed in the presence of the family, and by comparison the position of housekeeper in the country was one of a good deal of trust.

According to the Trentham accounts, in 1826 Mrs Doar's annual wages and board wages amounted to £62 14s, compared to 24gns as recommended for a country gentleman's establishment in 1825 by a popular household manual (the last figure did not include board wages).[26] Mrs Cleaver, her replacement in mid-1832, was paid almost £88 p.a.[27] Yet it must be remembered that the Sutherlands were much higher up the social scale than a mere gentleman, so the housekeeper's responsibilities would have been that much greater. Mrs Doar's half-year's remuneration up until the end of May 1832 was £47 2s 4d (this included six months' salary, board wages and sundry small payments), an amount which might have included some extra severance pay, though nothing was ever put down in writing. All in all, as housekeepers go, the Sutherlands' were not doing too badly.

Employing a married housekeeper at this level of society was extremely unusual. As Lewis pointed out, 'it is attended with many bad consequences', mainly arising from the fact that housekeepers had to live in their workplace and be on call twenty-four hours a day.[28] Their responsibilities were such that employers expected total loyalty – they became in effect part of the family for the term of their employment. Why the Sutherland family employed a married housekeeper is a puzzle; they were surely in a position to take their pick of London applicants. This is especially strange since at the time of the marriage in 1818 Mark Doar was only a footman, and according to servant tradition any male servant in livery was not allowed to marry, presumably on the basis that their salary was insufficient to support a family.

Another question is why Mrs Doar's pregnancy caused such a problem for her employers, as she had already gone through one such occasion before, in 1820. Presumably this was considered acceptable then as she was only a casual employee who must have been living at home with her husband in London.

An obvious though unrecorded problem was that Mrs Doar was encumbered rather than helped by her husband – she was in fact the family breadwinner. There are several references in the correspondence to his debts, a result presumably of his unemployment. But maybe the problem went deeper than this, for there is a record, dated 20 January 1830, of a baptism of an illegitimate child, Eliza Doar, whose mother was stated as Elizabeth Hayward (a servant), and father one Mark Doar, born in a London workhouse infirmary. Had Dorothy's husband, left alone in London, been playing around? Was Dorothy Doar's absence from Trentham in 1830 the result of her having to return to London to try to sort this crisis out?

There was also a third person in this family, the daughter Emma. In 1832 Emma would have been aged twelve; according to Dorothy's letter to Loch she was paying for her education, presumably in a board school somewhere, likely to have been at Hanford, just a few miles north of Trentham, in an establishment run by a Miss Wilmshurst, mentioned in Kirkby's letter as one of the places Dorothy was sending packages to and where she had arranged lodgings for herself.[29] Another place to which she was sending parcels was Whitmore, where, according to Lewis, her husband was lodging.

What happened to the Doars after 1832? At one point in the correspondence there is a reference to her 'friends in the North', and there is a burial record for a Dorothy Doar of the right age, dated September 1832 from Long Benton, Northumberland (she left Trentham in June 1832). Moreover, nine years later in the 1841 census, an Emma Doar, aged twenty, unmarried, was lodging in the same area with a couple called George and Elizabeth Steel – he was a colliery agent, well enough paid to be able to keep also a young girl servant. Ten years later Emma was still there but the wife Elizabeth had died, and Emma was described as niece and 'house servant'. In effect Emma was the widower's housekeeper. The family relationship is clarified by the record in 1824 of the marriage between George Steel and Elizabeth, whose maiden name was Parker, the same as Dorothy's. So Dorothy's daughter at least found a home of sorts as kin servant to her aunt and uncle; she died in Long Benton in 1858, aged thirty-eight, almost the same age as her mother.

There are two ways of interpreting this story. Mrs Doar was a servant with an unblemished record for hard work and loyalty who must have felt she had reached the pinnacle of female achievement in domestic service, but all her plans started to unravel after her miscarriage. Perhaps post-natal depression or other similar illness, then of course unrecognised, combined with family pressures – what seems to have been a useless and unfaithful husband, a child to support, a living to earn, a home to find. On the other hand, there is a touch of vindictiveness about her burning of the cleaning materials, at least an act of act of desperation, trying to remove the evidence of her thieving which began before her miscarriage with the theft of the sweet wine.

After her terrible time at Trentham, Mrs Doar must have taken her young daughter Emma on the week-long, bone-rattling journey over the Pennines from Staffordshire to Northumberland to seek refuge with her younger sister. The experience must have been the final nightmare precipitating her end a few weeks later.

As for her husband Mark, he at some point went back to London, where there is a record of his death in 1845 in Westminster.

To a modern reader many of the issues raised by this story are familiar. Mrs Doar was caught in the classic balancing act between work and family which is the experience of so many wives today. But in the 1830s she received a woman's wage, by common acceptance then up to a half of the amount for a male servant of equivalent responsibility. Despite this, she was the sole breadwinner in her family and with all the responsibilities attached to that role. She fell victim to the fact that society was not then ready to acknowledge, let alone deal with, the problems of the working wives of this world. Yet stories like hers must have been far from unusual at the time.

The Girls

Clearly a major concern about the affair of Mrs Doar was its effect on the rest of the female servant household. Country houses had long-standing and well-recognised problems with unlooked-for pregnancy – not surprising when large numbers of young unmarried women were sharing a household with men who were themselves usually young and single. One solution was of course to separate living accommodation. Traditionally female servants had their own bedrooms in the attics, well away from the male quarters which might be in a basement or separate block. Whole areas of the house and even staircases were thus genderised. In 1831 Loch was made aware of Lady Gower's desire to have a separate entrance at Lilleshall for the female servants, primarily for 'the morality and convenience of the Laundry Maids – who undoubtedly would not gain any thing from communication with my stable servants'.[30]

The house steward but more especially the housekeeper was responsible for the supervision of this system and for setting an example in their behaviour. Not only had a housekeeper to be of impeccable reputation, but under the terms of her job she had to put the convenience of her employers before herself or her family. A housekeeper who was morally lax could result in a host of social issues – the sudden departure of staff, highly charged emotional scenes, people driven to dishonesty, to say nothing of the ruined lives of young women and the possibility of babies deliberately smothered at birth.

It is impossible to give a general idea how common was the problem of servant girls becoming pregnant, as so many instances were probably hushed up. In the early 1840s, however, Walker, the new house steward, must have wondered what sort of household he had entered for there seemed to be a spate of problematic events. It is interesting to see that it is the Duke rather than his Duchess who dealt with them. His solution, standard at the time, was simple and straightforward.

The first involved one of the Attwoods' girls. She was one of three children of old George Attwood, a man who had served the family at Trentham for many years. The Attwoods probably thought themselves lucky in 1841, for all three of them were working in the very grand Stafford House. The wages book for that year show that one of the three children, the son George Attwood, aged twenty, born at Trentham, was the house porter-cum-second underbutler, earning between £23 to £25 a year plus food and board. Mary was second laundry maid, earning 16 guineas, and Ann was the fourth laundry maid, earning 10 guineas.[31] Mary had left by 1842, and George and Ann both left in 1843 during a stay at Trentham. A letter dated 1843 from the Duke at Trentham to Loch in London was about one of these departures:

> Here is Walker – to tell me that Anne Attwood in the Laundry gave warning lately and that it was said she was with child by William Aston the good [?] looking Porter – Walker sent for him and he does not deny it – does not mean to marry her. She is going to her Mother's and I have told Walker to give him warning – they will be no loss ... Walker is much concerned that such things should happen – especially considering the good example which he thinks that both Mrs Marsh and himself give.[32]

Another instance of sexual overfamiliarity in 1842 involved an expensive French chef and his second kitchen maid, Anne Tomlinson. It was described graphically in a letter from the Duke to Loch and was especially vexatious to them because it resulted in the loss of a talented cook (the wages book lists him as Louis Auvory salary £136 10s). It also reveals that at this time the sleeping quarters of the kitchen maids were not far removed from those of the male cook, which was perhaps asking for trouble even though the girl in question, Anne Tomlinson, shared a bedroom with another kitchen maid.

The Cook and the Kitchenmaid
6 March 1842, Duke of Sutherland at Trentham to James Loch in London:

Walker will write to you about a domestic occurrence which is vexatious – he reported to me this ... that the upholsterer Thomson had informed him last night that on Friday he saw the Cook and Anne Tomlinson, kitchenmaid, improperly connected in the cook's bedroom, that Thomson was ready to swear to it, that he had seen the Cook who hotly denied it – at his desire I have seen Thomson – his room is near the Confectionary – he saw ... in the passage under the wing a female take off her shoes and walk on, he lost sight of her at turning the corner from the passage – but heard the Cook's door lock – his suspicion and curiosity urged him to go through the confectionary door and look in at the Cook's window, the shutter of which when closed leaves about a foot free from the top and standing on a ledge one can see in – she was then sitting on his lap, he thinks the noise of his step was heard and he went away for 4 or 5 minutes and returned and saw them on the bed together – he says he was disgusted and went. He has since asked the carpenter whose workshop is next but one to the Cook's and whose door must be passed in going to it if he had seen anything to occasion any suspicion about his conduct and the Carpenter said and has since said to me he had observed A T several times pass his workroom the door of which opens to the passage and that he had seen her go into the Cook's room and from the noise of the steps ... he thinks she took off her shoes and that the room in which she and another kitchenmaid sleep is beyond the Cook's so that she proceeds to her own afterwards. This has happened at different times in the last fortnight.

I told Walker that he might tell the Cook that he had been reported to me and that I did not wish to interrogate him but was ready to see him if he wished – he came and denied the charge- and said that she had come to his room to show him a French grammar as they were all learning French for the Bill of Fare and repeated the verb '*je suis*', that the door was open all the time and that nothing wrong had passed.

We purpose to send A. Tomlinson to her mother – the Cook will be a loss professionally – but must go too ... I write to the Mother today and send her by coach tomorrow.

7 March, 1842. Duke to Loch:
Poor Ann Toml. has been sent to her mother with Mrs Marsh. She protests that she is not guilty and is very unhappy. Dauvray also protested yesterday. Today he has written to me that the

dismissal of the kitchenmaid proves that he is condemned – that it will be useless now to protest …

I have answered Dauvray that I must accept her dismissal, that the circumstances allowed me no alternative, that we had been always perfectly satisfied with his services, with his talent and disposition to suit our tastes and wishes. It was best that he should thus go of his own movement without waiting for my writing or announcing it to him.

Even though Anne Tomlinson was not pregnant, the punishment was never in any doubt – both parties had to go. Both protested they were not guilty of doing anything wrong and both were very unhappy at how they were treated. As was usual in such cases, the housekeeper Mrs Marsh, also relatively new in post, accompanied Anne home to her parents in Shropshire. Auvory the chef asked for an interview with the Duke, which was granted, and he also wrote a letter protesting that the sending away of the girl proved that he was condemned already and it would therefore be useless to claim his innocence. The Duke replied that the circumstances allowed him no alternative, and that it would be best if Auvory went of his own accord rather than be formally dismissed. The family had been perfectly satisfied with his services, which suited their tastes and wishes, but neither party was given a reference. This would have affected the chef much less than the girl. He was still highly employable in London society whilst she was taken home to her mother in disgrace. Even the Duke seemed to have felt some sympathy for 'poor Anne Tomlinson'.[33]

The Tomlinson family's trials were not over, however. Three years later, Anne's sister Sarah, a nursemaid with the Sutherlands, got into trouble with William Wykes, footman to the Duke's daughter. The Duke and Duchess had gone to Castle Howard in Yorkshire, leaving the rest of their family and household behind at Lilleshall. Sarah was in the habit of going into Donnington to see some friends, and William would go to meet her on her way back. On one occasion William also met with some friends who gave him drink, 'in consequence of that I very wrongly had connection with that girl on our return'. A couple of months later it transpired Sarah was pregnant. William immediately proposed marriage. As was the accepted rule for footmen he asked the Duchess for permission to do this, through the Duchess's maid, Mrs Penson (according to tradition, menservants in livery were not supposed to marry without permission). The reason for the haste was not explained. All was agreed and the couple were married in London in 1845. Sarah, of course, had to leave her employment on marriage.[34] Unfortunately the Duchess happened to hear of Sarah's confinement later in November and immediately dismissed William. He felt this was very severe, given his record of nine year's exemplary service with the family and the fact that the marriage had taken place a good seven months before the birth of the baby. William wrote to Loch to ask him if he could help; no reply has survived but the wages book records a new lady's footman being set on in June the following year, so presumably William had to leave.[35]

It might be thought that the Duchess was following a hard line in this case, but a telling point would have been the fact that William was personal footman to the Duke's daughter and that Sarah herself was one of the children's nursemaids. Both therefore had especially close contact with the younger, impressionable members of the family. By modern standards regulations about relations between men and women and the degree to which they were implemented seem strict. Yet research work on illegitimate births amongst Welsh servants in the nineteenth century – corroborated by case after case reported in newspapers of the period – show how devastating the result of unwanted and hidden pregnancies could be in the world of service.[36]

Twenty years after the Sarah Tomlinson case in 1862 a more difficult case was landed on the desk of Henry Wright, the Duke's secretary, for this was an instance of a homosexual relationship. Only one letter regarding this has survived, written to the Duke by Henry Wright, showing that the household was anxious to keep the situation as private as possible, for such a relationship was illegal. (The law relating to homosexuality had in fact been recently reviewed under the Offences against the Person Act 1861, which recriminalized it.) It must have been an unnerving task for Henry Wright, who was newly in post when the Duke asked him to examine a stableman's sheets.[37]

The Stableman and the Footman
5 February, 1862.
Henry Wright (personal secretary) to Duke of Sutherland:

My Lord,

I find I can only obtain the evidence of one more witness related to the affair of the Stableman and the Footman at Trentham.

The man who was in bed at the time of their coming upstairs has left before I had the opportunity of seeing him.

The other witness who came into the room and struck a light was Thomas York, Helper in the Stables. He says he went up to bed about 11.30 and struck a light when his attention was called by the man in bed to something going on in another bed.

On pulling aside the curtain they found the two men together – the Footman had on his waistcoat, shirt and cravat and stockings. When asked what he was doing there he said he was going away directly. He then got out of bed, put on his breeches and coat and left the room.

The man left in bed <u>would not allow the sheets to be examined that night</u>. The sheets were examined in the morning and found in a horrible mess <u>but dry</u>.

I think, my Lord, the Footman might have the benefit of the doubt, as the 'mess' might have been produced after he quitted the scene.

Yours most obedient sert.

Henry Wright.

7

The Incomer

'You never did know me – but half' – The House Steward

Most of the servants mentioned so far have arrived at Trentham and the other houses with fairly conventional English or Scottish backgrounds, often from families with a long history of service behind them. Yet there was another fashionable type of employee favoured by the Sutherlands, the exotic stranger from abroad. Vantini was very much of this tradition, but for whatever reasons – perhaps extravagant mannerisms and language difficulties – he found problems 'fitting in'. His origins lay in a world which had disappeared spectacularly, yet his arrival within a month or so after the death of the 1st Duke places him at the beginning of a new era for the Sutherlands, with their new aristocratic title, a brand-new London house, several newly refurbished country houses and new expectations all round. In a wider context, it was a world which was rapidly changing its technologies and embracing its new industrial potential.

As the house steward to a rich and sophisticated family Vantini was the head of their domestic household, wherever that might be. This involved the recruitment, training, discipline and supervision of all household servants. Through a staff of upholsterers, groom of the chambers, footmen, housekeepers, housemaids, chefs, kitchen maids, butlers, stable grooms and coachmen he was responsible for all the family's house interiors, their furniture, furnishings and maintenance, for the overall purchasing of goods and the financial records of the household, for the day-to-day servicing of family needs and family spending, and for the organisation of special events such as balls or receptions – whether they be at Trentham or London. An important part of his job was arranging family travel: buying carriage and riding horses, booking post horses, travel accommodation and shipping.

The Italian Zenon Vantini began his employment as house steward with the Leveson-Gowers in late summer of 1833. Vantini was then aged thirty-six and his wife Jeanette had recently given birth to twin girls. It was an eventful year: in January the seventy-five-year-old 2nd Marquess of Stafford was made Duke of Sutherland, only to die in July of the same year after catching a chill at Dunrobin. Also in July, Vantini's employer, George James Agar-Ellis, Lord Dover, died unexpectedly, in his thirties, probably following rheumatic fever. The widowed Lady Dover (*née* Lady Georgiana Howard) wished to reduce her household, so Vantini had to look around for other employment.

It was very close at hand, for Lady Dover was the sister of the wife (*née* Lady Harriet Howard) of the 1st Duke's eldest son, who on the death of his father became the 2nd Duke of Sutherland. In addition, Stafford House being without its own stables and laundry, the Duke rented suitable premises nearby, which happened to belong to Lord Dover. So by the early autumn of 1833, Vantini had become steward to the new household of the 2nd Duke and Duchess of Sutherland and was receiving his first instructions from James Loch. At this point it seems Vantini had built up a considerable expertise and reputation with the Dovers. It was this status and the close connection between the Howard sisters which made him an attractive employment proposition to the Sutherlands.

Presumably one of the attractions of a steward born on the Continent, apart from sheer status, was a fluency in both French and Italian languages and custom, with an ability to cope with the complexities of prolonged stays in Europe, which trips the family enjoyed in the 1830s. During the 1838–9 trip abroad, for example, Vantini was paying out bills of 2,000 to 3,000 francs each time, twice a month, far more than the Duke's secretary. Vantini's abstract accounts for that year listed his outgoings in a bewildering range of currencies, each of which he translated into English currency:

| The Roman States | paoli |
| Tuscany | francs |

Rome	scudi
Naples	ducati
Austrian Estates	paoli
Bavaria	zwanzigers
The Rhine	florins
Prussian States	dollars
France & Netherlands	francs [1]

The timing of Vantini's employment with the Sutherlands did not make for an easy beginning. Shortly after the death of the 1st Duke, Loch wrote to Lewis at Trentham warning him:

> It now becomes necessary to do what I have often hinted would be required upon a new successor to review the whole of the establishment at Trentham with the view of seeing what portion of the outlay which would be maintained and what portion of it should be diminished.[2]

There immediately followed a flurry of letters from Loch to Vantini asking for detailed records of household expenditure during the periods of the two previous stewards and an estimate of the staff which would be needed in future.[3] Vantini's calculations were to be made on the basis of the family being in London seven months and in the country five months:

> I should like to have a list of the Establishment such as you think it will eventually be, including Grooms of Chambers, Confectioner etc – and a guess for it can be no more, of what you think His Grace's monthly expenses will be under the various heads of Butcher, Baker, Brewer etc.
> You need not include those servants who are constantly resident at Trentham and Lilleshall but calculate the expense of living there as included in the annual sum. I am aware as I have already said that you can only give a guess as yet, but I should like to see your notions of what it might be.

Loch was concerned at the lack of records of household income. There was no value put upon supplies to the family or servants from the farm, garden, deer park, poultry yard and dairy at

Trentham. Vantini was to rectify this, making sure that the fruit and vegetables be brought up from the garden to the house each day by the same man, so that an accurate record could be supplied to Vantini who was to include it in his monthly report. He was to include even those vegetables allowed to various employees living on the estate. The gardener Woolley would not like this but Vantini was to make it clear this was not a comment on his honesty but a means of putting the household on a firm footing. Not even the deer in the park were safe from Loch – were they a saving in terms of food?

Plunged straight into a detailed review of the expenditure of a household about which he knew nothing, Vantini saw difficulties right from the start. This was how he began a letter to Loch later in 1836 in reply to a series of complaints then made against him:

> The first day I enter, I saw the difficulty I had to encounter. But I said what have I to fear, I understand the service better than any of them, I shall do them justice, I shall consider the best way of making economy in the Establishment without depriving them of their comfort, and soon their prejudices will be over.[4]

In the same letter, Vantini went on to deal with each subsequent complaint, which he was sure did not originate with either the Duke and Duchess or Loch, who had shown him nothing but kindness, but someone else amongst the servants:

- He had set on too many extra servants: he had set on only two extra, one a second steward's room boy to give a proper service to the senior staff at Stafford House; the other was a third coachman at the specific instruction of their Graces.
- The other servants could not understand him and he was too lenient towards them: this was not now the case – they could understand him. Perhaps he was too good towards them, but 'I think that a man is more brought to his duty more by kindness then by rigueur.'
- His accounting system was difficult to understand: he used the same system he had used with Lord and Lady Dover and they understood it without difficulty. He had shown his system to

both his Grace and Mr Loch separately when he had started work and they had all understood it.

- He bought in supplies in too great bulk, a system which would be wasteful: this was cheaper and would not be wasteful because he issued all stores himself. He was then told he must weigh out each supply himself and enter it in a book. This seemed to him to be a ridiculous waste of his time, and in fact Mr Loch later said he need not do this.
- The family trip to Paris had been too expensive and especially there was too lavish consumption of lamp oil in Paris: the family's journey and stay cost only £5,665 and the rest of the total cost of £9,867 was spent on purchases ordered by the young ladies and their Graces.
- He had overcharged on the servants' allowances at Trentham: he had checked and there was nothing of any consequence overcharged.
- Finally, he found it difficult to manage people older than himself: 'I care little of what age are the persons put under me.'

No doubt many of these problems were the result of difficulty with language, culture and character. Vantini never lost his heavy Continental accent, especially when excited, and his spelling, grammar and his small handwriting must not have helped. Though some of the senior staff at Stafford House were themselves of Continental origin, used to sophisticated international ways of arranging things, many were younger men and women recruited from the English countryside in Staffordshire and Shropshire.

The accounting problem was more fundamental, however, and proved a long-standing point of argument, especially between Vantini and the Duke's private secretary, Jackson. The latter was a powerful if discreet figure in the household at Stafford House, trusted by both the Duke and Loch. It was perhaps almost inevitable that a clash of personalities should develop. Vantini's letters were very different in style from the careful, measured tones of the secretary, and no doubt he was a bit of a fiery character, difficult to manage. Jackson complained that Vantini was 'impossible to reason with'. As early as April 1834, the house steward became involved in a public dispute at Lilleshall with a member of the estate staff, apparently about whether Vantini was allowed to ride one of the family horses. The Duke heard of it and had to refer the matter to his man of affairs, Loch: 'There has been,' he wrote, 'a breaking out on the part of Browne against Vantini and an inquiry will be necessary, as the insult was at supper and in public.' In this instance Vantini was in the right for he had been given permission by the Duke to use the horse whilst at Lilleshall, where he would be without the twelve-year old bay horse called Wallace, one of the fifty-three horses kept in London, and the one allocated to Vantini.[5]

Not all Vantini's relationships were stressed. Both the Trentham agent, William Lewis, and the clerk, William Henney, seem to have developed a good working relationship with him. Lewis offered him every sort of help whenever he came up to Trentham, and in fact Vantini acted as a sort of liaison officer between town and country, so that when he was due to travel to Trentham Lewis asked him to look in on his son in London before setting off so he could report back to him; and Henney made a point of thanking Vantini for the trouble he had taken over his wife's mother. Moreover, Vantini had complex social and financial connections with individuals and servants of other families, some of them immigrant. There is, for example, a letter in Italian from someone who appears to be lady's maid to Lady Howard de Walden, then living in Portugal; Vantini was running financial errands in London for her, receiving thanks from her for his kindness as well as a somewhat obscure assurance that 'you could count on me in adverse circumstances'.[6]

Problems with the household accounts continued. Those for 1836 were so confusing that Loch could not understand them. A major difficulty appears to have been caused by mixing two different accounting systems – one based on receipts and payments, the other on income and expenditure.[7] Loch's cashier tried to resolve the matter, with the result that there was a gentlemanly reconciliation between Vantini and Jackson, much to Loch's satisfaction. As a result of an approach by Vantini, reported Jackson, they had arrived at 'a perfect understanding' with 'all bitter feeling removed'.[8]

It was, however, a short-lived truce in the war. In 1838 Jackson commented that expenditure of the home farm at West Hill was extravagant and wasteful. Keeping sheep was not profitable even when the family were around to eat them, which they often were not; it would be better to let the land for stock grazing.[9] Vantini's name was not mentioned in this letter but later correspondence makes it clear that he had heavily involved himself in the running of the farm in order to make it a supplier of food for the household, even to the point of taking the poultry yard under his personal direction and hiring extra labour and draft horses for the harvest.

The amount of oats consumed by horses became a bizarre point of argument, Vantini complaining that the person who said they ate too much (i.e. Jackson) knew nothing about horses, and he asked Loch to put the issue to an independent expert. Loch being Loch, he took him at his word and asked the advice of officers of the Household Cavalry. Their answer supported Jackson rather more than Vantini, who responded, probably fairly, that army horses on ordinary duty would require a third less than working horses, especially coach horses; a fairer comparison would be with other landed estates.[10] His project of making the home farm a substantial producer of food was not deemed viable, however, and during an absence in Paris with the family, Loch quietly relieved him of that responsibility.

Late in 1838 the family and entourage set off on a major tour of France and Italy. Goodness knows what the atmosphere between Jackson and Vantini was like. In his previous letter Vantini had suggested that he cancel his own attendance on the tour in order to have time with Loch at home to answer the charges made against him, even though this meant missing a visit to his homeland. The Duke and Duchess, however, felt they could not manage without him so the two combatants, steward and secretary, were in close proximity throughout the trip. Whilst they were away Loch received letters from both of them complaining about the extravagance of the one and the deviousness of the other.[11] Whilst in Rome Jackson had even spoken to the Duke about the bills coming in from Vantini – besides the usual English servants they had employed sixteen extra Italians and hired ten horses. Jackson had told Vantini he had spoken to the Duke, but 'it is worse than useless to discuss these matters to him and besides the money was spent before anything could be known about it'.

On his return from the Continent, Vantini was dispatched out of the way up to Trentham to report back on the progress of Barry's rebuilding project. It is clear from a promise made by Loch to

Vantini that he need have nothing further to do with Jackson now that the row was becoming increasingly open.

Several of Vantini's account books have survived, and certainly his accounts for Trentham for 1838–39 seem incomplete, muddled and deteriorating in quality, though some of this may have been due to the retirement of Martha Cleaver, the Trentham housekeeper, which meant that Mrs Kirke, the Lilleshall housekeeper, took over the job of keeping the Trentham accounts alongside her own.[12] Vantini also cut administrative corners, for example ordering stable supplies direct from the producer – usually a tenant farmer – not through the office.[13]

Things came to a head in early 1840 when a major disagreement arose between Vantini and Jackson, with the result that Loch could not sign off Vantini's accounts for 1839.[14] The point at issue was the discrepancy between Vantini's version of the accounts, which he said would be not more than £28,000, later modified to £32,000, and Jackson's reckoning that they would amount to not less than £40,000. This represented a huge increase from the beginning of the years of Vantini's tenure, for in 1834 the equivalent sum had been £22,000. Loch asked his accountancy staff to compare year with year. They brought to light incomprehensible minor mysteries, such as why there had been a huge increase in the use of gas lighting at Stafford House between 1837 and 1838 and why the new cook had spent £400 on coppers in the kitchen. Vantini's explanation of the general increase in expenditure was that during these years the family did not stay regularly in England but spent months abroad each year; the only year in which they had stayed in England they spent most of the time in London rather than Trentham. This unsettled existence was much more expensive than if they had followed the usual seasonal routine of seven months in London and five months in the country. Jackson went through the bills and was scathing in his response.

By now the servant household was becoming openly divided. On Jackson's side there was Mrs Galleazie, the Stafford House housekeeper who gave Jackson the keys to the wine cellars, normally sacrosanct to the house steward; and George Woodhouse, the groom of the chambers whom Vantini accused of making up stories about him in the local pub. On Vantini's side was the chef Napolion Biney, the upholsterer George London and the confectioner John Cranham – noticeably all high-status positions requiring the consumption of expensive goods. There is certainly a touch of paranoia about parts of Vantini's later letters as these individuals became embroiled in argument.

Jackson's charge was of extravagance and incompetence rather than criminality, at least as far as the record survives. Vantini was obviously extremely upset, as can be seen in one of his letters in March 1840. This began normally enough – using formal language and spelling with good handwriting – saying he was sorry that business had prevented Mr Loch from seeing him yesterday when he called by appointment (Loch was probably avoiding him). Vantini's feelings quickly got the better of him and the letter deteriorated into a misspelt, shakily written and emotional outburst:

> Vantini humbly remembering to Mr Loch that he has <u>Naver</u> been find faulty – thow severall times the aptent as been made to find him so. Of this Vantini is proud – and it is a marit that no bady will be able to take way from him as it will go to his Grave.

The letter finishes abruptly – no 'humble servant', no 'yours most obedient'.

The row rumbled on, one focus of the investigation still being the supply of fodder to horses; this time it was hay at the Trentham stables. As late as July 1840, after Vantini had left, a clerk in Loch's office wrote to him asking for details of his financial breakdown of the expenditure on horses over several years. Vantini's response was dismissive: 'The only thing I shall say it is that every thing has been done with <u>intelligence</u> and <u>integrity</u> and as I am much engaged with things of more consequence I decline to do such thing.'[15]

Ironically, later that year, in December, Loch's own assiduousness and sense of fair play led him to contact Lewis about a paper that he had found, which 'led Mr Jackson when arranging Mr Vantini's accounts ... into the mistake that produced all the disagreables that occurred in respect to them and of which you were partly a witness'. A mistake had been made in the stables cash book, which was not kept by Vantini. This implies not only that the row between Jackson and Vantini was decidedly heated and took place in front of others but also that, at least on this point, Vantini was not to blame.[16]

Reading the rambling letters which Vantini wrote to Loch, one can almost see the latter pushing them impatiently to one side. Loch was in a difficult position, partly of his own making. On the one hand, in the early years of the 2nd Duke's tenure he had repeatedly impressed on the household the necessity for economy, especially bearing in mind the loss of the Bridgewater income. On the other side, the Duke and the Duchess clearly appreciated the attention to fine detail of an international aristocratic lifestyle as provided by Vantini. The Duke and Duchess were 'inveterate shoppers' whilst on the Continent, especially for architectural items to incorporate in the décor of Stafford House.[17] It is therefore hard not to feel sorry for Vantini, caught as he was between these two conflicting imperatives.

Vantini also clearly felt ill at ease, surrounded by petty regulations and people who did not like him, people who discussed him with the Duke behind his back at Trentham as well as in Rome, thus damaging his reputation both in England and abroad, which he valued highly. He was obviously not efficient at accountancy and had problems in expressing himself fluently in what to him was a foreign language, but he never at any point blamed Loch whom he repeatedly thanked for his kindness.

Eventually he had no hesitation in asking Loch for a reference, for he had other irons in the fire. A personal note from a friend dated September 1839 refers to Vantini's 'speculation' and a 'new establishment here in London'. This proved to be the solution for everyone's embarrassment. In a letter dated November 1839, Vantini asked Loch: '[H]as Mrs Loch mentioned Euston hotel ... Mr Loch will hear with pleasure the success of that enterprise is such to gave great satisfaction to my friend and the Directors ...'[18] By July of the following year Vantini had left the Sutherlands. Duchess Harriet wrote to Ralph Sneyd at Keele: 'Vantini has left to manage a large hotel in Euston Square, we are very sorry to lose him. We have seen a great many pretenders but none I like at all, the English do appear to me very vulgar.'[19]

Unlike the Duchess, Loch must have heaved a sigh of relief at the departure of Vantini. By September 1840 Vantini was installed at the Victoria Hotel, Euston, writing to Loch to thank him for his kindness and to tell him 'what I know you will be pleased to here – we have taken also the other House from the company – and we are drawing immense business'.[20] The 'other house' was a reference to the Euston Hotel opposite the Victoria, the two hotels linked to each other by an underground passage; Vantini was involved with both. Loch replied with some advice which was answered politely but ambiguously.

Interviews took place at Stafford House over the summer, and by autumn a new steward had been appointed, Richard Walker, an Englishman who went on to serve the family for twelve years. In September 1840 Loch sent him instructions to meet Vantini in London as the latter wished to hand over to the new man in person. The two then arranged to go to Lilleshall by the overnight mail train for two days and then to Trentham to prepare for the return of the family there. Loch assured Walker he would be given every help from the existing staff. There was also a note of warning: 'I need not say that every change in such a household as the Duke's, especially of the head, will give rise to many stories and reports – I advise you to attach no credit to any, but to judge entirely for yourself from what you shall see for yourself hereafter.'[21]

Vantini's parting with the Sutherlands was not without a postscript. Early in January the following year, Vantini wrote from the Victoria Hotel to Loch saying he had changed his mind about not replying to the charges against him and was ready to prove before the Duke and Duchess 'the conduct Jackson [h]as adopted to tourment me'. He wished for a formal hearing calling as witnesses a number of servants who had left around the same time, as well as his new business partner. Loch's reply to this letter has not survived.[22]

Later Life

So, what happened to Vantini? In fact, there is a good deal more to his story, for he had at least three very distinct, extraordinary careers, only the middle one of which was as house steward to a great English aristocratic family.

The correspondence in the Sutherland papers implies that he was involved financially as well as managerially in the Euston hotels venture. This was not his only project, for early in 1840 he answered a *Times* advert placed by Peter Hesketh-Fleetwood for a proprietor of the hotel at the northern end of the same railway, the North Euston Hotel, Fleetwood. By January 1841, Vantini was established in Fleetwood and, according to the Duke of Sutherland, had taken with him some friends from the Sutherlands' – the cook, confectioner and upholsterer who wished 'to try their fortunes under him'. Walker, the new house steward with the Sutherlands, was highly indignant about this poaching of staff, but he was positive also: 'It is the means of stimulating me with double energy as I feel they are all desirous to upset the establishment as far as they can ... If I find there are any more looking to Fleetwood I will take your advice and send them off.'[23] In the census of that year Vantini was described as proprietor of the Fleetwood hotel, heading a huge list of staff, one of whom was twenty-five-year-old Napolion Biney, the Sutherlands' French chef.

Fleetwood might seem an unusual choice for such a hotel and such a man as Vantini, but the town was an extraordinary place at that time. It was a new model town, planned and developed by Peter Hesketh-Fleetwood. An important part of the plan was the building of a grand hotel, intended as a stopping point for rail and boat passengers between London and Scotland. The project was partly based on the premise that the railway would terminate south of the Cumbrian hills and Shap Fell, Fleetwood thereby becoming a major transit port. The railway from London to Fleetwood opened on 15 July 1840, building of the North Euston hotel began in 1840 and was completed in 1841.

It certainly must have been a magnificent, spacious and sophisticated hotel with all sorts of luxurious facilities.[24] Yet there were plenty of problems – not entirely of Vantini's making. There were at least three other hotels nearer to the boat dock from where the ferries to Scotland or Belfast left, and the approach road to the hotel was left unmade for several years. The hotel had been so expensive to build that prices were astronomic.

Nevertheless Vantini threw himself into the developing life and culture of the new town.[25] After a couple of years Vantini felt the Fleetwood project needed a boost to its finances, not least because the railway engineers had succeeded in conquering Shap Fell, thus enabling the railways to bypass Fleetwood entirely. The solution seems typical of Vantini's idiosyncratic thinking. In order to put Fleetwood further on the map and encourage the development of the town, what was needed was a first-rate school. This seems to have been his original idea. One of the other founders of the school, W. M. Lomas, was generous in his attribution: 'The idea had its birth in a conversation between myself and Mons Vantini, and he,

I think deserves the sole credit for inducing it to palpability and form.' On 1 July 1842 a meeting of the provisional committee of the Fleetwood Colleges Association was held at the North Euston Hotel, at which Vantini gave an address outlining his proposal to fund two colleges, each for 500 pupils, one for boys and one for girls, on opposite sides of the estuary ('for ze proprieties!' as he said), to be funded by the novel means of life insurance. In the event Vantini persuaded the Revd St Vincent Beechey, the new vicar of St Peter's, to take up the project.[26] The boys' school was reduced to 200 pupils and the proposal for a school for girls was dropped altogether, much to Vantini's chagrin (Beechey said Vantini's reaction was 'You have dropped my 500 girls in ze river!') The project was named the Northern Church of England School and survives today as the Rossall School.[27]

As a further interesting postscript to Vantini's experience with the Sutherland family, in the archive is a letter dated 1844 from the 2nd Duke to his secretary, Jackson, which included a question:

> Vantini's Education Scheme has had a wonderful degree of success as ... this Northern Church of England School is founded on his suggestion. My brother says that the B[ishop] of Chester patronizes it and has asked him to be an 'office bearer' and I believe he will be V. Pres. I wish you to consider whether I should agree to give my name in any way.[28]

Jackson's answer has not survived!

Vantini did not stay long enough to see his idea materialise. Around the time the land for the school was to be purchased, after a poor summer in the hotel trade, Vantini and his wife had done a 'moonlight flit', quietly packed their bags and departed, leaving the hotel closed and deserted.[29] It was reopened in July 1845 under new management.[30]

Neither Vantini nor Biney appear in the 1851 census, though by 1861 Biney was running another hotel in Spring Gardens, Manchester. Vantini does not appear in any English census after 1841. It is clear, however, that by 1843 many other interests occupied Vantini's energies. Though not relevant here, it is possible to follow a variety of newspaper articles and advertisements appearing over the following few years to chart the progress of his projects in some detail. Working with at least two different partnerships, Vantini established the first ever railway refreshment rooms, at Wolverton, which were visited by Queen Victoria and Prince Albert in 1843.[31] More followed at Manchester, Rugby, Leicester, Folkestone Harbour and at least two other sites. There were also major hotels in Folkestone and Paris.

Vantini's interest in hotels and railways was not limited to England. According to Loanne Vajda, his idea of guided all-in holidays in France (several years before Thomas Cook ventured abroad with his holiday packages) were part of an even grander idea on the part of Vantini, a formal pan-European railway-hotel network which 'includes the creation of transport infrastructure, accommodation facilities, meeting venues, and leisure and commercial facilities'.[32] As in Lancashire, his ideas were brought into reality by others.

Earlier life
An interesting question is where did Vantini come from? Where did he gain his experience in aristocratic household management? A family of the status of the Sutherlands took great care in appointing its senior staff, and he himself pointed to his reputation as steward since 1823. But where was his employment before the Dovers?

Of Vantini himself, there is a complete lack of information between 1815 and 1825. 1825 was the year in which he and Jeanette Peters were married in the parish of St George's, Hanover Square, Bloomsbury; their first daughter was born in 1826 in Geneva, Jeanette's home. They were back in London before 1830, for the Westminster Rate Book of that year records them living in a house at 52 Westbourne Terrace, St Marylebone, not a million miles from the London home of the Dovers, for whom he was working at that time.

As for the period before 1815, in his book on the history of the Rossall School, its founder the Revd Canon St Vincent Beechey included an intriguing piece of gossip: that Vantini had claimed he 'had been a courier to Napoleon, and was himself a Corsican'.[33]

One can see that given Vantini's character some might have taken this with a pinch of salt, but it turns out to be true – though he was probably Elban, not Corsican. French genealogical websites enable us to discover Vantini's family: his father, Vincenzo Paulo, had been mayor of Portoferraio, the main town on Elba, and a member of one of the leading families on the island. He was married to the daughter of an army lieutenant, by whom he had a daughter Henriette and at least two sons, the eldest of which was Zenon Ruffino Gio Battista, born 18 October 1797 in Portoferraio.[34]

As a boy, Zenon was listed in the 'Almanac Impérial' (the Official Directory of the French Republic) as a page in the household of Elisa, Princess of Piombino, Grande Duchess of Tuscany (Napoleon's sister, 1770–1820). Along with a number of other pages he was schooled by no less than eight tutors, in maths, history and geography, Latin and French, drawing and fortification, fencing, writing, dance, and equitation.[35] As a teenager Zenon was present at Napoleon's famous, highly emotional arrival on Elba as an exile. Zenon's father Vincenzo was amongst the nobles and officials gathered to greet him, and Zenon himself was one of the officers of Napoleon's personal guard on that occasion, dressed in a uniform of sky-blue threaded with silver.[36] Zenon was in fact an aide-de-camp, one of six young men appointed by Napoleon to accompany him around Elba, riding with him wherever he went and monitoring incoming information from the European mainland. Other members of Zenon's family were closely involved with Napoleon's occupation, and the modest Vantini house was taken over as accommodation for Napoleon's mother and sister Pauline.[37]

Vantini was also involved in the preparations for Napoleon's escape from Elba. An account of his leaving published in a British local newspaper in 1895 includes the following:

> In order to keep his preparations a profound secret, Napoleon, two days before embarking, laid an embargo on all vessels in the harbours of Elba, and cut off all communications with the sea. He then ordered his ordnance officer, Vantini, to seize one of the large vessels lying in the port, and by this, with the Inconstant of twenty-six cannon and six other smaller craft, making in all seven vessels, he secured the means of embarking his 1,100 men and four pieces of field artillery.[38]

According to a memoir of the captain of the port on Elba, Zenon Vantini not only accompanied Napoleon to France as part of a group of Elbans but was also present at the Battle of Waterloo, but almost certainly did not fight.[39] Where Vantini went subsequently is unclear, though it was certainly not to St Helena.[40] In his will written on St Helena Napoleon made many bequests to those who remained loyal to his service, and one codicil instructed his executors to make payments to those members of his staff on Elba who were still alive, one of whom was Vantini. Most of the bequests were not actually made because of long-standing disputes over Napoleon's will.[41]

Vantini's family

What of Vantini's wife and family? After the first child, Cornelie, was born in 1826 in Geneva he and Jeanette had five more girls, including a pair of twins, all of whom were born in London. None of them were born during the period when Vantini worked for the Sutherlands, when he must have been away from home for long periods.

His family was not with Vantini during the 1841 census in Fleetwood. His wife, helped by the fifteen-year-old Cornelie, was running the Victoria Hotel, Euston. At that point their other children, Mathilda, aged ten, and twins Josephine and Frederica, aged eight, were residents in a music school in Church Street, Hampton, London. Despite periods of separation due to work, his family seem to have been a great practical support to him, and throughout his career Madam Vantini was recorded as being present at official events. According to Canon Beechey she was 'an excellent woman', a Lutheran who became a constant attendant at the local church in Fleetwood. Vantini by contrast was only a nominal Roman Catholic.

In 1843 Cornelie was married at Willesden to Alfred Denny Blott, the clerk-in-charge of the new railway station at Wolverton, where Vantini opened his first railway refreshment room. By 1851 Blott had become the station master at Wolverton, but later that year he was moved to the Rewley Road, Oxford station – not as a promotion but almost certainly as a punishment because he had left his wife and eloped with a young woman. He returned to Cornelie, however, and the family settled in Oxford; by 1861 he had left the railway and was working as the Deputy Steward of Christ Church, Oxford. They had five children.[42]

We can trace another of Vantini's daughters, Josephine Marian. She never married but seems to have inherited a little of her father's entrepreneurial spirit. She went into partnership with an older woman to found the Newlands School for Ladies in Sherborne, Dorset. This occupied what was then known as Newland House, now called the Manor House and currently the home of Sherborne Town Council. By 1867 the partnership was dissolved and Josephine became sole proprietor and head teacher. Like her father before her she threw herself into the local social scene, providing a supper for the choristers of Sherborne Abbey after a charity concert in aid of a local hospital and becoming a member of the archery club as well as secretary of the Cambridge local examination board. She left both school and town around 1880–81, the whole contents of the school being sold by auction in August of that year.[43]

By that time both her father and mother were dead. Zenon Vantini died in Paris in 1870, after a long illness, aged seventy-three. His widow Jeanette died in Geneva in 1877, also aged seventy-three.

Legacy

Zenon Vantini is an interesting example of how an individual can reinvent himself several times but still retain his basic character. Looking at his life as a whole one can see continuing threads running through it – his energy and original thinking, a willingness to take a risk, to keep trying in adversity, to use charm and humour to persuade people to back him. Although he also appears to be an opportunist, as well as a bit of a buffoon, Loch must have had some respect for him. Loch was not faint of heart at finding ways of getting rid of people if he thought them unworthy of employment or tenancy, and he was obviously reluctant to do this to Vantini, probably simply hoping he would go away of his own accord. He seems to have earned at least some degree of Napoleon's trust and Canon Beechey thought him spirited, humorous, shrewd and clever.[44] Most of his ideas were both imaginative and realistic (albeit not realized by him) and his appreciation of the revolutionary effect that railways would have on trade and tourism was serious and long term, born from his own experience. Though he knew when to walk away from a sinking ship, his determination to keep trying seems endless. Is it fanciful to imagine he took the example from Napoleon that one needed to make one's own luck? We do not know what happened to Vantini in the ten years after Waterloo (he probably went into the new French army) but whatever it was it cannot have been easy.

To what extent did his employment with the Sutherlands direct his interest in railways? Vantini, of course, had years of experience in relation to horse-drawn travel, since part of his job with the Sutherlands was to arrange accommodation and food at the various posting inns. It may well go deeper, however. At one point the Marquess of Stafford had been the largest single holder of railway shares in England, to the extent that the Sutherlands can be said to have played a formative influence on railway development. Throughout the 1830s and early '40s the dilemmas posed by the family's support of the new form of heavy transport, which was then in competition with existing canal networks, was an important issue entangling the family finances.[45] Did this also play some part in forming Vantini's imaginative vision of European railways, which to some people would have appeared ridiculous.

It is also interesting to speculate to what extent the Sutherlands knew of Vantini's origins, for the family archives make not a single reference to it. Judging by her comment about the vulgarity of English house stewards, the Duchess at least was attracted by Vantini's appearance and manner – his exotic past perhaps also would have been a grand talking point around the dining table. Did the Sutherlands know of his connections to Napoleon? At first sight it might seem they did. It seems unlikely that the issue did not crop up at least during their stays in Paris and their trip to Versailles. We should also remember that the 2nd Marquess (later the 1st Duke) had been the English ambassador in Paris at the outbreak of the French revolution and thus presumably had many French contacts.

Attitudes towards Napoleon in Britain after Waterloo were complex, but generally speaking the radical end of the political spectrum was sympathetic to his plight, and indeed had long been so. According to Stuart Semmel, Napoleon on St Helena became something of a cult object, transcending the 'mundanely political' to become a 'moral, tragic and aesthetic figure'. Objects associated with Napoleon became sought after and as early as 1816 his carriage, horses and wardrobe were made into a public exhibition complete with his Dutch coachman.[46] For a family with Whig

Above: 1. Lilleshall Old Hall, Lilleshall, now the centre of a sheltered housing site. The older part of the building, where Mrs Tungate was accommodated, is to the left. In 1817 the Old Hall was the subject of a letter from Harriet, Countess Granville, to her sister: 'I am delighted with this place and could pass months here with the greatest delight. The house is an enlarged farm with substantial airy rooms, large beds, and a commanding view ... ' (Leveson Gower, F., ed., *Letters of Harriet Countess Granville, 1810–1845* (London, 1894) vol. 1 p. 128.)

Below: 2. Lilleshall Hall, Shropshire, built in 1829–31, by Jeffry Wyattville.

3. Dunrobin Castle, Golspie, Sutherland, Scotland, refurbished by Sir Charles Barry in the mid-nineteenth century.

4. Trentham Hall, Staffordshire, in the mid-nineteenth century, after the rebuilding by Sir Charles Barry.

5. Stafford House, St James's, London, built by Benjamin Dean Wyatt, Sir Robert Smirke and Sir Charles Barry, 1827 to 1840.

6. View across the front of Trentham Hall, looking towards the west, and taken after the gardens were opened to the public in 1906.

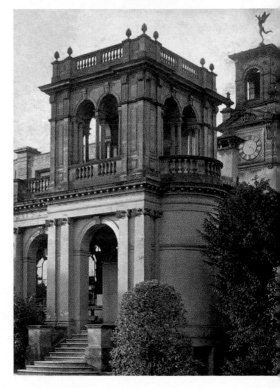

7. The south-east corner of the orangery which backs onto the service yard. These buildings survive but are now in a poor state, awaiting restoration. The service yard is behind, marked by Barry's distinctive clock tower, the time-keeper for servants and estate workers.

8. A view of the front terrace of Trentham, demolished in 1911, showing how elegant and finely finished the hall must have been.

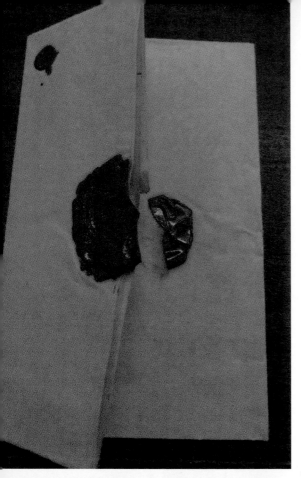

9. Letter from John Mackay to James Loch (see chapter 11), showing the damage inflicted by a wax seal before the new postal system was introduced in 1840.

Above: 10. The clock tower from inside the service yard, photographed in 2016.

Below Left: 11. Row of four thatched cottages in Ash Green, built Trentham employees. Both ends had two bedrooms, the middle cottages had one and three bedrooms. All had large gardens and toolsheds and pig sties. They were demolished in the 1960s and the site eventually became a petrol station.

Below Right: 12. The head gardener's house, now demolished, built in 1841 and occupied by George Fleming.

Above: 13. Elevation of the kitchen built by Barry at Trentham. Country-house kitchens were invariably of double height to improve ventilation and often had some form of louvred opening in the ceiling.

Below: 14. Barry's plan of the basement, the main servants work areas. In the event the layout was slightly different from this.

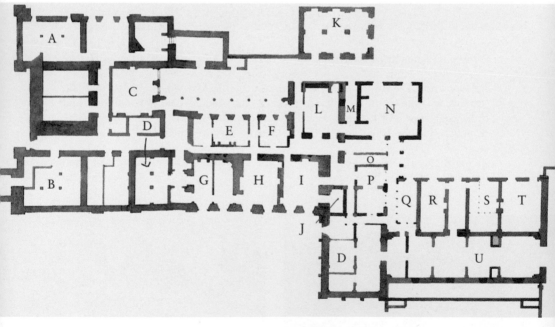

A Ale cellars	H Housekeeper's room	Q Pastry larder	RED INDICATES BARRY'S
B Beer cellar	I Butler's pantry	R Confectionery	INTENDED CHANGES.
C House steward's sitting room	J Plate closet (silver)	S House steward's office and stores	
D Wine cellars	K Servants' hall	T Footman's room	
E Stillroom and scullery	L Scullery (new)	U Open space under family's private appartments	
F Butler's sitting room	M Coal pit		
G Housemaids' room and store	N Kitchen (new)		
	O Dinner service stairs		
	P Larder		

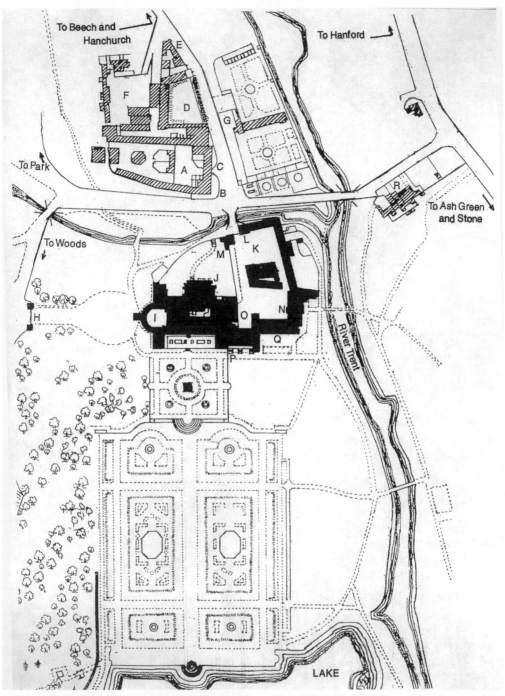

15. Plan of Trentham farm and house layout, taken from the map provided for a fund-raising bazaar held in 1908, adapted for the 1840s, after Barry's alterations.

A Farm yard with sheds, bailiff's office, piggery and cowsheds
B Brewhouse and bakehouse
C Land steward's house
D Laundry drying green with adjacent laundry, calf and cart sheds
E Blacksmith's shop
F 'Wood' yard with slaughter house, carpenter's and paint shops, surveyor's house
G Poulterer's house and poultry sheds
H Formal entrance gates leading to Tittensor
I The west court and formal entrance
J Parish Church of St Mary and All Saints
K Service/stable yard with coachhouses in the middle
L Office block
M Porters' lodge and dole house for the poor
N Clock tower
O Entrance to the house basement with servants' offices and workplaces
P Private wing and dining room
Q Orangery
R Employees' cottages

Above: 16. Barry's planned elevation of the west end, the formal entrance of Trentham from his book of plans, 1834.

Below Left: 17. The ceremonial porte corchère where important guests would be met from their carriages was at the western end of the house. It was designed as the formal entrance from several directions including the main drive from Tittensor and the south.

Below Right: 18. The entrance to the park and the service yard, looking outwards. To the left of the archway was the brewhouse with a louvred roof lantern for ventilation. Further to the left was the bakehouse, and further still, out of sight, the malthouse. To the right of the archway was the agent's house and further to the right was the washhouse.

I hereby certify that Ann Pinson is suffering from St. Vitus's Dance and consider her a proper patient for the Infirmary

Banford
June 3 '51

J. Hargraves
Surgeon

NORTH STAFFORDSHIRE INFIRMARY.

July 28th 1851

I beg to inform you, that Ann Pinson recommended by you as an In- Patient, has received all the assistance which this Institution can administer, and is now discharged cured.

To
His Grace The Duke of
Sutherland

Bragg
SECRETARY

Above: 19. Nomination for an employee at Trentham to be admitted to the North Staffordshire Royal Infirmary for treatment. Costs would be paid by the Sutherland estate.

Below: 20. James Loch's letter to one of his contacts asking for suggestions for a housekeeper for Trentham in 1840 when the post was being filled temporarily by Agnes Henney, the wife of Trentham's head clerk. (D593/K/1/5/36, June 16, 1840)

Mrs Douglas
Edinburgh

12 a.s. 16 January 1840

I am desired by Mr Loch to request that you will have the goodness to inform him if you are acquainted with any person whom you could recommend as housekeeper for the Duke of Sutherlands House Trentham It is not necessary that She has been in a large family before, but the Duchess wishes a person of active habits & competent to look after the internal management of the house, and at the same to have had the benefit of rather a superior education —

It is necessary also that She should understand the proper placing of furniture in the House —

GR

Above: 21. Kirkhaugh Rectory, near Alston, Northumberland. This was the original home of the Kirkby brothers.

Below: 22. The main entrance to the family quarters and the service yard. This gateway was controlled by porters working in the block tinted yellow. To its right was the site of the building where the poors' doles were issued. Further to the right is the gateway to the parish church. To the left of the picture is the edge of the office block, the workplace of the estate clerks. Above the whole scene looms the house and its belvedere tower.

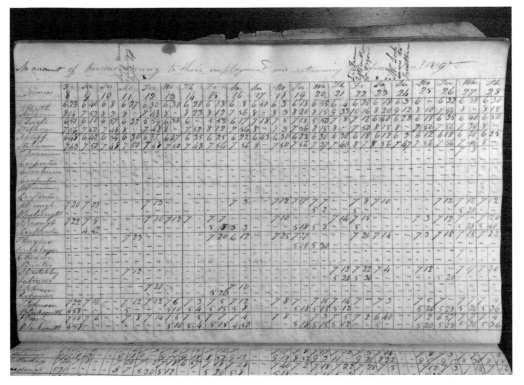

Above: 23. The lodge-keeper's time-keeping book. Page after page records times in and out of various workers such as gardeners, carpenters, painters and blacksmiths.

Below: 24. Villa dei Mulini, Napoleon's formal house on Elba and the young Vantini's workplace as courier.

Left: 25. The entrance to the courtyard of the Rossall School, Fleetwood, built early 1840s, after an original idea by Vantini.

Below: 26. The front entrance to the North Euston Hotel, Fleetwood, opened 1841. The first manager was Zenon Vantini but later it become a regimental barracks. It was reopened as a hotel in 1898 and survives today – a fine curved building overlooking Morecambe Bay.

Above: 27. Tittensor Lodge, home of John Penson senior and his family. It was built in 1775 to control the entrance to the parkland from a road running south along the present Monument Lane in Tittensor.

Below Left: 28. Tittensor Inn, first licensed as a public house in 1811. A plaque on the wall at the side carries the date 1831, the date of a rebuild. It was occupied by John Penson junior from 1836 until the 1840s. After it lost its license it was called Tittensor Cottage.

Below Right: 29. The estate office block from the inside of the service yard. Inside on the first floor was a floor-to-ceiling cage enclosing a large safe. This was where all the income from the Trentham estate along with the deposits from the Trentham Savings Bank would be stored prior to deposit in a bank.

Above: 30. An example of the sort of handwriting which Loch encouraged in his clerks – large and very clear. This notification about the Trentham Savings Bank written by William Day Kirkby, Randal William Kirkby's son.

Below: 31. One of the deposit books from the Trentham Savings Bank. This example belonged to James Kirkby, son of Charles Kirkby, the lodge porter.

Above: 32. Portrait of James Loch, chief agent between 1813 and 1855, when he was succeeded by his son George Loch. (Portrait by James Postlewhite after engraving by George Richard)

Middle: 33. Image of a view of a ploughing match at Groundslow Farm held in 1837. In the early decades of the nineteenth century, ploughing with a reduced team of two horses was encouraged by agricultural improvers on the landed estates. Lewis is probably the gentleman in the centre. From a painting by A Chisholm.

Below: 34. Front view of Groundslow Farm, taken from the estate sale catalogue of 1918, where it included 257 acres and three cottages.

Above Left: 35. Trentham in 1911 showing the partly demolished belvedere tower and the back wall of the parish church. As early as 1788 the lake south of Trentham Hall was polluted with 'tar water' from Hanley, and throughout the 19th century the housekeeper complained of dirty smuts on the furniture.

Above Right: 36. Many of the employees featured in this book – including the Kirkbys – were interred in the cemetery adjacent to the family mausoleum on the opposite side of the A34 to the hall. Unfortunately this part of the cemetery is now (2016) badly neglected.

Below: 37. The interior of the parish church showing the memorial encaustic tiles on the north wall. Most of the individuals were long-serving outdoor servants or other employees or tenants of Trentham, whose families contributed money for the tiles.

sympathies the employment of the emperor's aide would have been a statement of status.

Yet we are left here with a beguiling mystery, for there is amongst the correspondence files that highly ambiguous farewell letter from Vantini to Loch, thanking him for his interest and advice after he had left the Sutherlands' service to run the Euston Hotel:

> Thank you sincerely for your advice – But you never did know me – but Half – and that half under cover – An avery thing Sir that I did settle in my mind, I did always see clear – as I do see clear in what I mean to do now – with this difference – that when with you – my foresight was always contracted by my position, or the elements that did surround me. Now I am free, and surrounded by differing elements. When I shall have the honor of seeing you I will explain myself and you will see as clear as I do.[47]

Vantini's several adventures span a period of amazing change, and his life changed with it. He moved naturally from a traditional upbringing as a page in an imperial court to personal service to an emperor who brought upheaval to the whole of Europe, then to the management of what was reputed to be the wealthiest noble household in England, and finally to the life of a Victorian entrepreneurial businessman envisaging physical pathways between Britain and the Continent, aiming to link the two great world centres of London and Paris. His most enduring memorial, however, lies in none of these but way off on the windswept Lancashire coastline, in the buildings of the Rossall School.

8

Staying for the Long Term

'Entitled to a more than usual consideration'? – One Family

As with the Hemmings, the Penson family's service to the Leveson-Gowers can be measured in centuries rather than decades, one of those families whose loyalty, or perhaps more realistically whose expectations and dependency, earned them a special place in the traditions of Trentham.

Possibly the Penson connection began on the Levesons' early estates in Willenhall, as their family history may go back to Wolverhampton. By the seventeenth century some had moved to the Shropshire estate, and the generation of the family with which this story is concerned can be traced back to a great-grandfather, James Penson, who was born at Lilleshall in 1696 and married a girl from Ashbourne. This couple moved to Trentham sometime before 1741 when the birth of their son was entered into the Trentham parish register. Traditionally the Pensons were head forester and park-keeper; they filled that post at Trentham for a large part of two hundred years, possibly longer. One of James Penson's grandsons was John Penson, who had ten children, all born at Trentham, most of whom retained strong links with the Leveson-Gowers. This story revolves around individuals from this family.

John Penson
John Penson senior, the father of the ten children, was born in 1775 at Trentham, and married Elizabeth Stanley at Trentham on Boxing Day 1797. In 1803 he was a park-keeper living rent-free

in the Tittensor Lodge but renting an additional 15 acres of land to the value of £20 p.a. (see Illus. 27). By 1824, according to the Leveson-Gowers' annual tax return, he had reached the status of head park-keeper at Trentham.[1] He must have been doing well, for in 1827 he became the tenant of the Upper Ley, over 200 acres valued at £430 a year, where he pastured cattle and horses in the summer and sheep in the winter. A few years later he took on yet more pasture, presumably working the land with the help of his sons. This continued until 1836 when he reverted to the original acreage worth £20 – he was over sixty by then. By 1841, Lewis described him then as being very infirm.[2]

As far as his place in the estate hierarchy is concerned, Lewis's letters occasionally referred to 'Penson's men'; he had several men to supervise, including his own sons. He was a highly trusted member of the senior staff, expected to attend on special occasions.[3] One occasion, however, has left us with a different and much more vivid picture.

One of Penson's responsibilities was the security of the park and woodlands, a job which was no sinecure in those days – there are several accounts of occasions when poachers attacked keepers in the area. There was, however, another side to this problem. Local people had long been given permission to walk in Trentham Park when the family were away, and it was on one such stroll in the early summer of 1833 that an anonymous letter-writer had a sudden and rather frightening encounter in the woods. He was suddenly confronted and

> barbarously insulted by a dirty fellow on horseback of the name of 'Penson' who in an insolent manner commands all persons to confine their perambulations to the carriage road ... on pain of being horse-whipped ... 'Penson', seizing the hapless wanderer roughly demands, 'where are you going? There is no road this way, what business have you here? Come, move off.'[4]

The anonymous letter greatly offended the Duke's image of his family establishment and resulted in a reprimand for Penson. Lewis reported, 'I told him very plainly that he must conduct himself with more civility to all visitors both high and low

and neither to stand nor set to watch over respectable people
... Penson is a well meaning man but where he can bully he
certainly does. I have been very severe upon him.' Lewis also
undertook to ask amongst 'the Pottery folks' who the writer
of the letter might be and to apologise to him. He would also
place a watchman in the park on Sundays in order to check the
security of property, not to 'haunt and dogg after' respectable
people.[5]

John Penson senior, of course, had a difficult job, balancing the
requirements of a genteel park to which the public had access with
the job of keeper of an estate positioned on the edge of a poorly
paid but growing industrial area. In 1838, for example, he saw two
men crouching on the ground in the park. When he approached he
saw they were skinning a deer; they ran off but Penson ran after
them and took them into custody – he was obviously a tough man
in a tough job.[6] For this reason Penson kept his place until he was
physically unable to cope. By 1841 he was a sixty-five-year-old
widower still living at the traditional park-keeper's house, Tittensor
Park Lodge. Described as a forester, by then he was semi-retired.
Living in the same lodge were his two youngest sons, Reuben, aged
twenty-nine, assistant to his father, and George, aged twenty-seven,
foreman to the park labourers. Also in the same household were
daughter Mary, aged twenty-three, nephew Thomas, aged ten, and
niece Elizabeth, aged five. There was also a twenty-five-year-old
female servant born in Ireland.

Fortunately the lodge was fairly sizeable and Penson's other seven
children were absent. Three had moved away from the parental
home: the eldest son, James, was working in the Potteries, and
another son, John, was married with his own household locally.
Daughter Elizabeth (aged thirty-four) had worked at the Hall as a
housemaid but by 1841 had moved on elsewhere. The remaining
four children had died, Joseph and Ann in infancy, Thomas and
Richard killed in accidents whilst working on the estate. Their
father's death was registered in nearby Stone in 1847. He was then
aged seventy-one.

We can follow the outlines of his children's stories from parish
records and census returns, but in two cases the skeleton can be
fleshed out by correspondence in the family papers. Each casts a
slightly different light on the world of the Sutherlands' great country
estates and in particular on the long-term dependent families.

> ## One generation of Pensons at Trentham
>
> JOHN, SENIOR, born Trentham 1775, head park-keeper, died 1847, m. Elizabeth Stanley, died 1845. Father to:
>
> JAMES, born Trentham 1799, Lilleshall wood ranger, stonemason, died 1877, m. Ann Jenks
>
> THOMAS born Trentham 1800, estate quarryman, died in Beech Cliffe Quarry 1823, m. Mary Wright, born Standon 1801, nursemaid, Duchess's lady's maid, died 1865
>
> JOHN, born Trentham 1802, groom, publican, clerk, died 1857, m. Betsy Latham
>
> JOSEPH, born Trentham 1806, died 1806
>
> ELIZABETH, born Trentham 1807, housemaid, died ?
>
> RICHARD, born Trentham 1809, assistant park-keeper, died 1839 in fall from horse
>
> REUBEN, born Trentham 1812, head park forester, farmer, died 1873
>
> GEORGE, born Trentham 1814, head park-keeper, died 1889
>
> ANN, born Trentham 1818, died 1818
>
> MARY, born Trentham 1820, housemaid, schoolmistress at dame school in Hanchurch from 1836–1877, died 1880

James Penson

Not every Penson was prepared to touch their forelocks to the Leveson-Gowers in return for a secure rural existence – and John's eldest son was one such individual.

James was born in 1799 at Tittensor Park Lodge, Trentham, but not baptised until three years later. He was brought up to help his father working in the park at Trentham, so by the time he was twenty-one he had been given a responsible job of wood bailiff on the Lilleshall estate and was married to a local girl, Ann Jenks. Over the next eleven years they had five children, but by 1831 he was no longer in favour with Earl Gower, the Marquess's eldest son and heir, who ran affairs at Lilleshall. The reason was not made plain in the correspondence, Lewis simply passing on the fact that in January 1831 the Earl had decided to part with him, as 'he is unworthy of his kindness'.[7]

James was certainly heavily in debt, having gambled or drunk away his livelihood. His wife's family were local publicans, and both Earl Gower and the Marquess were concerned at the levels of drunkenness in the rural communities on their estates in both Staffordshire and Shropshire.

There was a particular problem at this time in relation to the Beerhouse Act of 1830, which allowed anyone to brew and sell beer on payment of a two-guinea licence fee. This had been introduced by Parliament in an effort to encourage competition between brewers and to help wean the working population off stronger drinks, particularly gin. It was fairly quickly criticised as encouraging drunkenness and was unpopular amongst many large landowners such as the Leveson-Gowers, who wished to retain control over their tenants. The new legislation saw a flowering of informal beerhouses, which in themselves were no problem but which in some areas, such as Ketley in Shropshire, encouraged drunkenness and sports such as dog fighting. Even more importantly, in 1830 there was an outbreak of rioting and rick-burning. Of the village of Himley in 1831, Loch wrote to Lewis that 'the whole village is drunken'. All of the incidents of incendiarism were related to pubs, and Lewis and his staff were to 'check regularly all personnel who attend Public Houses frequented by agricultural labourers'.[8]

Both Loch and the Duke were adamant about reducing the number of beerhouses amongst the tenants on the estate. In a letter to William Smith, the young Shropshire agent, Loch instructed that not only were applicants for licences to be refused but they were to be given notice to quit their tenancy. For existing licence holders, in future their rent would be increased in order to discourage them.[9]

It was perhaps not surprising, therefore, that in May 1831 the local vicar in Shropshire wrote to Loch, then at Lilleshall, to complain of rumours that James Penson, having lost his job, was about to open a beerhouse in his cottage, which of course belonged to the estate and was tied to the job which he had just lost. 'Two such houses recently opened in Shenstone,' wrote the vicar, 'and I am continually receiving complaints about noise, drunkenness, battles and cock-fighting.'[10] Loch on a visit to Lilleshall was outraged by James' audacity and immediately wrote a letter to his father, John Penson senior, back at Trentham, to ask him to encourage his son to embark on what seemed to Loch to be a convenient solution:

> I am sorry since I came here to hear of the continued ill conduct of your son.
>
> It will be quite impossible that he should remain here an example of profligacy. I hope you may have the influence with him to induce him to go to America where he may yet retrieve in some degree what he has lost and by doing so he will preserve to his wife and her children the means of livelihood.
>
> He must not open a Beer Shop without first obtaining leave.
>
> I am sorry to be forced to write to you thus, but my duty obliges me, lose no time in seeing or communicating with him.[11]

A month later James' wife Ann went to the Lilleshall sub-agent to ask for permission on her own behalf to open a beerhouse in their cottage, from where she already ran a small huckster's business, selling small items door-to-door. She thought a beerhouse appropriate since her father, licensee of a public house, had left her several ale barrels and she had a good cellar room. James, her husband, was 'about leaving the country' and she didn't know what to do to fend for her five small children. Mrs Webb, Ann's sister and licensee of the Lion pub, was due to retire, so she thought she'd try it before she gave up her huckster's shop, especially as Mrs Webb said she made enough to live and retire on. A couple of days later when William Lewis was paying one of his visits to Lilleshall, he was faced with a repeated request by a distraught Ann Penson. Lewis treated her with characteristic kindness: 'I told her that I was pretty certain that you would not object to her making the most for her poor infant family who are now entirely dependent upon her own exertions for their maintenance.'[12]

Lewis in this instance was mistaken and no permission was forthcoming. James and his family were given notice to quit. He was still there twelve months later, under notice but in dispute with the estate. The clerk reported that there was around £480 owing from James for sales of bark and timber off the woodlands (an amazing income) but he refused not only to hand over this cash but also to render his account books. His condition for doing so was that he and his family should be allowed to stay in their house and open a beershop. The clerk was gloomy about recovering the money owed: 'There will be some loss ... as he is much in debt and has disposed of most of what he had to convert into money.' In fact he was already selling ale even though he had been strictly forbidden to do so.[13]

This impasse continued for at least two years, during which time James and Ann had a sixth child, at whose baptism in February 1833 James was described as 'publican'. Loch did not want to take James to court for the money owed, simply because he wanted rid of him as quickly as possible out of the district and out of the local limelight. Unfortunately, for some reason this decision had not reached the lawyer used by the estate in such matters, and James ended up in the debtor's prison, much to Loch's irritation. Lewis himself went to see James Penson, who promised 'faithfully to leave the country immediately if he could only rest satisfied he would not be followed'. Lewis described him as 'destitute' and his wife and children existing on parish relief.[14] The Leveson-Gowers were usually prepared to take tenants to court for non-payment of rent, but were less keen on suing their employees. All charges were withdrawn at Loch's insistence.

The idea of James taking his family to America never came to fruition, and it is impossible to trace from the correspondence where he and his family went in the short term. By 1841, however, they had all moved away from Shropshire, sucked into the industrial area of the Potteries, at Shelton. According to the census James was lodging in a household which included two other men, one of whom was a stonemason. James himself was described as an agricultural labourer, and Shelton at that time was still a farming area; in fact the last livestock pasture, attached to a slaughterhouse, was not built over until well after the 1950s. His wife and family were not with him during the census; they were living at 16 Pinfold Street, Macclesfield. By then Ann had given birth to two more children: one was born in Shelton in 1837 and the other in Macclesfield in 1839.[15] So the family must have lived at Shelton for some time in the 1830s before moving to Macclesfield.

The 1851 census shows James and his wife together again at 73 Pinfold Street, Macclesfield, according to the census enumerator the parents of a hard-working urban industrial family. James gave his occupation as stonemason, the eldest daughter said she was a dressmaker, and two of the younger daughters and an eleven-year-old son were working in the silk industry. Another son was a coal-carter and another a bread baker. The mother, Ann, must have been pretty well occupied with two young grandchildren who were living with them.

So it remained for well over another quarter of a century. Occasionally changing resident children or grandchildren, and moving house within Pinfield Street at least twice during the following years, James and Ann stayed in Macclesfield, James working as a stonemason until he was at least seventy-one, and the silk industry providing work for the younger members of the family. The couple died almost together, James in the spring of 1877, his wife during the summer, both aged seventy-eight. However profligate he had been as a young man, he and his wife appear to have succeeded in bringing up a large, extended, working family, one among thousands of such families that populated the industrial towns of the Midlands and the North of England, but a far cry from the world of ancestral deference of his forebears.

John Penson

John Penson senior's third son, also called John, was born in 1802 and went to work in the stables at Trentham, firstly as 'helper' (a term restricted to work in the stables), then in 1821 as groom. In 1833 he was away at Dunrobin with the family when James Wood, his boss and head of the stables at Trentham, was unexpectedly promoted to a new post of farm bailiff, assistant to Lewis. In his absence John Penson was chosen to succeed him as head groom. In 1834 he married Betsy Latham, who had worked as a housemaid at Trentham since 1821, and a year later the couple had their first child, a girl. John and his wife were found a rent-free cottage in Ash Green, and though his job must have meant he was away from home for long periods, he kept their home in good repair and even coloured the outside.[16]

In June 1836 he presented the 2nd Duke with something of a dilemma. When the Sutherland Arms public house in Tittensor became vacant, Penson applied for the tenancy. The pub (also sometimes referred to as the Tittensor Arms) was on the main through road south from the Potteries and a good proposition for a man who clearly wanted to settle down with his young family in a more static job than that of head groom. The pub had nineteen acres of land attached to it.[17] William Lewis was keen to see the tenancy filled as soon as possible and recommended that he be given it, but of course this meant the Duke losing his head groom.[18]

What would have normally been a straightforward matter left up to Lewis's discretion became a major irritation to both Lewis, who wrote a fairly curt reminder to Loch that he was awaiting a decision, and Loch, who sent a snappy letter in return, saying the Duke should be given more time to consider the implications.[19] The Duke wanted reassurance, firstly that a replacement head groom would not be difficult to recruit, and secondly that if John Penson was not given the tenancy, he would not feel disgruntled towards his employer. Lewis agreed with him on the former but would give no comment on the latter. The Duke decided that John Penson be given the tenancy and thus the matter was resolved.[20] The rent records for 1837 show him giving up his rent-free cottage, and instead taking on the inn rental.

Lewis, however, had been upset by Loch's shortness, which threw him into 'a great flutter'. He wrote one of his rambling paranoid letters justifying his actions. In return Loch, clearly exasperated by what he considered to be a trifling matter, nevertheless sent Lewis a generous apology: 'I have been so overloaded with business of such magnitude and such a variety that I was out of sorts altogether – so you must not mind this.'[21]

This minor spat did not bode well for Penson's tenancy of the Tittensor Inn, however. It was only two years later that the house steward, Vantini, received a request from John Penson:

> I understand that Mr Hitchcock [the replacement head groom] is going to leave the Duke's establishment. And in consequence of the Railroad being open it has tuck traffick off the road. And the trade his so very bad in the Potteries that I am doing nothing as like where I am. It certainly has been a very unfortunate speculation for me coming here. But we cannot foresee these things. And the only alternative I have left his to go to service again and I should very much wish to be placed in my old situation again providing it should meet with His Grace's approbation.[22]

This turnaround, prompted by a situation which was met by many proprietors of coaching inns which had the misfortune to be replaced by a nearby railway line, did not meet with the Duke's approval. Another man was appointed. A second opportunity came up two years later, in 1840, this time created by another unexpected death, the terrible fall off his horse by the second Penson brother, Richard, who worked as assistant park-keeper under their father. Then aged sixty-four, the father took news of the accident very badly. His son lingered for at least ten days but eventually Loch wrote to the Duke:

> My Lord Duke – I have to assure your Grace that we all here sincerely regret the death of poor Richard Penson. I saw at the first glance at him after the accident that he could not live, he was pitched off and fell heavy on back of his head, his hat went off which made the fall much more severe. I had every assistance and advise to him. The funeral will take place Sunday next at 10 o'clock. The old man is very much cut up. I believe this the most severe trial he ever had in his life and besides he is not well and has not been for some weeks.[23]

A week later Lewis received a letter from John Penson at the Tittensor Inn, who had approached his father to ask what he thought about John's applying for Richard's place. The father was pleased with the idea, for he wanted the post to stay in the Penson family. The Duke, however, had taken against John Penson. He asked Lewis 'whether you are of the opinion that John Penson having kept a Public House in no way unfits him to be his father's Assistant and Successor, either as to habits, authority over people or otherwise'. He was also concerned as to whether he could be trained to do the wood ranger's work, in which he was not experienced. A few days later he wanted to know whether there were any other younger Penson sons and how old they were, obviously searching for alternatives. Loch also suggested a rationalization of the responsibilities of the gamekeeper, wood ranger and park-keeper, enabling the amalgamation of the two latter posts, presumably on the retirement of the old man.[24] This was done, but it took a further two months before the reorganized post of park-keeper was filled – not by John Penson but his younger brother Reuben. Thus began John's long slide into serious penury.

At first, perhaps, the true situation was not obvious. The local newspaper carried glowing reports of various society meetings at the inn; yet the rent books showed John Penson to be drifting into arrears, even though his rent had been reduced to £20 a year.[25] They were still there during the census of 1841, but in 1843 the situation became critical. Lewis, though by now retired, reminded Loch not to forget the Pensons; in May 1843 John himself wrote directly to the Duke, his landlord:

> I am very sorry I am now compel'd to state the very serious situation that I am now placed in – for through the effects of the Rail Road and the Depression of Trade I have now been compl'd to make over for the benefit of my Creditors an assignment of all that I am possessed of.
>
> I have now got the Bailiffs in the House but next week I expect they will sell that which we have both worked Hard and Honestly for – I have been anxiously waiting for this 4 years in hopes that something better would have turn'd out ... And without the Assistance of some kind Friends myself and Family shall be left to the Mercy of the World. For after I have paid all that I owe I can assure your Grace that I shall not have one penny in the world, and God only knows what his to become of us ... I hope your Grace will find me employment so that I can maintain my Wife and Family– which I hope and trust that that our conduct of 16 years work in the Family will induce your Grace to sympathy with us ...[26]

The Duke, however, was no more help than previously, and four days later Loch informed Lewis's successor, William Steward: 'John Penson has received his answer from the Duke as far as his Grace is concerned and I have nothing to offer him.'[27] Loch still felt obliged to help, and somewhat in desperation asked advice of Lewis, but Lewis could be of little help:

> I am really at a loss to know how to advise in his case. I cannot help thinking he should have done better ... I am quite satisfied that the rent of both house and land is fair and reasonable, and what will be cheerfully given by any competent and industrious

tenant. I feel very sorry for the poor wife and family. I am of the opinion that the best thing for him to attempt is to get into service again. He is young and active and I believe sober.[28]

Loch asked William Steward to pass on this piece of advice to Penson. Steward went to the inn to tell him this and to sort out his eviction for non-payment of rent. He reported back that Penson had got someone to buy most of his furniture and was still anxious to stay in the inn, but Steward told him that if necessary the estate would take the fixtures out of the house and buy the manure from the stables. The Duke remained adamant that a new tenant be found.[29]

No one, however, seemed anxious to carry out the eviction. The months dragged on, so that it was March the following year when the Duchess first appeared in the correspondence, expressing great concern about the imminent eviction. She seems to have persuaded the Duke that they had a special responsibility towards the Penson family:

> Could we not offer him a cottage till he finds employment, it would not become a precedent on account of the family serving us. The Duke was displeased with one of the brothers and he was not allowed to remain in the Hanchurch Lodge cottage, but in this case he is anxious to show the difference. You are aware what constant satisfaction Mrs Penson has given us, she says John Penson was in most distressing distress.

In reply, Loch agreed: 'I have always felt that any branch of the Penson family was entitled to a more than usual consideration and still feel this to be so.'[30] From then on, the estate's agents seemed to bend over backwards to help the Pensons, largely as a result of the Duchess's concern rather than the Duke's. In April the Trentham steward had a suggestion with regard to the new tenancy:

> A very likely man ... has applied for it and I have thought it might be well to let him the place, at the same time stipulating that J. Penson should remain in the House for a few weeks until something can be had for him, and we could easily make the incoming tenant a little allowance in the first half year's rent to make up for the want of the House and its profits for a short time.[31]

As a result, Loch's instructions to William Steward was to allow the Pensons to stay at the inn in the short term but in the longer term to try to place them in a cottage, if necessary as lodgers, and find him some employment on the estate.[32]

A month later it seemed that a solution might have been found. John Penson was under consideration for a job with the Bridgewater Trust, which ran the Bridgewater Canal in Lancashire, an opportunity found for him by Loch who had long been a co-director and in 1837 had become superintendant. William Steward was in the position of having to give Penson a reference. Loch advised him:

> If Mr Fereday Smith should apply to you for John Penson's character and fitness to take charge of the horses and ostlers upon the Canal, you must state to him truly your belief as to his knowledge of horses, as to his power of keeping the ostlers in order, and above all as to his personal activity.[33]

This last comment seems to have been at the heart of the problem. The Duke and his agents all thought John was honest and good-natured but not exactly energetic, perhaps unduly affected by drink since his tenancy of the inn, so that even though one of the grooms at Trentham was dismissed for misconduct at this time, they did not replace him with John. Even recommending John for a place with the Bridgewater Trust gave Loch cause for reservation:

> I hope that John Penson may fit a place in the Bridgewater Trust but do tell him that he must be active and zealous in the discharge of his duty, honest I am sure he will be. But I cannot keep any man in that service who is not quite alive ...[34]

Maybe it was with relief mixed with some irritation, therefore, that Loch explained that the Bridgewater Trust job had not worked out and that the Pensons were still at the inn despite a new tenant having been chosen: 'I have done all I can for John Penson and am sorry that the present tenant should be so inconvenienced by him.'[35]

Shortly after this, in March 1844, another member of the Penson family stepped in to plead John's case. Mary was the widow of

Thomas, another of the Penson brothers. Since her husband's death in an accident back in 1823 she had made a successful career as nurse and lady's maid to the Duchess, with whom she was a great favourite. She had been to see John and reassured him that the Duke and Duchess would not turn him out but would let him stay until he got another situation, though in reality she had no right to give this promise and was scolded by the Duchess for making it:

> He said how grateful he feels, but ... he cried and was in a sad state of mind ... I am quite sure it is not in his powers to pay [rent], if he could he would, he is very honest and wishes to pay everyone ... he is much respected and only wants a situation where he could work to keep his family.[36]

The Duchess forwarded Mary's letter to Loch, including with it one of her own, casting around for ideas. Of course the Pensons could not stay at the inn as it needed a proper tenancy, but

> the Duke and myself wish that some lodging should be provided for him and his family ... believing that there is no fault in him – and on his Father's account ... if [Mr Steward] had no lodging in view perhaps the most economical plan of disposing of the family would be to send them to the Stables at Lilleshall ... I do feel that in common humanity ... I cannot turn them out.
>
> It seems singular that no situation can be found for a man whose character stands high and who is an able-bodied well looking man – at all events I feel he must remain in our care till something is found.
>
> Is there nothing at Dunrobin that would do for him – the care of the stables and his wife to take charge of the men's rooms ... Might they do for the house at Loch Inver. His wife was housemaid at Trentham when I married and a very tidy person. I think his family only consist of two little girls.

Perhaps amazingly, eight years after the problem with the inn first arose both Loch and William Steward were still suggesting solutions. Perhaps Penson could work as one of the porters in a wharehouse run by the Bridgewater Trust? But the work was hard and irregular.

Another position was ruled out because it would mean displacing people even poorer than Penson – but even then Loch persevered:

> If he will think of a porter's place I will enquire if there is any vacancy ... If I find ... that John Penson can have an opening I will not forget him. But I dread to [recommend] him for if he is not most alert he would have to be parted with which would be very unpleasant.[37]

This situation seems to have dragged on, with the Penson family presumably camped out in the back of the Tittensor Inn until at least 1848 when the correspondence on the subject gradually peters out. Up until then the Duchess was still writing letters to Loch about it; Loch must have persevered, because the 1851 census shows John Penson was living in Blackburn Road, Hulme, Manchester with his wife Betsy and their two girls, registered on the enumeration sheet as a merchant's clerk. This was close to the terminus of the Bridgewater Canal and its offices, so there seems little doubt as to how the family came to be there.

A notice of Penson's death appeared in the *Staffordshire Advertiser* for 24 May 1856: 'At Altrincham near Manchester, on the 15th instant, aged fifty-four, Mr John Penson, son of the late Mr John Penson, park-keeper, Trentham.' His death certificate described him as 'a coal agent', presumably associated with the Bridgewater Canal.

As for his long-suffering widow Betsy, of whom the Duchess always had a high opinion, there is at least a possibility that she helped her out too, for according to the 1861 census there was an Elizabeth Penson, widow (i.e. not a Penson by birth) of the right age and the right birthplace, working in the household of the Duke and Duchess of Argyll in Kensington. The Duchess of Argyll was the eldest daughter of the 2nd Duke and Duchess of Sutherland.

Mary Penson

By contrast with John, the Mary Penson who tried to console her brother-in-law was most successful insofar as service to the Sutherlands was concerned. She was not a Penson at all by birth but was born Mary Wright, the daughter of another of the Trentham long-serving families.

Three other Pensons

John Penson's two youngest sons had successful careers at Trentham.

Reuben was born in 1812 and automatically went to work under his father. Perhaps he had other ambitions, however, for in May 1832, when he was aged twenty, his father and he took the rare step of asking for permission for a day off to go to Chatsworth to arrange for the instruction of his son under the Duke of Devonshire's gardener.

He must have stayed there for a short while for by 1841 he was living at home again with his father and had been appointed as his successor. A couple of years later, he was faced with disappointment when Barry's alterations to Trentham were advanced to the stage of planning the ornamental tree planting in the woodlands. The Duke decided that Reuben, as forester, had not enough knowledge for planting 'with taste', so his various tasks were reallocated. The management of the tree planting became the direct task of Fleming, the gardener, and Reuben became the foreman over the labourers as well as attending to the park and estate draining. He was still paid his previous salary of £52 10s.

He lived with his family on a small holding at Tittensor.

Reuben's younger brother George became first one of the lodge porters but was eventually promoted to head park-keeper.

Their younger sister Mary became a housemaid.

In many ways she represents one of the core employees, joining two of the families who had served the Leveson-Gowers for generations as well as holding a position close to the Duchess, right at the heart of the household. Unfortunately, because of her intimacy with the Duchess, she figures little in the correspondence.

We do know, however, that she had a most tragic early life. She was just twenty-one when she married Thomas Penson in June 1822, the second son of John Penson senior and quarryman on the estate. In August the following year she gave birth to a daughter Frances, who died before she could be baptised, and was buried on

18 August 1823. One month and one day later Mary buried her young husband, killed in an accident at the estate's stone quarry at Beech Cliffe.

Widowed so young, she inevitably fell back on the dual family tradition and went into domestic service. The inscription on her tombstone at Standon says she served the Sutherlands for forty years, which would make her twenty-five when she began employment with the family. The log of servants kept by the house steward Vantini records that she was set on as 1st nurse with the Marquess's family in 1825. Fourteen years later in 1839 she was still there as first nurse on a salary of £26 5s. She served in this capacity until 1846.[38]

Duchess Harriet of Sutherland (the 2nd Duchess) had a lady's maid who left her service in 1843. For a while the Duchess seems to have had problems with her maids, for she had four different women in three years, none of whom seem to have been suitable. In 1847, after only a few months as nanny, Mary became the Duchess's personal maid on an increased salary of £31 10s. This move obviously suited both parties, for she appeared as lady's maid to the Duchess in the 1851 census and in the wage list of 1854. She was still in that position during the census of 1861 when she was with the Duchess staying at Cliveden House as part of a huge family and servant gathering. She was then aged fifty-nine, the Duchess fifty-four.

As they both aged, the Duchess became more and more dependent on Mary Penson, who in effect became a minor part of the Sutherland family, in the tradition of long-established, faithful retainers serving in the great aristocratic houses. According to memoirs of one of the Duchess's younger sons, Lord Ronald Gower, Mary was taken ill whilst travelling on the Continent with the family in 1865, when she would have been aged sixty-four.[39] She was carefully taken back home to Stafford House, the whole European trip was cut short and the family returned home in August. By September their 'dear old friend Penson' was dead.

Evelyn, one of the children to whom Mary had been nanny, had rushed back from Ireland on hearing news of Mary's worsening state, only to be greeted by her coffin. This was, after all, the woman who had, in effect, brought her up along with her brothers and sisters. She wrote to her brother Ronald: 'You will be deeply grieved for this sad loss to us all. There never lived a more devoted, unselfish being, and I cannot bear to think of Mamma without her loving care.'

Mary's body was escorted back to Staffordshire, Evelyn and other members of the family attending the funeral and burial at Standon, in a quiet graveyard amidst the pleasant Staffordshire countryside, overlooking the village duck pond. The tombstone, alongside the Wrights' family graves, was paid for by the Sutherlands. The Duchess visited the grave with Ronald later. Mary, widowed most tragically at twenty-two, had been in service with the Duchess for most of her life, had accompanied her everywhere in her travels to all the exotic countries of Europe, had seen the family children grown into adulthood and had cared for her mistress in old age and increasing frailty – a potent testament to the strong relationship which could grow between mistress and maid. For a working woman she did well financially, for her effects at death were valued at around £600.[40]

9

Keeping the Records Straight

'I am to be fed with a teaspoon' – The Clerks

The clerks' role at Trentham and Lilleshall was theoretically straightforward: they provided the office backup for the agent who managed the Trentham home park and farm and the wider Sutherland estates in three counties. From 1840 the estate administrative work was carried out in the office block opposite the lodge at the gateway to the service yard (see Illus. 29). The work involved a great deal of road and property maintenance, but above all Lewis was responsible for the estate finance in the form of purchasing new properties and maintaining rental income: collecting tithes and rents at quarterly 'collections' or 'audits', keeping records in the rental books, setting rents (farm and small holding rents were set anew each year, based on that season's market price of wheat), preparing monthly and annual reports, working out future estimates, chasing defaulters, issuing notices to quit, and enforcing evictions. It required experience in valuing both property and harvests.

Most of the rental work was done by the clerks, but in practice both at Trentham and Lilleshall the distribution of responsibilities is often unclear. This blurring of job demarcation became a real issue, especially at Lilleshall in the early 1830s. The head clerks seemed to vary in responsibility; much of their work was legal, processing the paper work for purchases and leases. Yet the more experienced clerks could also become involved in rent collection, property inspection and repair, land assessment, fencing disputes, road construction, even woodland and livestock management. In these cases, therefore, very different experience and abilities were needed in addition to office administration skills. In extreme cases the clerk became in effect a bailiff. We therefore can see the post of clerk as being a means of recruiting and training potential sub-agents and agents.

The administrative interdependency between Trentham and Lilleshall is clearly illustrated by the clerks. Difficulties in the Trentham office were mirrored or exacerbated by problems at Lilleshall, and vice versa. Individuals were moved between the two; sometimes an endemic insecurity seemed to be contagious, often with good reason. In the 1830s, times were tough; widespread shortage of work and general poverty, especially amongst the cottagers, meant poor rent collections and the Sutherlands' determination to rebuild almost all its houses in that decade saw Loch pushing for cuts in salaries, retirement annuities and general expenses.

This was at a time when Loch himself had many other commitments, including those of an elected Member of Parliament. Lewis, his man on the ground, was busy building up his own tenant farm as well as nursing a sickly wife. Both to some extent gave the estates less attention than was needed. The period especially between the years 1831 and 1836 reveals a complex and in many instances desperately unhappy picture of the life of the administrative clerks on the Sutherland estates.

The clerks were educated, highly literate and numerate men, with professional writing skills that were usually better than those of the agents, and most were not slow at writing letters. Some expressed their feelings in passionate, poetic language. Their skills provided an excellent platform for upward social mobility.[1] Social or professional disappointment would strike very hard.

Randal William Kirkby

Of the four Kirkby brothers who came down to Trentham from Northumberland the eldest, Randal William Kirkby, became an important mainstay of the estate administration at Trentham for well over twenty years. Randal was baptised at Kirkhaugh in 1782. He was aged twenty when he married a local girl in his father's church, but five years later the parish register in Kirkhaugh recorded her death whilst giving birth to their only child, Thomas, who survived. Kirkby started work at Trentham probably around 1810. His second marriage was entered in the parish register of St Mary's, Trentham in 1813, to Elizabeth Day of Trentham, by whom he had seven children, two of which died in infancy. He appeared in the rent record in 1815, when he paid just over two pounds a year for a small cottage. He was then working as lodge porter with his brother, Charles.[2] In 1818 the couple moved to Trentham Lodges, which was rent-free, indicating that by then R. W. Kirkby had been promoted to the position of clerk in the estate office.

It is not clear whether Thomas, Kirkby's son by his first wife, came down to Trentham with his father, but if he did he eventually went back north to work as a clerk to the Earl of Carlisle's estate at Castle Howard in Yorkshire, probably through the long-standing connections between the Leveson-Gowers and the Howards. Thomas stayed at the office at Castle Howard for the rest of his working life, marrying a local girl, raising a family, able to employ a governess and a general servant, and eventually retiring in a cottage on an annuity from the estate.[3] He kept in touch with his father at Trentham and was present at his deathbed.

After Kirkby's promotion to clerk, many of the letters to Loch during the years up to the late 1830s were written out in his handwriting. He was seen as a middle manager par excellence – honest, loyal, energetic, a safe pair of hands for the estate. By 1821 he had been given the associated appointment of clerk to the Trentham Savings Bank, which meant he received depositors' cash as well as keeping the minute book up to date.

Trentham Savings Bank
Trentham Savings Bank was opened in 1818 as a result of an idea by Thomas Butt, vicar of St Mary's Trentham. It was aimed at the lower end of the Trentham parishioners and the nearby estate tenantry, with the intention of encouraging thrift. By 1827 it had 316 depositors rising to peak of 410 in 1841. Most of its users were domestic servants, journeymen, mechanics and agricultural labourers. It was made redundant by the Post Office Savings Bank Act 1863, but it was still there

in 1876 when consideration was being given to its future. It closed in 1880.

Each depositor was given a bank book inscribed with their name and usually their occupation, which recorded deposits, withdrawals and interest payments. The bank books were returned to the bank when full or when the bank closed, so they survived along with the declaration forms when opening the account and the minute book. If the depositor was a long-term subscriber a rough picture of the individual's prosperity or otherwise can be built up from the bank book.

According to the minute book, in 1821 the patron and treasurer of the bank was the Marquess of Stafford, the vice treasurer was the Trentham agent, the clerk was the estate head clerk, and amongst the six trustees were Earl Gower (the Marquess's eldest son and heir), James Loch, the Revd Butt, and Fenton, the estate solicitor in Newcastle.

The rules of the bank stipulated a minimum deposit of a shilling and an interest rate of 4 per cent. The bank was open between two and four o'clock every other Saturday, in the estate office. Up until 1839, the bank clerk was the Trentham head clerk, Randal William Kirkby. After his death the post was divided in two: the cashier and auditor was William Henney, the estate head clerk; the actuary and bank clerk was Kirkby's son William Day Kirkby, another clerk in the estate office. In 1839, for their work for the bank they were given a set salary of £20 and £30 respectively. This changed the previous arrangement under which the clerk received an annual payment of £5 plus a further five shillings per £100 of total deposits.

Apart from the obvious uses of the bank, its close connection with the Trentham clerks strengthened the ties which bound the estate to the local community. It was the clerks who attended every fortnight to receive and sign in deposits and give out withdrawals, so they would build up a fair picture of who was who in the area. It was also they who sent the cash to Drummonds' Bank, and arranged for it to be certified as being offset against the national debt following the Napoleonic War. A similar savings bank was set up by the estate at the Lilleshall office.

Until around 1827 R. W. Kirkby was also parish clerk – the parish registers bear his writing and attest to his presence at parish ceremonies. Between 1813 and 1827, for example, he was formal witness to over eighty-four marriages in the parish church of St Mary's, Trentham. He was also overseer of the poor, reporting that in February 1830 the weather was very cold, the poor suffering greatly, and that he had given relief to seventy-two families in the Trentham parish, all of them out of work and solely dependent on the parish relief.[4] The fact that both these last positions were traditionally held by the estate clerks shows the degree of social control wielded over the village by the Leveson-Gower family. Trentham was the archetypal 'closed village', sewn up by the family as tight as a drum. The estate administration even ran the village school, appointing the schoolmaster who was sometimes a member of one of the estate service families such as the Kirkbys or Henneys.[5] The curate of the parish church was also private chaplain to the Duke and the house.

In his later years Kirkby acted more as an assistant to Lewis than a mere office clerk. He was one of a small number of seniors who were called on to help organise important family events. In March 1832, for example, he helped Lewis and the head park-keeper John Penson to arrange the funeral of little two-year-old Lady Blanche, one of the Marquess's granddaughters. The family being away, the three men acted as chief mourners, meeting Blanche's body which was brought from West Hill to Trentham. Lewis described the occasion: 'The remains of the dear child have arrived ... every arrangement is made for the funeral tomorrow ... Penson, Kirkby and I met the carriage and followed it to the house. Both the nurses were much affected on their arrival, the coffin is placed in the State Bedroom.'[6] Only two of the three men were needed to carry the tiny coffin.

Kirkby was also named as a substitute for Lewis to meet the newly inherited 2nd Duke at Darlaston Bridge, on his way to the important first visit to Trentham after his father's death in 1833. If Lewis was not available because of illness, wrote Loch, Kirkby was to arrange for the Duke to be greeted ceremonially by the Yeomanry and to sit down to a meal with them in the new west entrance hall to the house.[7]

Sometimes national or regional emergencies penetrated the apparent country idyll of the estate. In one letter to Loch, dated

2 February1831, Kirkby gave an account of the outbreaks of riots and property burning in Staffordshire and the precautions taken at Trentham:

> The feverish state lately felt here with respect to incendiarisms have in some measure subsided yet the utmost vigilance continues on the part of the Farmers and others in order to detect and prevent the proceedings of these diabolical villains – Mr Lewis, Emery, Fenton, Woolley, Hunt and myself have been sworn in special constables – the fire engines are put in the best possible state and are standing in the Coach House fully equipped for a moment's notice.[8]

In August of the following year the possibility of the spread of the first ever outbreak of cholera in England again galvanised the senior staff. Lewis reported that several people had died in Newcastle, all 'dissipated characters'. He, however, had formed a special board of health at Trentham composed of three local clergymen, plus Lewis himself, Kirkby, Dr Goddard and two others: 'It was proposed to have the Barn in the Upper Ley converted into a Cholera Hospital but that I decidedly objected to, that being too near the Hall, but I have found a cottage suitable at the far side of the Parish, and it is now ready if wanted for a limited number.'[9]

Kirkby's routine work was varied, but an especially important job was keeping an eye on income and expenditure and collating information to be used in the monthly and annual reports, which the Trentham agent had to send to Loch. Kirkby accompanied Lewis to 'collections', set days when they went to a convenient inn on each estate, requiring the tenants to bring their rent to them. It was Kirkby who kept the record of defaulters and often Lewis delegated to him the task of sending out the notices to quit. He needed to become familiar with individual tenants and their problems in order to judge whom to pressurise. In some circumstances he was sent on his own to other estates to collect rents, as when, after the death of the 1st Duke, the rents of the Yorkshire estate of Stittenham were to be sent to the new Duchess as her 'pin money'.[10]

On legal matters, Kirkby worked closely with Fenton, the Sutherlands' lawyer in Newcastle, especially on the seemingly endless purchases, sales and lettings of freehold and leasehold property. Given the nature of the relationship between Loch and Lewis, frequent reporting back to London was critical, and whenever Lewis was absent or extra busy, Kirkby would send detailed but fluently written letters. Several reports, for example, were taken up describing the improvements that the agent and his office staff had made to Tittensor: purchasing freeholds, rebuilding houses, draining and fencing Tittensor Common and preparing the site for a new lodge at the south end of the Common.[11]

Sometimes a letter from Loch, ever on the lookout for ways of maximising income, must have caused Kirkby to raise a quizzical eyebrow; but only for a moment perhaps – as when he was instructed to write a full account of how to make washballs out of ferns, and exactly how and why they could be used in laundering. This presumably required a visit to the Trentham laundry, when no doubt his somewhat bewildered inquiry would have been answered in full. This account was to be sent urgently to the Sutherland agent at Scourie, part of the Highland estates, where the land was overrun with ferns.[12]

Occasionally Kirkby played a personal, active part in events. It was he, for example, who wrote the warning letter to William Lewis in 1832 about the gossip which was abroad about Mrs Doar sending parcels of goods away from Trentham. He was worried that the whole sorry situation would blow up and Lewis would be left holding the proverbial baby. On that occasion, Loch's warning to Lewis about Kirkby gives us a first glimpse of one side of the clerk's character: 'He is as honest a man as breathes, but he is a man of strong passions and liable to be prejudiced and he never liked Mrs Doar, for she resisted his authority.'[13] Here we have a hint of the tension which must have existed between the two hierarchies of the domestic and the estate management, the one resisting the 'authority' of the other. Kirkby was certainly no paragon of virtue; he did not like giving way to women or to men whom he considered his inferior and he certainly thought Lewis too lenient regarding rent arrears, a true stickler for rules and regulations. With his personality, authority and experience it was almost inevitable that he would be used by Loch as a troubleshooter, but also that he would himself become involved in the occasional highly charged dispute.

The Emery affair

Lewis depended on Kirkby a great deal. As far as the tenants were concerned, perhaps he provided a touch of steel to reinforce Lewis's softer approach. On several occasions Kirkby agreed with Loch that 'something ought to be done to enforce more punctual payments'.[14] Despite such comments, the two, Lewis and Kirkby, had worked happily together for over fifteen years, yet everyone in the Trentham office was not on such good terms. Kirkby's personality was at odds with that of his junior clerk, Thomas Emery, outwardly a much quieter character who had worked in the office since the 1820s. Lewis must have been aware of troubled relationships but it is not until early 1833 that there appears evidence of a deep rift. It was a situation that was to throw the office into chaos for months, adding to the stress of what proved to be a difficult year for the Sutherlands.

The surviving record begins on 2 February with a disjointed but heartfelt letter of resignation from Emery to Lewis, giving as his reasons disagreements with Kirkby. Frustratingly, Emery's letter was suggestive but not specific. The two clerks' tempers, he wrote, 'are very opposite as regards our fellow servants'. If he were forced to leave, he might have to sell the last piece of furniture in his house and, if so, 'another victim will be added to the catalogue of destroyed servants'. Was this a veiled reference to Kirkby's intervention in the Mrs Doar affair, which had come to a head during the previous summer?[15]

Unfortunately, Emery also said in his letter that he was going to write direct to Loch. This angered Lewis, who replied with a personal note which has not survived. The next day Emery delivered him another letter, apologising, saying he had been overwrought: 'I scarcely know what I wrote from the excited state of my feelings at that moment.' Apparently things had come to a head when Emery was late with preparing the monthly report, but as Emery explained:

> I did not know what I had to do as first one thing and then another were taken out of my hands. The Duke of Sutherland could not have come into the Office with half the consequence Mr Kirkby did to demand of me an explanation.

Kirkby had accused Emery of shamefully neglecting the accounts and of being a liar. Emery went on dramatically:

> But stop, did he think I was to be treated as he treats by fits and starts the Noble Duke's poor work people under his charge in the same negro manner – if he did he was never more wrong in his life – my blood boiled and I told him plainly [what] my opinion of him was ... After better than twelve years service I am to be fed with a teaspoon ... as though I was a Schoolboy or a Child ... I know not whether I am legible, I write hastily and it is the language of my soul.[16]

On receiving this Lewis had a sleepless night. The next morning he forwarded Emery's letters to Loch with the request that he find another situation for Emery and replace him with a junior clerk from Loch's own office, whom he called 'little Plank'. A second, simpler idea had come to him in bed, however: that Emery be moved to Lilleshall and the Lilleshall clerk come to Trentham. All this was because he did not want to lose Kirkby who, when told of Emery's threat to leave, had stated that he himself would leave if there was any further unpleasantness. This Lewis could not countenance as Kirkby took so much of the burden of the agency on his shoulders: 'I can never give my consent to part with him.'[17] Unfortunately, the second and simpler solution was scotched when Loch put it to Lord Stafford, who ran the estate in Shropshire and who thought Emery had 'a bad and difficult temper'.[18]

Loch was driven to the ultimate sanction at this point – a discussion with the Duke. On 14 February, there followed what was in effect a final written warning sent to both clerks. The covering letter from Loch to Lewis reads: 'The Duke desires to say he regrets that such altercations should exist between two otherwise respectable persons, as they receive such a different example from you. Such scenes must cease as they value his favour.' He expected them to go on with their jobs, but if the unpleasantness did not cease 'he will part with both as he conceives that such conduct among the Superiors is derogatory to his service'. He required 'mutual forbearance towards each other – temperate though firm conduct towards those under them and very strict and inviolable secrecy as to the matters they have to transact'.[19]

If this was intended to settle everyone down to work together, it was not successful. Though it clearly frightened Emery into the full realisation of his vulnerability, he was not cowed. The next day he wrote to Loch, pleading his cause, apologising for his rash conduct in writing 'strange' letters to Lewis, explaining that he was hurt and confused by Kirkby's taking one piece of work after another from him and giving it to his young son who was helping out around the office. Neither did he appreciate having his stool kicked from under him many times, just to annoy him: 'I have a wife and four small helpless children dependent upon me, these to Kirkby are light considerations.' In fact, his wife gave birth to their fifth child later that same year and he was also helping finance his aged parents. He went on to recount his family's long history of service to the Leveson-Gowers, on both his father's and his mother's side, pledging his sincerest loyalty and good intentions:

> Do I want zeal? No my life if required in the cause of my noble employers would be a willing sacrifice – I have been better than twelve years in the Office and had I not have been so situated under the control of such a person as Mr Kirkby whose temper and violence exceeds everything I can possibly describe I should have been truly happy ... deal with me as seemeth best to you – whatever decision you arrive at I will not murmur.[20]

Kirkby also reacted decisively to the Duke's admonishment. His letter was a simple resignation delivered to Lewis at home, provoking the latter to send a panicky early morning note to Loch from Groundslow: 'Emery can never fill his [Kirkby's] situation with me. I am just going down to Trentham and if I cannot arrange matters I will certainly take one of the first coaches for London to see you ...'[21]

Lewis seemed not to have 'arranged matters' and Kirkby remained determined to resign. No record remains of the meeting in London, but judging from subsequent events Loch managed to calm Lewis down and persuade him to part with both clerks from Trentham. Emery had not impressed Loch with either his efficiency or the emotional tone of his letters, so he was to be given notice as soon as the clerk from London, George Plank, was available. As far as Kirkby was concerned, he proposed to move him upwards to an extremely onerous position, the post of bailiff and clerk at Ketley, part of the Leveson-Gower estates in Shropshire, which position was shortly to become vacant.

A few weeks later Lewis reported that Kirkby rather liked the idea of moving to Shropshire and, on 18 March 1833, he formally accepted the offer.[22] By this time Lewis was also reconciled to his moving: 'The sooner Kirkby goes to Shropshire the better,' he wrote, and set about finding a suitable replacement. The post of head clerk was an important one, effectively Lewis's eyes and ears locally, and it required a person of 'respectability' and sufficient perspicacity to pick up early signs of trouble.[23] Lewis also seemed happy to be rid of Emery as office clerk, probably with the idea that Loch would find him a post elsewhere. He repeatedly expressed a wish to have Plank, possibly as head clerk.

It was not to be so simple. Perhaps after discussions with his wife, perhaps for other reasons, Kirkby changed his mind, turned down the offer of the Ketley position and resigned. After some negotiations he was allowed to keep the subsidiary post of clerk of the Trentham Savings Bank and his cottage in Ash Green rent-free, so he retained some income and a home for his family.

To add to Lewis's troubles, Plank's transfer from London was delayed because his younger brother needed to be given time to take over from him. On 18 June 1833 Emery was told he had to leave when Plank was ready.[24] Inevitably there followed a final sorrowful letter from Emery: 'In taking a retrospective view of my past life I cannot help observing that I have been truly unfortunate.' After promising to help Lewis and his successor in the office all he could, he made a request: could he have the tenancy of an estate property, the New Inn Mill in Hanford?[25] A couple of months later he disappeared from the correspondence, and in September George Plank was sent up to Trentham as the head office clerk, with Kirkby assisting on a part-time basis.

There is something of a hole in the correspondence in the second half of 1833, partly perhaps because the office system was in some chaos, but mainly because in July the 1st Duke was taken ill at Dunrobin and died shortly afterwards. Loch rushed up to Scotland leaving his son William Adam Loch in charge of his London office. Lewis followed shortly afterwards to attend the Duke's funeral. Thereafter, of course, the management was taken up with the arrangements for a smaller household for the Dowager Duchess, now to be called the Duchess Countess, and a larger one for the new Duke at Stafford House. Several of the long-serving servants retired at this point, and Loch began his overhaul of household expenditure.

The Plank affair

Kirkby also recedes from the correspondence for a time and the story of the Trentham office does not reappear in the letters until early 1834, when, confusingly enough, Emery's successor, George Plank, was working temporarily in the office not at Trentham but at Lilleshall, where he was suddenly taken ill with inflammation of the bowel. For a few days he was considered by the doctor to be in serious danger and Lewis insisted on frequent bleeding. A fortnight later he was recovering well and soon returned to Trentham, where a son of Kirkby's had been asked to help out.[26]

The next we hear of Plank is in July of that year, 1834, when there was a routine letter from him about the cash accounts which were slightly delayed but were shortly to be with Loch.[27] A few days later, however, there was a major scare. The Revd Butt, vicar of Trentham, in a hastily scrawled note to Loch explained that Plank had been missing for over twenty-four hours; it was raining heavily; Lewis was exhausted in body and mind, out searching for him.

Lewis himself reported to Loch later. Plank had left his lodgings at seven in the morning but had not turned up at the office as usual. Mrs Cleaver at the hall thought he sometimes went for an early morning bathe in a local pool. Lewis and the farm bailiff went out to search for him, and in a secluded spot in the woods near to Hargreaves Pool they found his greatcoat. Lewis had two boats and a number of men with dragnets brought and the dragging of the pool continued until night. Some of the water was drained off and the next day Lewis sent a line of men, holding hands, into the water. Nothing was found.

Later Lewis had gone to Plank's lodgings and had broken open a lock to find a letter addressed to him from Plank, explaining that he had been driven to leave Trentham because he was £700 out in his accounts; in his trouble he had arranged for Mr Kirkby to come in and help him yesterday, but instead he had gone out with a friend, a man called Thomas Davidson, and had wasted the time.

He resigned his post. The letter ended dramatically: 'Comfort my parents.'[28]

Plank's friend Davidson had been helping Lewis with the search when Plank's letter was found and later felt moved to explain the circumstances of his visit. He had stopped at the Trentham Inn on his way home to Dudley from a holiday in the Isle of Man. He intended to call on Plank and perhaps see the hall and park. He met him in the office about two in the afternoon. Plank said he had to go to the Potteries on business for Mr Lewis, but that Davidson could come with him. They did this and on their return to Trentham they spent the evening in the Housekeeper's Room at the hall, presumably talking with Mrs Cleaver, who seemed to have befriended the lonely young Plank. The two then went for an hour and a half to the inn, where they parted. Plank had nothing to drink at the inn and was perfectly sober and cheerful when he left to walk back to his room at one of the lodges. They arranged to meet the following morning to walk through the park, but he never turned up.

Davidson was amazed at Plank's letter. Plank had never confided in him about worries over the accounts or the meeting with Mr Kirkby, and this greatly distressed him. It was unaccountable – 'nothing short of insanity could have prompted him to take the rash step he had done which had been the occasion of so much trouble and anxiety to hundreds at Trentham'.[29]

All this time, Plank's whereabouts remained a mystery. It was still thought he was probably dead, though Lewis had sent messengers to contacts in Liverpool and Manchester and also to some of the local towns to search for him. He had gone off wearing his best clothes.

Plank, however, turned up at Lewis's house at Groundslow Farm at midnight, wet through and exhausted. He was 'extremely absent' but after something to eat agreed to go to bed, though he did not sleep much. Lewis called the doctor the next morning and arranged for someone to look after him. Lewis thought Plank had not 'been himself since his illness' in Shropshire. It appeared that he had walked to Whitchurch where he had gone into a church and then retraced his steps to Groundslow.

Lewis wrote to Plank's father to ask him to fetch his son home, and Plank's younger brother came up to Trentham to help. In the meantime, Kirkby was sent for in order to go through the accounts to find the problem that had caused his panic, though Lewis had no doubts about Plank's honesty. Lewis himself was very unwell and would not be going into the office for day or so. Dr Mackenzie sent a report to Loch on the results of his examination of Plank. His mind, wrote the doctor, had been over-excited 'and has largely lost its tone – Rest under such circumstances is clearly the best remedy – The time required to recover the tone of the mind is always uncertain and depends very much on the extent of loss of memory, absence, slowness of reply'.[30]

During all this, Loch was at Dunrobin, leaving his son to run the office in London. Away in Scotland, he was clearly exasperated over the whole affair, thinking Lewis had overreacted. To Lewis he was moved to make a joke about Plank, a poor youth 'more fit for your neighbour's habitation than yours' (the nearest neighbour to Lewis's home at Groundslow, across the fields, was Spring Vale, the farm which Thomas Bakewell ran as a lunatic asylum). Loch went on, 'I cannot think he is fit for so responsible situation as your head clerk, nor do I see how the Duke should be burdened with him.'[31] To his son Loch confided, 'Lewis seems as daft as poor Plank.'[32]

With the departure of Plank and Emery sacked, the Trentham office was in trouble. Kirkby had resigned and was now merely helping out part-time. Loch's advice was level-headed: get Kirkby back full-time on a temporary basis, an arrangement which was accepted readily enough. The Duke, Loch and Lewis discussed his long-term replacement in the office. Lewis preferred to keep Kirkby, but the Duke seems to have been adamant about bringing in an experienced clerk, William Henney from Lilleshall, who had recently been served notice to quit by Loch. But there was a serious issue to be resolved – William Lewis was not happy with Henney.

The William Henney Affair

William Henney was one of three brothers, the sons of old George Henney who had been the clerk at Trentham for many years and, as was traditional, the guardian of the poor of the parish; he was also the postmaster, collector of taxes and teacher at the Trentham boys' school run by the estate. George was born in 1767 and his son thirty years later. Both Loch and the Marquess, as he was then, had a very high opinion of the father and therefore took on the young William as a junior clerk in 1813.[33] On his father's death in 1816 William was thought responsible enough to be made a committee member of the Trentham Savings Bank. In 1818, he was given a rent-free cottage, probably at Ash Green. In 1820 Lewis thought him honest and trustworthy but 'almost unpardonably slow' in working on the accounts. Perhaps this had something to do with his being moved over to the Shropshire office in 1822 to help out as cashier.[34] There he lived in a small but reasonably comfortable cottage which was extended when he married in 1830.[35]

William proved satisfactory there, at least to Loch, who stood surety for a sizeable sum of money for one of Henney's brothers who had applied for a job in the Birmingham branch of the Bank of England. His reference for John reads, 'His father was long under me as the Office Clerk at Trentham. His brother is in the same situation now in Shropshire – all are persons most faithfully and zealously, most honestly discharging their duties.'[36]

In 1830, however, the Lilleshall office, like Trentham, was in trouble. Realising that Lewis could not run the Shropshire estates adequately from a distance, a new Lilleshall-based sub-agent named Thomas James was appointed for a trial period, to work as an assistant to Lewis. As the clerk who had largely been keeping the office afloat, Henney did not like the way he was treated by the new man, especially the way he was forbidden to give instructions to workmen and order materials.[37]

To make matters worse, Henney had recently married and instead of waiting in the office in the evenings to check the day's work with James and make out orders for the following day, he preferred to take his evening work home. Loch mightily disapproved of this, especially as it meant Henney working in the living room in the presence of his wife, Agnes. He wrote to Agnes herself, explaining why this was not acceptable:

In my own case I never do my business in the same room with Mrs Loch and she is now after 19 years as little acquainted with Lord S's affairs as she was when I first undertook them ... and during the sitting of Parliament I often leave home after breakfast and never get back until between one and two in the morning.[38]

This might seem an extraordinary thing to do but there was something of a personal relationship between the Henneys and Loch. Later, when he visited Lilleshall he sometimes took his daughter with him and left her in the care of Mrs Henney.

In the matter of staff disagreements Lewis blamed Thomas James, and Loch was inclined to agree: 'I have remarked what you say about James and could not help seeing his temper was hasty, perhaps a little peevish – not entirely calculated to manage mankind.'[39] By June 1831 he had decided that James was 'not fit for the job', his trial employment was a failure and Lilleshall should return to the structure as before. He proposed to divide the responsibilities for land improvement and house repair between existing staff and to promote Henney to do more outdoor supervision work with the help of a boy in the office at a low salary, all under instruction from Lewis. This would come to less than James' salary and they needed to save money.[40] By October that year a highly indignant James had received notice that his services were no longer required because he could not keep on proper terms with other staff. By November Lewis was happily going round the farm and plantations with Henney, pointing out where improvements were to be made.[41]

The year 1832 seemed to progress fairly quietly, but 1833 was a different matter. Problems began with a letter from Lewis to Loch saying he had found the tradesmen – painters, plumbers and glaziers – who were still working on the improvements to Lilleshall Hall were 'at their old tricks' of not turning up for work until after eight in the morning. This was a sufficient hint for Loch to write a sharp letter to Henney, whose job it was to oversee such matters: 'I find that you are not so active in a morning as is requisite for a person in your situation and that in consequence thereof advantage has been taken … to neglect their duty.' The letter concluded with a thinly veiled threat of dismissal.[42]

A flurry of indignant letters followed. On one Sunday morning Lewis dashed off an infuriated note to Loch complaining that he had received 'what I call a very impertinent letter' from Henney, only to send another letter by a later post on the same day saying he had received an apology from Henney, so Loch was to 'think nothing more of what I wrote this morning'.

Henney could hardly believe what was happening. Though he was careful not to voice directly his suspicions, it is clear that he thought Lewis was trying to manipulate his dismissal, partly out of jealousy of Henney's wife Agnes who had been taken particular notice of by the Duchess and partly to make way for Lewis's son, who needed a job as a clerk. Having been reassured by Lewis on this point Henney wrote an apologetic letter to Loch, and things seemed to settle down.[43]

Such a relatively minor dispute did not bode well for Henney, however. Early in 1834, Loch was complaining of Henney's slowness in understanding a problem in the accounts and the fact that he was having difficulty in collecting rents from cottages. By March he had decided on another reorganisation. As Lewis wanted to be relieved entirely of his duties over the Shropshire estates, Henney was to revert to being simply a clerk, and a full-time experienced agent was to be appointed who would report directly to Loch. Moreover, Loch had someone in mind, a Scotsman called William Smith who used to work in the employ of the Duchess Countess, a young man Henney would get along with. Henney, of course, did not think so and complained not only that he had been doing outdoor work for the last two years with no increase of salary but also that he had been promised the position of agent himself.[44] This was not true, wrote Lewis to the Duke, for Henney was 'quite unfit for the situation, knows nothing of land, but has turned very conceited'.

By June Henney had been given his notice: his duties would cease as soon as Smith arrived, except insofar as the clerkship of the Lilleshall Savings Bank was concerned. Loch would, however, do all he could to help him find a new post: his own clerk in London had recently got a position as accountant in a new bank opening up in Manchester, why not think of the same? To the Duke, Loch wrote of Henney that 'a more painstaking and honest person cannot be'.[45]

Naturally Henney was unhappy: 'I must say I am very unjustly delt with. I feel that my conduct has merited a better reward.' Because he had no children and was optimistic about getting another post, there was perhaps not the same appalling anxiety of the other clerks. In July he closed his rental accounts and was anxious to get away from Shropshire to take his wife on holiday to the seaside as her health had been worsening for some time.[46]

Only he probably did not do so, or at least not for long. The administration at Trentham being still in disarray, the Duke and Loch, against Lewis's preference, offered the office clerk's position at Trentham to Henney, the only obstacle to this being the ill will that had developed between Henney and Lewis. On 8 August Loch, before setting out from Dunrobin to the Reay country, forwarded letters from the Duke to both men.[47] Henney received the Duke's letter late one evening and the next day set off to Trentham to talk to Lewis; they had a good conversation, after which Henney accepted the offer with slightly stiff-necked gratitude. He would be absent, however, for about ten days, as he was about to set out for Portsmouth to visit his brother whose wife had recently died.[48]

It was a while before all the details were sorted out. In December 1834 Henney sent a memo listing his salary and perks received at Lilleshall, which were to be used as a basis for his new remunerations. By January 1835 he was hard at work, closing the Trentham rentals for the end of the year.[49] Though spurned by Loch at Lilleshall, largely at the behest of Lewis, Henney, largely at the behest of the Duke, became the slow but steady accountant, one of the main supports of the Trentham office for many years to come.

The aftermath

Randal William Kirkby's death and after

It is not clear to what extent Kirkby remained working at the Trentham office once Henney was appointed. He seems to have been part-time or just filling in, probably the result of deteriorating health. There are records of this from 1830 onwards, when he had had a stroke. At that time Lewis had reported that 'Kirkby has taken a paralytic attack whilst drawing on his stockings. He is getting better though confined to bed.' A few days later Kirkby was up and about again, 'not a pin the worse' though 'his mouth was a good deal twisted about at first but is now quite right'.[50] Kirkby must have made a reasonable recovery for he survived nine years after his first stroke.

It was in the winter of 1839 when Kirkby had another attack. In a letter to Loch, William Lewis wrote that 'poor old Kirkby still remains very ill. I saw Dr Mackenzie today and he has no hopes of his recovery.' Henney wrote shortly afterwards: 'Poor Mr Kirkby cannot survive many hours longer – this is the third day that he has neither spake nor taken anything.' Two days later came the news from Trentham that Kirkby was dead: 'He suffered much, his son from Castle Howard remained with him.'[51] He was aged fifty-six; the record of his burial in the parish register described him as churchwarden and yeoman.

Randal William Kirkby was the most successful of the brothers in terms of his own achievements at Trentham; an important man, well known and respected locally, obviously with a temper, not a man to be crossed, indeed probably feared by some. In many ways he appears a stronger character than his boss, Lewis. He signed himself 'yours faithfully', never 'your obedient servant', in his letters to Loch and he did not seem to write the passionate letters of some of the others. The correspondence about his brother James showed he had a genuine respect for Loch and hoped that Loch returned that respect; but he never lowered himself to beg.

Randal William's sons

One of the issues which had so infuriated Emery had been Kirkby's introduction of his young teenage son into the office. This was William Day Kirkby, the eldest son by his second marriage. The experience proved useful, for in 1834, aged seventeen, after his father had left full-time work in the Trentham office, William was appointed full-time junior clerk under the newly arrived Henney.[52] Three years later, after his marriage, he moved into a small rent-free estate cottage in Ash Green. He was aged just twenty-two when his father died and passed to him the mantle of head of the Kirkby family at Trentham. By then he had one young daughter and was still living in Ash Green.

Randal William Kirkby and his family had lived rent-free in an estate cottage which would be needed by other workers (it was next occupied by the assistant park-keeper Richard Penson). His widow Elizabeth and her dependents were allowed to stay on rent-free until the next half year, but from then on the extended Kirkby family had to find homes for them. The family's solution was to spread them around amongst small cottages in Ash Green, most of which were already overcrowded; Kirkby's widow Elizabeth lodged for a while with her brother-in-law, Kirkby's younger brother Charles, though she very quickly moved into her own estate cottage which she occupied until her death in 1844. William himself found room in his cottage for one of his younger brothers, George, who also worked part-time in the Trentham office.[53] One of his sisters went to live with the family of the Trentham baker and brewer, Robert Wright. The eldest sister had already left home to marry, and another brother Randal had possibly also already left Staffordshire.

Accommodation was not the only problem caused by Kirkby's death, for the family was short of cash. Any pension paid to him would not have been passed on to his widow although it is unlikely the estate made no payments to her. Kirkby had given the matter some previous thought, however. A letter from Lewis to Hathorn, one of the London clerks, warned: 'William Kirkby has just informed me that there is 1 year's interest due to his family by his Grace, it had better be paid, they are in want of money, remind Mr Loch of it.' After some discussion as to the exact details, it emerged that Kirkby had held a mortgage of £2,000 on Spring Vale, the farm which had been opened as a lunatic asylum. Situated right on the edge of his estate, the Duke wanted this closed, and so the estate had arranged a transfer between Spring Vale and Oulton Abbey, which the Duke had purchased a few years back. On completion of the transfer the mortgage was released, but the loan remained with the Duke as an investment for Kirkby who received 4 per cent interest per annum. William had found the note in hand securing this loan in his father's papers. The interest due was paid thereafter half yearly (i.e. forty pounds each half year). Eighty pounds a year was a good income in 1839.[54] In addition, immediately following the death of his father in 1839 William was formally elected as clerk at the Trentham Savings Bank at an additional annual salary of thirty pounds.[55]

William's first wife died in 1846 having borne him four children. Two years later he married a woman from the nearby parish of Wolstanton, by whom he had a further three – thus three successive generations of this line of Kirkbys lost their first wives fairly young, remarried and generated large double families. William appears in all the censuses as 'clerk' or similar, until the 1871 census. He died in April 1880. One of his sons, William, appeared in Kelly's Directory between the years 1880 and 1900 as running his own business, two large flint mills leased from the estate at Strongford.

Randal William's youngest son, George, also seventually followed
in his father's occupational footsteps. In the 1841 census he was
lodging with his elder brother William and was recorded by the
enumerator as an agricultural labourer. He was certainly also doing
odd jobs around the office and estate generally, but in the same
year the sudden retirement on health grounds of William Lewis
as well as the appointment of a new Trentham agent not all that
many years older than himself in the following spring all seemed
to galvanise the young man into a realisation that he should make
something more of himself. Hence a letter was sent to Loch asking
for assistance:

> I have no situation or prospect in view without an intercessour. I
> am 21 years of age I feel myself quite ashamed at not being settled
> before this time but it is not the fate of all to do well, but why
> should I despond? My time is not at hand ...[56]

Busy though he must have been Loch almost certainly took up his
cause, if only for the memory of his dead father whom Loch had
held in great respect. By the next census in 1851 George was living
in the heart of a busy industrial and trading centre in Toxteth,
Liverpool, with a wife and a six-month-old baby, working as a
bookkeeper.

Thomas Emery
The chaotic reorganisation of the Trentham office in 1833–34
would sound farcical if it were not so tragic. Though rambling
and disjointed, a very real despair colours Emery's letters. What
happened to him?

Emery's deep-seated fear was not only for himself but for his wife
and family – five children by the time he was sacked from his post
at Trentham, and an aging father. The Trentham job had brought
in a secure but not particularly generous salary and a rent-free
cottage in Ash Green, which he occupied from 1823 onwards. His
income was barely sufficient to allow him to rent two small areas
of land, presumably for food production. Finances were very tight,
especially as his eldest son, a bookkeeper in a large pottery concern,
had been laid off due to lack of trade, though Lewis set him on
temporarily to help in the office at a busy time.[57] By 1833 Emery

was in arrears of rent on his land, so he was obviously struggling financially even then.[58] His comment about having to sell his furniture if he lost his job was not fanciful.

When he was sacked by Loch in August 1833 he asked if he could have the tenancy of a corn mill in Hanford called New Inn Mill. This was a vacancy caused by yet another man's heartache, for Henry Cartwright had been given notice to quit by Lewis for non-payment of rent; he even had a traumatic unannounced visit by the bailiffs to seize his furniture. It was here that Emery thought he could make a reasonable livelihood for his young family, but the mill needed a lot of repair which he could not afford and he hoped the estate would take this on. Loch must have gone along with this suggestion for a month later his office received two estimates for the wholesale repair of the mill.

According to the rent books, Emery started paying rent in 1835, which must have been for the mill. The Emerys had two children after leaving employment at Trentham to add to the five born previously, and both baptismal records, dated 1837 and 1839, give Emery's occupation as 'miller'. In the 1841 census he and his family were living in the same New Inn Lane, according to an estate valuation survey of that date still in the Mill House, though his occupation in the census was then given as 'farmer'.[59] Emery must have been struggling financially, for the rent records for 1840–41 show he was then owing a half year's rent (£45) on his business. The rental shows his payments ceasing altogether after 1843.

It seems that Loch had not washed his hands of the Emerys, however, for by the next record we have of them, the 1851 census, we see a great change: Emery had gone back to clerking, this time working for the Manchester Ship Canal Navigation Company in Preston-on-the-Hill, Cheshire. He and his wife lived in a cottage with fourteen-year-old son Alfred, who worked as a probationary clerk, and with twelve-year-old Dorothy. In 1861, the couple were still there with an unmarried thirty-year-old daughter, Elizabeth, who worked as a dressmaker. Dorothy, by then aged twenty-two, was working as a servant, and they also had staying with them a young grandson. By 1871, Thomas had died and his widow Jane was living in the same area with another daughter Mary and her husband, who was a police officer.

Though the family had survived, did Thomas ever reflect that they had not perhaps done as well as he might have hoped when he was happily working away for the Marquess of Stafford in the early days at Trentham? On the other hand, he may well have thought himself extremely lucky in that, once again, James Loch's influence and position within the Bridgewater Canal Trust had borne fruit. A case of guilty conscience, perhaps.

William Henney

Of all the clerks involved in the difficulties of the 1830s, William Henney lived the longest and certainly ended the richest. He died aged seventy-seven in 1875 and was buried at Trentham. In the 1871 census he had described himself as 'retired estate office cashier'; in the three previous censuses he was called 'office clerk' or 'accountant'. As well as working in the Trentham office he had continued his post with the Savings Bank; in its minute book his last signature was dated 1864 when the bank was beginning to close down. He had worked for the Leveson-Gowers continuously for over forty-five years, at both Lilleshall and Trentham. Whatever afflicted his wife back in 1834 was serious because she died aged forty-nine in 1845. He never remarried and had no children, but continued to live at Hanchurch.

The house which Henney occupied in Hanchurch is further evidence of his relative wealth. Loch had suggested the old farmhouse be made good for him. Although the rent books carry no entry for him (the rent books usually included even rent-free occupiers), a survey and map of 1859 records William Henney's tenancy of Hanchurch Manor House – over eleven acres including a large farmhouse with orchard and garden, two other houses and gardens and over eight acres of meadow. In the 1841 census he and Agnes, who may have been an invalid by then, could afford to keep in their household not only two young female servants but also a twenty-five-year-old manservant. Moreover, the rent book for 1844 shows that a rent-free cottage in Hanchurch was let to one John Bennett, described as 'Mr Henney's man'. This continued after Agnes' death, occupied by a Samuel Halmarack, again described as 'Mr Henney's man'. Thus it seems that Henney's rent-free entitlement included not only his own house but also his manservant living adjacent, perhaps as a gardener and groom.[60]

After Agnes' death in 1845 the next census showed that Henney's household included a housekeeper who was his unmarried niece, Mary Eleanore, aged thirty-six, as well as two young women servants.

Henney's effects upon his death in 1875 were valued at just under £8,000, which seems a good deal. Before she married Henney, his wife Agnes had been the widow of a reverend gentleman, so he probably inherited money from her which might have contributed to his wealth. Henney had maintained that his wife's wealth and social status were the reasons Lewis felt so jealous of him. Alternatively, Henney may have bought property or invested otherwise very wisely, both of which would have been possible, given his professional position.

10

The Parting of the Ways

'My blood was shed and nearly my life sacrificed' – The Cottage Agent

After the excitement of helping to sort out the Plank affair in the summer of 1834, Randal William Kirkby might have been forgiven for looking forward to a quiet life of retirement from Trentham office politics, especially as it is likely he was suffering from long-term hypertension. As things worked out, however, he was next to be plunged into the middle of the longest and most bitter defensive fight of all – that waged by John Mackay at Ketley in Shropshire, whose job Kirkby had previously refused. This was an affair which rumbled on for years, and it not only illustrates the extent to which Loch relied on Kirkby as a troubleshooter but also explains how the two administrations based at Trentham and Lilleshall, long ago centralised by James Loch under the agency of William Lewis, eventually came to be split under two agents, each reporting separately to Loch.

Ketley was a manor in central Shropshire, now a suburb of the town of Telford. The Leveson-Gowers owned it until 1894, when it was broken up into smaller parcels of land and sold. Much of the area was underlain by coal measures which here and there outcropped the land, resulting in some early small-scale mining exploitation. An ironworks was built in 1756, which became a major source of employment, thus drawing in population. Many of the colliers and ironworkers were poor, living in what Loch described as 'wretched huts'. Most of the settlements in the area were 'dispersed and impoverished', a characteristic which was not conducive to the development of a successful social infrastructure – with the single exception of beershops (of which there were many).

When James Loch was appointed in 1812, he determined to tighten up the administration of Ketley, pursuing a policy of house improvement and enlargement of the smaller holdings with enough land to keep a cow. From 1817 until 1834 it came under the supervision of William Lewis, based at Trentham. By its nature as described above, it was never going to be an easy estate to manage from a distance, especially through the difficult times of the recession of the 1830s.[1]

John Mackay

John Mackay was another one of Loch's protégées brought down from Scotland, this time a Highlander whose parents remained on the Sutherland Highland estate. His career in Staffordshire started at Trentham, where the rent book for 1814 shows him paying one guinea rent for a cottage.[2] He then moved to the Shropshire estate, first as clerk to the Lilleshall Savings Bank and then as assistant in the Lilleshall office. By the 1820s he had been promoted to the status of resident 'ground officer' or sub-agent on the Ketley estate near Ironbridge. He worked directly to Lewis back at Trentham but he had to do his own clerking. Mackay was given a good salary of £120 and a house and land in the area known as Ketley Grange, described by Loch as being 'as nice a house as any in England'.[3] By 1831 he was married and had four children.

By 1830, however, he was having difficulties with poor rent collections. The Shropshire estates were in trouble. Farm labourers were having their wages cut by the farmers and were thus in debt as to their rent. One tenant farmer received a letter signed 'Swing' threatening to break his machines and burn his ricks.[4] By June 1831 Mackay had earned Loch's particular disapproval because he had unilaterally given James Penson permission to keep a beershop, a decision which infuriated Loch who was committed to ridding the estate of both beerhouses in general and James Penson in particular. Clearly fearing for his job, Mackay wrote several long letters of excuse. It was the sort of mistake that Loch was liable to allow once but would never forgive or forget. Lewis for his part never seemed to like Mackay and described him as a 'confused and stupid man'.[5]

By March 1833 it emerged that Mackay was grossly behind-hand with the cottage rentals at Ketley – both collecting the cash and the paperwork. Loch wrote to Mackay saying he had long delayed sending him notice that his services were at an end and had tried to find an alternative position for him but failed, and he warned, 'You cannot expect to be continued in Lord Stafford's service after this.' Formal notice that he was no longer required was given him a few days later, including a promise that Loch's aid and his Grace's influence would be available to help find him a new post but that he must also exert himself in this direction. In the meantime he would have to settle with Lewis both the date of his leaving and the date when his books would be brought up to closure.[6]

Mackay's emotional letters in defence make for interesting reading, as they make Ketley sound like the Wild West. Indeed this may have not been far wrong. Because the estate was a developing industrial area, many of the farms sublet smallholdings and miners' cottages. When he started at Ketley, Mackay claimed he had inherited a rental book which was five years out of date and it had taken him much effort to try to rectify this. Getting the rent from the sublet cottagers had given him great trouble. Houses were in a very poor state, many well beyond repair, and he had made improvements which had not made him popular. Indeed, at first the estate was turbulent:

> For five or six years I was in danger of my life ... I have pulled down more than 100 cottages and destroyed more than 500 ferocious dogs ... I have been in danger many times and humiliated ... my blood was shed and nearly my life sacrificed, from open assaults and from ambuscades ... If I had been a single man I certainly would have fought a second Waterloo sooner than suffer the anguish which I then felt.

As a result largely of his efforts, he maintained, the estate was now 'peaceable and quiet', the Duke and Duchess more popular and the cottagers more comfortable. The letters show a man in deep shock and distress at being sacked and evicted from his home:

I do not know how to speak or how to act, but I hope and trust you will be mercifully inclined, for the sake of my parents and my wife and children, if you decide otherwise, I implore you not to let my father and mother know ...[7]

This is the period when Loch and Lewis were also struggling with problems in the Trentham office, the solution to which seemed to be to send Kirkby to take Mackay's place. Mackay got to hear of this and even asked to be considered for Kirkby's replacement at Trentham. Loch dismissed the idea in short order. In any case, Kirkby must have realised what a difficult estate he would be inheriting and turned the position down. Apart from any other consideration Lewis could never have worked closely with Mackay. His frustration with him was not simply that he was hopelessly behind-hand with the rents but that he had insisted over a long period in spending his own money in improving the house and farm, of which he was tenant. Lewis had warned him time and time again of the risks of the miserable situation in which he was like to find himself, all to no avail.[8]

Over the next few months several meetings were set up for Mackay to see Loch at Lilleshall, to which MacCay sent apologies for his absence, ostensibly citing various health reasons but probably also because he found it impossible to sort out his rentals. His health problems do seem to have been real – he had long-term trouble with his eyes and one of his hands. At one point his doctor, a Dr Webb, sent a letter explaining that Mackay was suffering a severe inflammation and 'watery effusion', caused by seriously injuring his left testicle on the pommel of his saddle whilst on duty with the Shropshire Yeomanry some years ago. The stress of his situation had worsened it and Webb was now preparing to operate on him the next morning, after which he would be confined to his house for some time.[9]

Having been dismissed from his post, Mackay was without income but remained at his Ketley house, even though he was liable to pay rent for it and was accruing substantial rent arrears. Though the list of people and institutions he applied to for work was long, nothing was available due to the depressed state of the economy. 'God knows,' he wrote to Loch, 'that such a change in my affairs could not possibly happen at a more inopportune period.' To add to the problems it appears that Mackay had taken to drink.[10]

Following Kirkby's refusal of the Ketley position, one of the tenant farmers, Skitt, was appointed instead. In what must have been an extremely distressing incident, Skitt arrived without warning to deliver his furniture to the Mackay house in order to take legal possession. He was greeted by Mackay's wife, who had to run upstairs to tell her husband what was happening since he was ill in bed. Skitt eventually took his furniture to a local inn for temporary storage, but a few weeks later his family took possession of the garden and orchard by planting potatoes in them and claimed possession of the surrounding pasture. They had also inspected the inside of the house, 'from the cellar to every room in it', which Mackay had allowed.[11]

To add public humiliation to private insult Mackay discovered that Lewis had circulated a leaflet in the area notifying everyone that Mackay was no longer in service with the estate and should not be given any money for rent. Why was this done, demanded Mackay of Loch, when everyone knew it anyway? Lewis was just trying to humiliate him. He denied resisting Skitt's taking possession of his house – the furniture had been moved to the inn before he could do anything. He would have accepted some of Skitt's furniture but not a wagon load, as his own was in the house awaiting sale.[12] He had never received a formal notice to quit and Skitt's possession of the land was 'irregular if not illegal' and had caused a great deal of talk locally: 'My cattle grazing on the land still keeps me in regular and legal possession.' He denied an accusation of receiving rents illegally: on appointed days when Skitt was supposed to attend at the farm to receive rents he did not appear, and some of the tenants had asked Mackay to keep the money for them to give to Skitt when he eventually turned up.

He also claimed once more that he, Mackay, had transformed the popularity of the Sutherlands in the area – did not that deserve some reward? He even showed Loch around the estate and pointed out places where he had been assaulted in the past: 'I should like the Ketley estate to be viewed and compared with the Ketley of 1816 and 1817.'

In addition, he had made many long-term improvements to his tenanted farm in underdraining, ditching and extending the buildings, and it would be hard if he was not allowed to have some financial reward for it. He wanted the improvements he had made to the house, for example the two new bedrooms he had added, to be properly valued and set against what he owed in rent: 'If this was allowed it would restore my health and make a new man of me. Sooner than leave the family I would serve them gratuitously, this feeling is peculiar to highlanders ...' Perhaps this was a dig at Lewis, who was southern Scots and who was firmly against him; Loch was now his only friend.[13]

In this judgement Mackay may have been correct, for it seems Loch was beginning to come around to the idea that they delay further action and perhaps give Mackay another chance: 'It is better to err on the side of leniency.'[14] How to answer such claims about rents and valuations, but to get an expert in? In May 1834 Loch called in Randal William Kirkby as an experienced but independent assessor into Mackay's affairs. Given all the rows at Ketley, Kirkby must have felt hugely relieved at having refused the permanent job. Now he was to go to Ketley, work on the rental books, assess the situation and prepare a formal settlement of accounts at Mackay's leaving. Kirkby possibly held the future of Mackay's whole family in his hands.

Kirkby's assessment of the Ketley estate carried on for the rest of 1834 and into 1835. It developed into a full-scale review of the rentals back to the 1820s and required many visits to Ketley and Lilleshall, spending a good deal of time with both Mackay and Skitt.[15] On one occasion Mackay failed to turn up at Lilleshall for a meeting, which infuriated Lewis once again. To Loch he wrote, 'I am sorry you should be troubled and plagued by one so totally devoid of every proper feeling.'[16] By January 1835 Lewis refused to have anything more to do with Mackay.[17]

The review involved visiting all the tenants to ascertain whether they were in arrears or not. At the behest of Lewis, Skitt was tasked with much of this investigation, which Mackay again regarded as a deliberate public humiliation – Lewis's behaviour in using Skitt to destroy his good name was 'vindictive and malicious in the extreme'. At one point he and Lewis met at Trentham but neither spoke to each other.[18] Mackay accused Skitt of including in the list of tenants from whom he was supposed to have collected rents illegally a woman who had been dead for seventy-two years and several cottages which had been knocked down years ago.[19] Kirkby was asked to look into these accusations too and his report was not 'altogether favourable to Skitt'.[20]

Mackay was always complimentary towards Kirkby, whom he described as 'indefatigable', 'rigidly strict' and 'equally impartial', but he became ever more incensed against Lewis, especially after a meeting in the nearby inn, which he thought Lewis had deliberately arranged like 'a Court of Arbitration' to humiliate him publicly. Mackay's letter to Loch describing this occasion was so angry that Loch sent him a warning about his intemperate and disrespectful language, and reminding him how kind Lewis had been in the past.[21]

Between Mackay and Henney, Lewis had had enough of the whole Shropshire estate. Throughout 1834 he expressed a desire to be relieved of its responsibilities. If Loch appointed a full agent over both Lilleshall and Ketley he could dispense with both Skitt and his own wages relating to Shropshire and thus save money. Loch did not need to be told twice. Skitt was given notice, and in May 1834 a young man from the Sutherland's Scottish estates, William Smith, was given a trial six months as the independent Shropshire agent working directly to Loch.[22]

By July 1835 Kirkby had managed to prepare 'a sort of abstract of Mackay's accounts', which concluded that the estate owed Mackay some ninety pounds; but when the various expenses were added – Mackay's rent arrears and Skitt's costs in moving furniture for example – Mackay was left with around seven pounds.[23]

The uncertainty as to what would happen to him and his family continued, Mackay being obliged to borrow from both his neighbours and even William Smith to avoid his goods being seized by a creditor.[24] Unsavoury disputes about money owed by various parties carried on throughout the summer. Mackay was in a state of great distress during this period, expressing his Highlander's emotional affiliation to the Sutherland family in a letter to Loch:

> I would not wish my greatest enemy to suffer as I have done for
> the last twelvemonth, being discarded and severed from a family
> to whom I bear filial affection ... What, could the most indifferent
> and the most callous to mental sufferings resist shedding a tear
> under such circumstances.[25]

It was a combination of the improvements which Mackay had made to Ketley as well as the public humiliation that had so angered him which ultimately saved him, for in May 1836 Loch was sent a remarkable document, a 'memorial' or petition. It was signed by twenty-four of the gentry of Ketley and district, many of them tenants of the Sutherlands, all people of worth whom the Duke could simply not ignore – landowners and doctors, a minister of the Church, a miller, and an ironmaster. They remembered the 'uncultivated state of the Country', the 'wretched Condition' of the cottages and the 'rude Manners' of the lower classes of Ketley before Mackay's arrival. They remembered also the 'Perils and Dangers' suffered by him 'from ill-disposed Persons waylaying him in Ambush' and regretted the deterioration 'of the Manners and Morals' of the people since his removal. They hoped that his Grace would restore him again.[26]

The memorial was presented to Loch for his Grace's attention by Mathew Webb, the local surgeon who tended Mackay. His covering letter was written in even stronger terms. Thirty years ago, Ketley was 'exceedingly vicious and disorderly'. During Mackay's residence things had improved greatly but were now deteriorating again, due partly to the growth of beershops but also because there was no resident agent. It was now 'scarcely bearable as a residence'.[27]

Not even the hardest-headed employer could have ignored this, especially a family who were extremely aware of their public image. Loch, however, was always anxious to have a third opinion before making up his mind, and again wrote to Kirkby asking for his honest opinion of Mackay's character. Given all the stress to which everyone concerned had been subjected over that last year, Kirkby's response was illuminating. He was entirely assured of Mackay's honesty, honourableness and humanity, but he was inattentive to matters of money and accounts. He had been impressed by the genuine respect and affection he had earned from the inhabitants of Ketley, the authority he held, and his knowledge and concern for the area. His conduct towards himself during the review of the accounts had been 'highly praiseworthy ... I think Mackay may be trusted again with the superintendence of the Ketley Estate subject to the exception of his having nothing to do with the disbursement of monies and of course under the control of the resident agent at Lilleshall.'[28]

The result was a formal meeting between Mackay and the new young agent at Lilleshall, William Smith: 'I sent for Mackay at the House where I do business at Ketley, and delivered him the Duke's letter, on reading which his feelings were almost overcome with joy ... as he will continue to occupy the House he is in, I think it would be well if he held the ley as formerly as it surrounds the House.' So overcome was Mackay that he had to read the letter three times and have Smith explain carefully what his duties would be.[29]

Mackay's previous salary and allowances added up to £146. This was now to be split – £52 salary for a new clerk who would handle all the cash and rentals for Ketley, and the rest for Mackay who was appointed resident cottage agent, all as recommended by Kirkby. Smith had asked Lewis's advice on what the exact amount of Mackay's salary should be, but he had refused to give an opinion. Smith also asked Loch to give Mackay an advance on his salary as he was in such difficult financial straits.[30]

Thus with the help of Kirkby, the whole affair of the administration of Ketley was theoretically resolved. Lewis would no longer have any responsibility for Shropshire. The new agent Smith would work directly to Loch supported by office clerks at Lilleshall; Mackay and a clerk would run Ketley under Smith. Kirkby remained at Trentham, working only for the savings bank and for the office on a casual basis.

There was a postscript to Mackay's financial affairs: he still owed the estate a substantial sum in back rent for his own house, but on Smith's letter referenced above is a pencilled note dated January 1837 to the effect that due to his total inability to pay these bills and others (one a medical bill) all were struck off – that is, paid by the estate. The same year William Smith recommended that the estate accept the fact that out of thirty-three cottagers in Ketley who owed back rent, thirteen were old, many infirm widows, who would never be able to pay and their debt should therefore be written off.[31]

Mackay's problems had gone very deep and were not all resolved overnight. He remained in serious debt for several years. In January 1841 he wrote a long letter to the Duke asking for help for his widowed mother back at the Sutherlands. It seems that the Duke and Duchess had visited her and found her ignorant of her son's troubles but in terrible poverty. They had written to Mackay reproaching him for not helping her. His reply described all the problems he had experienced over getting his accounts passed by the estate, and that he had kept in touch with his parents when there was good news but would not unburden himself to them, which he regretted now. He described how he had no furniture, for he had to sell all he owned. When the doctor had come to see his son they had brought him downstairs to conceal the extent of their poverty, for 'we have not a bed of our own to lie on, nor a chair of our own to sit on' but possessed only a mattress and some chairs which had been lent by some neighbours.[32]

This highly emotional letter was passed on to Loch, who wrote to William Smith asking about Mackay's family – how many children had he, had any been educated or been in service? 'He seems in great want and distress, you could perhaps ascertain for his Grace's information, in what way he could ... alleviate his distress.'

In early February, Smith reported a gratuity from the Duke to Mackay of ten pounds along with the suggestion that he wished to place Mackay's youngest daughter (then four years old) in a charity school in London. Smith thought this a good idea 'as it is painful to see the state the family are in without furniture or clothing of any description'.[33] Mackay had told him he was hoping to get some respectable clothing for the eldest daughter (aged twenty-one) and to get her placed in service soon. It is perhaps ironic that whilst previously employed by the Sutherlands Mackay had been one of the Guardians of the Poor for the parish of Ketley, by virtue of his job as bailiff. Given all the circumstances of his fall into debt and his family's long connections with the Sutherlands in Scotland, the Duke and Duchess do not emerge at all well from the affair.

Mackay continued his job as resident cottage agent in Ketley for the rest of his working life. He and his family – wife Hannah, children Marion, Jessie, Elizabeth and Charlotte and Alexander – remained in the same house at Ketley Grange, but John died in October 1851, aged sixty-two. His wife outlived him by sixteen years; in fact, she outlived her only son, Alex, who worked as a clerk in the ironworks at Ketley. The rift between Lewis and Mackay was never healed.

PART THREE

11

The Agent

'Not contented with half measures'
When James Loch was appointed as chief agent or commissioner
to the Leveson-Gower estates in 1812 he set about dismantling the
previous administrative system, with each estate having its own
steward or agent, replacing it with an administration based on the
centralising, specialising principles propounded by Adam Smith.
From 1814 onwards, a single English agency had been built around
one man, Francis Suther, who worked not through local sub-agents
but full-time professional experts – builders, surveyors, accountants,
bailiffs – who were responsible for a single aspect of management
over all of the combined estates and who had a network of assistants
and clerks, some of whom were part-timers. Suther was based at
Trentham, it being the most central site and the one most easily
accessed from London, where Loch set himself up with an office and
staff. Trentham also had an office of clerks and cashiers.

Suther remained in this post only three years, during which time
most of his efforts must have been taken up with consolidation
of the new management system. In June 1817 he moved to the
Scottish estates at an increased salary of £400 p.a. William Lewis
arrived as his replacement and was paid a salary of £250 p.a., plus
a free house and a free horse along with travelling expenses, which
brought it up to £330. As was usual with Loch's management style,
there was an overlap period of several months to allow William to
settle in. Suther became a major player in Loch's dealings with the
Highland estates, but later William confided to Loch that during
this period at Trentham he never trusted Suther, whom he thought

deceitful and who behaved very badly towards himself, so that he could not understand why Loch did not see him for what he was.[1]

William Lewis was a Lowland Scot, born in 1791 at Larbert in Stirlingshire, of a farming family. He became a professional land agent and was working as such on the Pitcairn estate in Perthshire when Loch recruited him as a new agent for the Leveson-Gowers' English estates. Landing the job at the young age of twenty-six must have been a huge and perhaps daunting rise in William's status and responsibilities.

In employing Suther back in 1814, Loch had got rid of a number of old employees. Until 1794 the Leveson-Gower's chief agent had been the Revd G. Plaxton and in the early years of the nineteenth century the Trentham estate had been part-managed by the local parish vicar, the Revd Thomas Butts. He was retired in 1814 for reasons of ill health but remained as an informal adviser for many years – Loch was always willing to use people's hard-earned experience. The services of separate agents running the estates in Yorkshire, Wolverhampton, Lilleshall, Lichfield and Newcastle-under-Lyme were also dispensed with, though in the last case Thomas Fenton remained in contact as a useful local solicitor.

Lewis was to spend the rest of his working life with the Leveson-Gowers, based at Trentham. He retired in 1841 after a stroke; his service lasted twenty-five years, during which time he oversaw the creation of much of the physical landscape and architectural heritage which remains today at both Trentham and Lilleshall.

Lewis's family affairs

Previous to 1817 William had worked as a land steward in Perthshire but had also been involved in a family enterprise, sharing the tenancy of Boglilly Farm near Kirkcaldy in Fife with his younger brother George, who ran the farm. The only other family members present at that time were a sister, Janet, and their widowed mother, Helen. William carefully kept the early correspondence between himself and Boglilly, partly because he retained both a financial and a working interest in the farm.[2]

It appeared that Boglilly was heavily encumbered with debt, and during his early years away at Trentham William was doing his best to increase productivity on the farm back home and also sending remittances home to pay off the loans, to the point where he himself was short of cash. His letters to George, of which he kept copies, were full of detailed instructions, and in some cases severe admonishment:

> What is your motive for travelling Blaze thro' the country when you are so well aware of your speculation proved so ruinous in former times? I am far from being satisfied at this affair and you must have known my sentiments long ere now, on that subject.'

('Travelling' here meant walking around the district farms with a stallion, receiving payments for covering mares.)

George must have objected to the tone of this letter, for shortly afterwards William again wrote to him:

> I have all along studied to give you my best advice in the disposal of the produce of the farm and if I have given you bad counsel at any time why not inform me of it ... I have no selfish motive in the great interest I have in the operation of Boglilly Farm, but a sincere desire to promote the prosperity and welfare of the whole family.

By the time he had been in post at Trentham a couple of years, William had learnt some of James Loch's ways and had adopted Loch's close attention to paperwork, for he went on to instruct his brother:

> I wish you to sit down as the nights are now long and make out an inventory of every article – Implements and Livestock (except Household goods) and put a value on them as near as you can guess and send it me. I am anxious to see how we stand as to property and also make a separate list of any debts that are owing.

Several of the letters William kept were from his mother, who sent him a box with bread and some oatmeal and pot barley, and later a small cheese. As mothers are wont to do, she worried about his shirts – 'I think your shirts will be thin by this time' – so she sent six fine shirts, two nightshirts and two flannel shirts, as well as six kitchen towels and a pair of stockings. In return he sent her some tea, that available in Fife being so bad that many people had given up drinking it.

Two years after arriving at Trentham, in a most matter-of-fact letter to his mother, William made an important announcement:

I sit down to inform you that I have been for some time resolved to change my situation in life by taking to myself a wife. This circumstance has not been decided upon without due and deliberate consideration on my part as in my present situation I am uncomfortable and my living attended with considerable more expence than I can well afford ... the young woman I have fixed on is of a most industrious and economical habit and some day will have a handsome property ... as soon as circumstances will allow we will pay you a visit ... Lord and Lady Stafford approve of my intentions ...

Notice that William had sought approval of his employers before telling his mother! He then went on to say:

I am quite willing to resign my interest in the farm if it is your and George's wish, this you can turn over in your minds and let me know your determination as it is my most anxious desire to do what is right ...

William had indeed been giving serious consideration to the problem of a wife, for not long after arriving in the Midlands he had written to a friend in Northumberland asking if he had seen any pretty girls lately. The answer arrived: 'Certainly I have seen a great many, they being more plentiful in this country than in yours ... I think if you want one, you may suit yourself here very well, there are some very fine girls and plenty of siller, which is a great object.'

William did not have to travel so far, however, for in August 1819, in the church at Trentham, he married a girl from Lilleshall, twenty-one-year-old Jane Pearce, the daughter of one of the Leveson-Gower's tenant families. The marriage was witnessed by the two Trentham clerks, Willim Henney and Randal William Kirkby, and by a brother of the bride. William and Jane raised three children: William (b. 1821), Helen (b. 1823) and John Pearce (b. 1830). Nevertheless, it took Lewis a long time to forget he was a 'foreigner'. In 1838, over twenty years since his first arrival in Staffordshire, he could write the enigmatic sentence: 'They are a queer set in the Potteries.'[3]

Work

When William was set on in 1817 Loch sent him a daunting job specification that required of him the superintendence of all the tenantry on all four English estates – in Mid-Staffordshire, South Staffordshire, Shropshire and Yorkshire; their buildings, fences and their methods of farming, especially their agricultural improvements.[4] Attention was specially drawn to the 'preservation of old Grass lands from the Plough ... a most important and distinguishing feature between English and Scotch farming.' This last was part of a reaction to the drop in national cereal prices following Waterloo, resulting in a widespread return of attention to good grassland management. This explains the enthusiasm displayed by both Loch and Lewis towards field drainage and manuring on both the Staffordshire and Shropshire estates; more than once they exchanged drawings of field drainage pipes. New projects such as road improvements were also in Lewis's charge, but only as approved by Loch. He was also responsible for the half-yearly rent collections, the completion of monthly reports, and the payment of wages and bills for all departments under him, which included the farm bailiffs, the park-keepers, surveyors, gardeners, gamekeepers, coal bailiff, and in some cases the grooms. He had charge of all his Lordship's title deeds (no mean responsibility in itself). In short, the document concluded, 'Mr Lewis's duty is to see that all the rest do their duties.'

Lewis got through a heavy workload, particularly with draining and improving both the home farms and tenanted properties, Tittensor and Groundslow in particular. He had help from the office clerks who kept the books, paid the wages and bills, drew up lists of rent defaulters, and arranged for the many newspaper adverts of land for short-term letting and mining leases. As a hands-on farmer, however, he never lost the need to get out on the land and see for himself.

Being an agent for a great estate might have been a financial necessity for Lewis but practical farming was his real love. The surviving correspondence of another land agent, Ford of the neighbouring Fitzherbert estate at Swynnerton, provides evidence that in the early 1830s Lewis rented over a hundred acres of land near Beech on the Swynnerton estate. Ford wanted to persuade him to take more land, most of which was in poor condition, for as Ford reported to Fitzherbert, 'Mr Lewis is a most desirable tenant for any land that he can be induced to take; whatever may be its present condition or quality, he would soon make it good.'[5] Ford and Lewis had developed a relationship which was part-professional, part-friendship, collaborating (one might almost say colluding) in Fitzherbert's purchase of a property at Blakelow, but certainly Ford had a high opinion of his fellow agent: 'I have not the least doubt of Lewis's sincerity.' A sale advert in the local paper also shows that Lewis used his local knowledge and contacts to buy a farm on the Shropshire–Staffordshire border, which he then let out himself.

Ross Wordie, an academic writing on land agents, has characterised William Lewis as an agent who was conscientious and efficient but deficient in the art of delegation and 'lacking in level-headedness and the strength of character of his predecessor', equating 'infinite hard work and endless galloping over the estate with greater efficiency'.[6] Such remarks may have a grain of truth in them, but at the same time Wordie's overall verdict is somewhat harsh, especially as far as the 'galloping' is concerned. The geographical area for which William was responsible was widespread and enormous – from Wolverhampton to Yorkshire, Staffordshire to Shropshire. At that time, it was commonplace for an agent responsible for several estates to spend seven or eight hours a day in the saddle. John Grey, the agent to the Greenwich Hospital estates in the north of England oversaw properties in Carlisle, Berwick and Tyneside: 'I was almost killed in the first year and a half; for I rode over every farm and every field and I made a report every night when I came home of its value and it capabilities.'[7]

There is no doubt about Lewis's enthusiasm, loyalty and energy, so much so that by February 1820 Loch had given him strict orders to stay home for a while at Trentham. In obvious frustration, Lewis wrote, 'You will recollect some time ago that you strictly forbade me leaving this place without having Lord Stafford's consent even for a day. I wish to know if you are still of this opinion, because I am at this time quite at a loss how to act.' He was needed urgently in Wolverhampton, wanted to go to Yorkshire and had not been to Shropshire for ages.[8]

His idea of a holiday was to travel by public coach to York, then to Hull to choose the timber for the new offices to be built in the stable yard at Trentham, before going on the next day to Stittenham and also to Castle Howard for a day, then across the Pennines to Manchester. At seven the next morning he took a trip on the railway to Liverpool, then a coach ride to see a large nursery, then home. This was all in February when everywhere was covered in snow. The trip obviously invigorated him; he described the railway as 'one of the most wonderful undertakings ever attempted in any country', and later took his children on a day out to see it.[9]

Lewis's own memorandum book gives an idea of the extent of his journeys. He seems to have thought nothing of riding from Trentham to Lilleshall and back in the same day, and on one occasion, around noon on 3 February 1835, Lewis was sent a message from his son's school in Stone (some five miles from Trentham) saying that Willie was very ill. He immediately set off to see him, returning to Trentham later that afternoon, returning back to the school in the evening. The next day he visited the school three times, each time driving back to the estate to work. Lewis spent the next fourteen days juggling work and visiting his son two or three times a day and sometimes staying overnight with Willie. Eventually, on 18 February, his son's condition was sufficiently improved that he hired a chaise and fetched him home to Groundslow. In his record Lewis gave no hint as to what was wrong with Willie, but obviously he was extremely worried and had prepared himself for his death.[10]

Local journeys like this were usually undertaken by horseback, but going to Lilleshall he sometimes borrowed a gig; the correspondence records numerous accidents on both. In 1832 he met with a frightening collision in a narrow lane with another gig 'being driven furiously'. He was taking his little girl to stay with Mrs Kirke in Shropshire. She was unhurt in the accident but he had the shaft of the other gig driven into his thigh; after this he was lame for some time. In May 1833 he was injured in the foot by his horse stamping on it, so badly so that a splinter of bone came out; Loch, though commiserating with him, also wrote that both he and the Duke 'expressed a wish that you rode horses less likely to do you injury'.[11]

Perhaps not surprisingly given the amount of time spent on horseback, Lewis suffered from haemorrhoids. In October 1833 these were so severe he cancelled a trip to Castle Howard but instructed his clerk Randal Kirkby to assure Loch that he would be well enough to be with the Newcastle and Trentham Troop of the Yeomanry, which was planning to greet the new Duke on his first visit to Trentham after inheriting the title. Loch's sympathy here was that of a fellow sufferer. He advised 'plenty of cold water, anoint the parts out and in with ointment, candle grease is as good as any'; he also recommended copious bleeding or cupping on the lower part of back. On another occasion Lewis had rheumatism in his thigh so badly that he could not 'mount on saddle for at least six days'.[12]

Lewis's relationship with Loch was complicated. The letters between them are usually fairly formal, especially on Loch's behalf, but there are occasions of intimacy. Sometimes Loch was clearly irritated with Lewis's ramblings. Perhaps the correspondence is best described as representing that between teacher and pupil. No doubt William felt enormous respect and gratitude, even fear, towards Loch, and there are no shortages of what appear, at least to modern eyes, to be instances of undue deference. Yet he could also stand up for himself if he thought he was being mistreated or if Loch was simply wrong. They did not always see eye to eye. For example, over the tenants on the Yorkshire estate at Stittenham, Lewis wrote to Loch:

> I feel sorry that you found it necessary to make such remarks on the condition and state of its improvement. I think it but justice to myself and to the present occupiers to state that at the commencement of my stewardship I found every tenant upon that estate insolvent ... since that period and during the worst of times for Farmers you will <u>now</u> find them all recovered from that state of misery except Mr Hornsey. It is true the Estate might have been cleared of these poor people and others' skill and capital introduced but that course would not have been in unison with my Lord's and your own feelings ... I certainly think well of Matt Hornsey ... you state that you are told that they are the worst tenants in the country. I cannot agree to the justice of such remark. It would have applied formerly but not at the present day.[13]

Perhaps because of his early years struggling with the debts of Boglilly, William often showed a degree of sympathy with genuine poverty which perhaps is unexpected in a man in his position. In 1818 he wrote to his brother that North Staffordshire was troubled with unrest and the gentry was preparing to increase the militia, 'but in my opinion it would redound much more to their credit if they would endeavour to find work & meat to these poor starving suffering creatures, their present condition is truly deplorable'.[14]

As the person ultimately responsible for rent collection, Lewis even voiced sympathy for the incendiarists of 1830 – rioters who were setting fire to ricks and other farm properties. He thought that there was no sign of riots in the Trentham area because most men were still in work and 'in a general way fairly paid'. In many areas, however, poor labourers had received 'barbarous treatment'; he was only surprised 'they have remained so long in quiet subjection. Their sufferings have been very great.' In another letter to Loch he reported that Lady Gower had ordered clothing and coal for many of the poor people in Lilleshall and warned, 'The country is certainly in a dreadful state of distress, pauperism every day increasing.'[15] He thought the situation worse in Shropshire where farmers had been reducing wages. The day after writing this, however, to be on the safe side Lewis set a night watch on the farm hayricks near Trentham, as there had been reports of discontent amongst the potters because of the truck system. He was confident, though, that 'my Lord's goodness' was appreciated locally and this was 'a grand shield over our head'. He would ask his Lordship whether he was to designate some special constables from the staff at Trentham – James Penson the park-keeper, Woolley the head gardener, Randal Kirkby the head clerk, Emery the under-clerk, Elliot the gamekeeper, James Wood the farm bailiff, and himself.

As an extra precaution he intended to organise a supper-dance for the labourers on the estate during the week between Christmas and New Year. He had done this before and it was always 'attended with good consequences. Poor creatures, it is the only treat they have during the year ... I have always through life been a strong advocate for shewing kindness to the poor folks around one – they have their feelings as well as the great.' He would arrange it at a time when Loch would be able to attend. The rent-day dances must have become something of a fixture, for in 1838 Lewis reported that the celebration had gone off very well, with 250 people, all connected to the estate, present. It was the sort of occasion which the convivial Lewis would love.[16]

Like most other sympathisers at that time, Lewis distinguished between the deserving and undeserving poor, and there was of course a tension between natural sympathy with those in poverty through no fault of their own and the pressure from Loch to reduce rent arrears. By 1833 this had become a real problem, Loch warning him that he needed to be tougher on late payers as Trentham was producing less income than would 'afford a livelihood to a very ordinary squire'.[17] Even as late as 1838 Lewis promised to do better as far as the individuals who were unworthy of his light hand were concerned; 'but there are some truly pitiable cases which I will lay before you ...'[18]

Another example of Lewis's soft heart occurred in 1834 when one of the cottage tenants at Lilleshall had his house burnt down. They had lost all their furniture and clothing and the family were now totally destitute. Lewis started a collection for them, contributing himself and putting in £5 on behalf of the Duke. The incident pointed to an ongoing problem on the estate: the cottage was sub-let by one of the estate farmers, who were putting up the rents and showing 'disgraceful behaviour' towards their subtenants.[19] It was not uncommon for Lewis to write to Loch asking for help for a retired employee in distress, as in 1841 when he reported that Chapman, the retired gardener, was in 'great poverty and wretchedness'. Ten shillings a week would be of great service to him.[20]

Resigning responsibility for Shropshire

Loch's centralisation of estate administration may have seemed efficient on paper but it put a great strain on the senior man at Trentham and explained to some extent Lewis's obsession with galloping around the countryside. By 1830 Lewis admitted it was all too much for him: 'For some years past I have not felt very comfortable', realising that Lilleshall needed its own land steward 'for all to look up to'. The problem of Lilleshall was a real burden to him; but for that, he wrote, he would be 'one of the happiest men in England'.[21] Loch had earlier appointed Thomas James as assistant agent at Lilleshall to help

Lewis, but Lewis had taken this as a hint that he was to give up his responsibility for the Shropshire estates – wrongly as it happened. The assistant was sacked for other reasons, and thereafter followed a couple of years of a make-do management structure.[22]

Lewis's continuing dissatisfaction with his own management of Lilleshall reached its culmination in 1833 when he announced he was feeling ill: 'I am feeling weak and feeble as can be.' His doctor accordingly had him confined to the house. Loch was sympathetic and sent him a kindly letter: 'I know your zeal and your extreme diligence in the execution of your duty and that you are not contented with half measures either as regards your own exertions or those under you.'[23] Lewis also talked to the Duke about giving up responsibility for Lilleshall: he was reluctant to continue but would do so if a clerk were appointed specifically for his own use in Shropshire, although this was not his preferred solution. A few months after the 1st Duke's death, when the issue was still being discussed, he wrote to Loch saying:

> I entertain the same feeling to his present Grace as to my late worthy benefactor and will do every thing in my power to promote his comfort and good name ... I am afraid that his Grace and you may think that I am getting above my work but the fact is not so. I care not what I do or where I go, so that I can <u>perform</u> and <u>see</u> my charge properly executed <u>to my own satisfaction</u> and for the credit of the family and not trust the integrity and despatch of others. Caution and great prudence are very essential qualifications to be possessed of to guide the conduct and government of so many individuals. Sub agents can never have that feeling that a principal ought to be possessed with, hence much mischief arises and that without any bad intention.[24]

Loch was of the same mind. In a letter to the 1st Duke's son, who had been running Lilleshall, he took some of the blame for the inadequate management of the estate on himself: 'I have since you went to Lilleshall permitted some of the detail of the estate to escape me, thinking it my duty towards you not to interfere ... but I shall soon regain my intimacy with its details so as to teach another.' This was, of course, around the same time as all the troubles with John Mackay at Ketley came to a head, which had upset and angered Lewis so much. The result of all these deliberations was the appointment of William Smith, thus relieving Lewis of his responsibility for Shropshire.[25] It was no mean event, for it marked the end of Loch's adherence to the principles of the specialisation and centralisation of his agents in two Midland counties, which he had so laboriously instituted back in the first years of his life with the Leveson-Gowers.

Although Lewis had suggested that some of his own wages could go towards Smith's, in fact Lewis's salary and allowances were continued at their previous level. Indeed, his allowances had been increased a couple of years previously, in 1831. Loch reported to the Marquess that Lewis had complained he was spending a fair amount of his own money on food and drink for people coming to see him on business, 'a glassful of Ale and some Bread and Cheese'. Could he be recompensed – it might amount to forty pounds a year? The response from the Marquess must have pleased Lewis: he was to add fifty pounds to his salary for the last year and to continue it in future, 'as a mark of his sense of your services'.[26]

Moving to Groundslow

In the earlier years of his tenure, much of Lewis's energy seems to have been concerned with extending the Staffordshire estate by the purchase of farms and cottages. This was especially true of the nearby village of Tittensor. The estate had enclosed Tittensor Common earlier in the nineteenth century and was gradually buying up the rest of the village properties in order to expand the existing estate of Trentham. In 1831 Randal William Kirkby, Lewis's head clerk, told Loch he was busy working on a conveyance of a widow's house that adjoined Tittensor Common, after which 'except for 1 or 2 items in the village, the whole of the Township of Tittensor now belongs to his lordship'.[27] One remaining problem was Spring Vale, situated right on the edge of the estate's southern boundary at Tittensor, a farm which had been converted by Thomas Bakewell to the first lunatic asylum in the county. The 2nd Duke disliked the presence of this establishment, especially as his father had given permission for the asylum's patients to walk on Tittensor Common, and on one occasion some young ladies from the hall had been frightened by the sight of some of the patients out walking in dressing gowns. Pressure was put on Bakewell to sell Spring Vale to the Sutherlands or exchange it for another property. Bakewell was no admirer of the Sutherlands or Loch and operated various delaying tactics for some time.[28] The converted farm was eventually exchanged for the house at Oulton Abbey, which became Bakewell's asylum for a few years.

1831 was definitely a good year for Lewis. In August an urgent letter arrived at Trentham from Loch, explaining that Lady Stafford was in need of a companion to go with her on the long journey to Dunrobin. She would be attended by her maid, her chambermaid and two footmen, but neither her son Francis nor Loch's own son George could go with her as had been previously arranged. Loch was sure Lewis would be delighted to oblige. Lewis must have made the best of this golden opportunity for long conversation, for a few weeks later Lady Stafford had told the Marquess how impressed she was with the amount of improvements made by Lewis at Tittensor and that she thought he should be offered the tenancy of Groundslow Farm.

This necessitated finding a new farm for Malabar, the perfectly satisfactory present tenant; the plan was to give him tenancy of a farm in Shropshire vacated by one of the Pensons who was being evicted for arrears of rent.[29] It was also proposed to lay Aston, a Trentham farm which was managed directly by Lewis, down to grass so that it would require less attention. So eventually, in 1833, Lewis and his family moved into Groundslow (see Illus. 34). Later that year Lewis paid another visit to Dunrobin, this time to attend the 1st Duke's funeral. On hearing of the death, Lewis had done what he usually did at times of great distress, taken to his bed, 'quite unfit for business'.[30]

During the later years of his time as agent Lewis became obsessed with improving Groundslow Farm. By 1833 he told Loch he was short of outbuildings at the farm – he needed a tool house, turnip store, a small cart shed and a boiling house, as well as a new rickyard fence. He would be happy to pay for the labour to build these if the estate would provide all the materials. Later that year he complained that the farmland was 'in an impoverished state', and that the kitchen chimney smoked so bad that the servants were nearly suffocated and unable to work.

He still owed the estate £849 for the stock on the farm when he took it over, and he intended to pay this off by investing money in the building materials taken from his savings. This would be 'an uphill fight', which he was sure the Duke never intended. The heavy hint was taken, for the Duke instructed Loch to excuse Lewis the payment of £849 'entirely to show his approbation of your services'.[31]

Six years later he had made great improvements to Groundslow Farm, but his wife's death in June 1839 concentrated his mind on the future – not only for himself but also for his children now they had no mother. He had spent in all £2,850 of his own money on farm improvements at Groundslow, which still required a further outlay of £500, yet he had only a short-term tenancy agreement. He needed to talk to Loch about changing this to a twenty-year agreement, 'not necessarily a lease, just a memorandum'.[32]

This time agreement was not immediately forthcoming. The Duke required more details about Lewis's personal expenditure on Groundslow, particularly what proportion of this had been spent on permanent improvements. Perhaps unreasonably, Lewis took offence at this inquiry: he was not asking for a favour, rather fairness, 'a small mark of respect', especially as he felt his 'helpless situation sensibly'. Eventually, agreement was forthcoming, greatly to Lewis's relief. His worry was for his family, particularly for the future of his eldest son, Willie, who wanted to become a farmer. In the long term it is clear he hoped Willie would take over from him at Groundslow.[33]

Mrs Lewis's death and William's second marriage

Throughout 1838 and '39 there were regular notes attached to letters from Lewis and his clerical staff regarding Jane Lewis's illness. By March 1839 it is clear she was dying, probably of tuberculosis: 'Dr Mackenzie has been very attentive but nothing he does affords permanent relief or abates the cough, with sleepless nights and now reduced to extreme weakness.' In May, Lewis himself was taken ill and confined to his room for three days. There is no doubt Lewis was something of a hypochondriac, worrying about his own health and periodically taking to his bed when greatly stressed, but on this occasion he had reason enough. On 30 May Lewis's clerk, William

Henney, reported to Loch that Jane had died that morning. In his letter a week later, Lewis described his frame of mind: 'Altho' my poor wife had been long very ill, yet her departure came upon me suddenly. She died calmly and without a struggle – the Funeral took place last Tuesday.' Unfortunately, only a week later came the death of one-year-old Lady Victoria, whose funeral Lewis had to organise at Trentham.[34]

In the course of Jane Lewis's long decline, a good friendship had developed between the Lewis family and Martha Cleaver, the Trentham housekeeper, who seemed to have helped care for the children during Jane's illness. In March 1839 Lewis reported that on his arrival back at Groundslow from a trip to Stittenham he found his wife no better, but the household was fortunately in the care of Mrs Cleaver: 'She can only stay a short time, which I regret much as she would be a great comfort to us all. She left a niece in a dying state and must return to her or she would have remained with us for a time.'[35]

Before his wife's death Lewis had begun to convey his worries about the children's care in letters to Loch, who sympathised, especially over his daughter who was too young to be her own mistress or simply left alone with servants. Perhaps Loch saw which way the wind was blowing: 'In case the sad event should happen, why not have Mrs Cleaver until you have time to nurse yourself round.' Even Mrs Loch felt impelled to write in the same vein: 'Mrs Cleaver will I trust return to Groundslow, she is so gentle and sensible that I think she will be a comfort to Mrs Lewis and you.'[36]

Shortly after Jane's death Lewis again confided to Loch: 'I now feel myself in the most trying situation on account of my dear children. Mrs Cleaver has been a most kind friend. I hope she will be able to remain a few weeks at Groundslow, the poor children cling round her, she was taken very ill yesterday but is much better today.' This must have been something of an exaggeration on Lewis's part, for at this date, though his youngest child was only nine years old, the other two were sixteen and eighteen.

Twelve months later, a year after Jane's death, Martha Cleaver was still paying visits to Lewis's home at Groundslow. On one occasion she was taken ill and had to stay longer than intended. Her brother Thomas was worried, it appears ostensibly about her health but possibly also on another unspecified account:

I quite expected to see poor Martha at Hanslope before this, I am fearful her whole frame is affected from that violent inflammation on the first onset in her Thumb. I am quite satisfied she cannot be in better hands than yours or Mackenzie. As soon as she can do without the Doctor and gathers strength sufficient to stand the journey I shall be happy to see her as I think a little fresh air will do great good ...[37]

If Thomas Cleaver was concerned at Martha's over-long visits to the widowed Lewis, he need not have been, for on 24 June 1840, a respectable twelve months and twenty days after the death of his first wife, Lewis married Martha in her home parish of Hanslope, a ceremony witnessed by her brother Thomas and his wife. Martha was entering on her first and only marriage at the age of almost fifty.

Loch had been informed a few days earlier, in a letter which sounds as if Lewis was reporting the recruitment of a new employee. Loch was quick in returning his congratulations:

I have received this morning your letter announcing your intended marriage and have shown it to Mrs Loch. We unite in wishing you every possible happiness and comfort, in the union which you are about to form and think that you have shown much judgement in the selection which you have made. I believe that you could have fixed on no one who will be more congenial to your own habits or who will take a more affectionate care of your children. Sincerely yours, James Loch.[38]

A few months after the wedding Lewis announced his intention of going to Fife to see his mother, with whom Lewis's eldest son, Willie, had been staying on holiday, growing 'hearty and getting stout'. He had come to a decision about him, and had made several requests to Loch to remember Willie if the tenancy of a suitable farm came up on his Lordship's estates, somewhere where he could learn his would-be trade, but nothing had emerged. Eventually he turned his ideas back to Fife:

I am anxious to get Willie settled under some respectable man in Fife ... I am determined he shall learn his business thoroughly in all the branches. He will then never feel himself deficient go where he

will … I should like to place him under some branch of the Family
if it can be done, if not under any other respectable landlord that
you may recommend. I expect he will be qualified in 3 years.

The visit to Fife eventually took place in early December, but things
did not turn out as Lewis had intended. Willie had been ill in Fife
but was recuperating well enough to travel back to Staffordshire
with his father, glad to be going home. Lewis stayed in Fife only a
day or so before undertaking the long journey back.[39]

Lewis's stroke and aftermath

It is perhaps ironic that, early in August 1841, Lewis wrote to Loch
commiserating the ill health of the team that formed the mainstay
of the Trentham administration. Henney had been unwell and had
gone off to Harrogate and Scarborough to take the waters; William
Day Kirkby was still 'weakly' and so could not yet get back to close
office work; and old John Penson was very infirm – 'so you will say
we are a crazy lot'.[40]

Only three days after the date of this letter, Dr McKenzie
reported to Loch that 'our friend' had suffered a stroke, which
paralysed the whole of his right side: 'It appears he had got out of
bed to ascertain the state of the Weather, & upon returning to Bed
he complained that something affected his head.' William Smith
over in Shropshire received reports of the stroke and that same
evening rode over to visit him, but he was too ill to see anyone.
Smith reported to Loch: 'The family are in a sad distress.'

A week or so later another letter from McKenzie related that
Lewis had been brought downstairs for the first time and that he
was pleased with the improvement in his leg. He had told McKenzie
that he could not live if he had nothing to do: 'It would make him
very miserable if he thought he could not continue in the Duke's
service. He could not do as much as he had done but his Head he
felt was as clear as ever it had been.'

By mid-September, Henney was writing letters dictated by Lewis,
saying he was getting back to business and outlining several of the
problems attendant on the arrival of the new gardener, Fleming.
Neither had he forgotten his concern with Groundslow Farm:
Lewis's brother, George, had come down from Fife to see him and
had made some observations on how much the farm had improved

since his last visit, which comments were passed on to Loch and the Duke. Sometime later there followed a report from Dr Broomhall to Loch: the patient was in excellent spirits and progressing satisfactorily; power was returning to his leg. By November Lewis was well enough to write a letter to Loch arranging to see him at Groundslow, albeit in a very unsteady hand.[41]

By November, though, it had obviously become clear to Loch that he would need to find a new land agent at Trentham, for he asked Henney to send him a detailed breakdown of Lewis's salary:

Mr Lewis's salary	£250 p.a. (same as set in 1817)
Extra for superintending drainage	£30 p.a.
Extra for managing home farm	£100 p.a. (set in 1827)
Extra for horses and gigs	£190 p.a. (set in 1832)
Total	£570 p.a. (same as in 1832)[42]

Although Lewis was up and about by early January 1842, he was extremely depressed, so much so that reports about him had worried the Duchess enough to make her call at Groundslow farm herself on her way to Lilleshall. It appeared that Lewis was worried about the farm and his debts:

It is a melancholy spectacle – he looks much more thin and haggard than he did. I found Mrs Lewis with him … He talked most despondingly – and that he felt he never should recover – that this blow had come upon him – after he had spent all upon his farm and where others had saved, he now found himself a poor man. He complained much of his servants. I urged upon him that he should put his trust in his sons, that it was a duty not to give way … I then went to her … and noted this state of low spirits. She told me confidentially it had almost approached to insanity, indeed, one cannot wonder for he told her he had been ten nights without sleeping. She then gave me to understand that he was [indebted] … as much as £2000, that he had hoped that all would have been well and that he would have worked it up but now that he was becoming in despair … that he had talked of letting Groundslow, that she had answered him how could he entertain such thoughts – that they could not be pleasing to us ... she has said to him that he would kill her if he talked as he did ... I asked about his son. She said his children were very childish, that he had not accustomed them to taking any management. When I urged his son's assistance upon him he said he ought to be gone away from home as he had done – I still think his circumstances would make it desirable that he should stay with him – particularly as his nature is suspicious and he will always distrust servants.[43]

During the same visit Martha reminded the Duchess that she had been offered a pension when she had retired but had rejected it on her marriage. But now this money (twenty pounds a year) would be convenient to her. The Duchess asked Loch to arrange this to be paid to Martha privately: 'I left the house with heaviness at the sight of all this gloom and unhappiness and I feel more satisfied now that I have given you a full account of it ... I am anxious to do all in our power to relieve such a state of distress.'

Though all concerned sympathised greatly with the Lewises, all were equally puzzled. The Duke wrote to Loch: 'I cannot understand how such a man as Lewis can ever got into the difficulties he finds himself in. The farm is not a very large one and one would have supposed him as capable of good management as any.' And a day later, 'The necessity of prudence in farming is again exemplified ... but where could one have expected to find it if not in Lewis ... I am really unable to account for his difficulties.'

The irony is that, assuming Lewis's account of his financial troubles was accurate, he had fallen into exactly the same dark hole as John Mackay, whom Lewis had warned so often in the past about the perils of putting his own money into a tenanted farm. Clearly he had been led astray by his delight in being given a longer lease. The correspondence ends with the Duchess making what seems a telling remark: 'Mr Lewis never gave me the impression of a strong mind – easily excited, easily hurt.'[44]

A letter written by Lewis to Loch at this time shows his physical distress and his state of mind. There was no doubt that Lewis had effectively given up management of the estate permanently, but Loch, thinking that Lewis might still also want to give up the lease of Groundslow, must have immediately contacted Lewis's brother George in Northumberland. Three days later Loch received a letter from George outlining Lewis's thinking. Ever since his illness he had thought he would have to give up the agency, but George was surprised to find that he had resolved to sublet Groundslow, since in their discussions he was always determined to stay there. He himself could not help physically with the farm work but was happy to find 'a qualified individual to superintend the practical details'. He was awaiting a report from Dr Broomhall, and after that he would be coming down to Staffordshire again.

A day or so later Lewis's wife Martha wrote to the Duchess to thank her for her interest and to say that William was a little more composed and that for the first time they had talked seriously about money. Unfortunately, the situation seemed even worse than he had told the Duchess, but for the moment he was determined to stay at Groundslow Farm. At this time, too, William Henney, the estate clerk who was very busy running the Trentham office in the agent's absence, wrote to say Lewis seemed to him a little better in the use of his limbs, that he had been very depressed because the wet weather meant he could not get outdoors and was also short of proper sleep, but that he was now more thankful than complaining.

What, if anything, was Loch doing about the matter of a replacement for Lewis? Before Christmas he had lost no time in following his usual practice of writing to personal contacts, and early in January the replies started coming in from a wide number of estate owners and agents. This could not have come at a worse time, for not only did the estate need to find a new factor at Scourie in Sutherland, but at the end of January Loch's own wife, Ann, died. For a little while many of the replies to his enquiries were handled by his son George.

Some of Loch's correspondents were completely nonplussed by his request for suggestions for a possible new agent for Trentham. John Henderson from Castle Howard could only reply, 'I do not at this moment think of a person whom I durst recommend to succeed my old and very much esteemed and ... sincere friend Mr Lewis.'[45] Most of the others were also negative. Taking on the Sutherlands' Staffordshire and Yorkshire estates was no mean step; they required a man of experience, enthusiasm and level-headedness, but Loch also wanted a young man whom he could mould to his ways. Very early on, however, he knew who his man was; the problem was the young man concerned was not keen to move.

William Steward (the early letters have him as Stewart) was a young (a mere twenty-three years old) assistant land steward employed by the 1st Earl of Durham, a Whig politician, friend of the Duke of Sutherland and Governor General of Canada, at Lambton near Durham, the family seat. Steward was highly recommended by the chief agent. If any of the Earl of Durham's estates were to need a new head land steward, wrote the agent, he would appoint Steward immediately.[46] At that precise moment Steward was away, working on the Scottish borders at Branxholm, an ancient tower and hunting lodge near Hawick owned by the fifth Duke of Buccleuch. When approached, however, Steward said he was very comfortable where he was and not prepared to move 'unless he is offered a very great inducement'.[47]

The inducement was forthcoming. By mid-February Steward was in Staffordshire, being driven around the farms on the Trentham estate by William Henney. He wrote to Loch explaining that he had spent time with Mr Lewis at Groundslow, who had been very kind and helpful. Henney had shown him the offices and explained the methods of accounting. He had discussed matters of drainage and manuring and been introduced to Mr Fenton, the Duke's law agent in Newcastle, 'who appears an exceedingly nice man'. He liked the area; it was more wooded and hilly than he had expected, and above all he was very impressed with the estate – 'there appears to be <u>a decided stir for improvement all over the estate</u>' – a great tribute to Lewis's hard work. He had not yet been appointed to the job, but he must have spent three or four days at Trentham, having long discussions with Lewis. During one of his visits to Groundslow, the Duke had called and he had been introduced. Mr Lewis, he reported, was rapidly improving in health and strength. He had gone for a drive with Steward in a low four-wheeled gig into every field on Groundslow farm, which 'is in very excellent order and the land in high condition, the fences are neat and remarkably clean'.[48]

Everyone seemed very happy with William Steward and he was immediately appointed. He returned to Lambton to serve his notice, and in March Lewis sent down to Trentham his own office and garden keys. Lewis spent much of April sorting papers at home. With young Kirkby's help from the Trentham office, he sent down two large boxes full of records and had many more to sort out. He promised to write a full report of the changes and improvements that had taken place on the Trentham estate during his agency. At the same time, he reminded Loch that he would be glad to receive the first instalment of his annuity as agreed with the Duke, which he took to start from Lady Day 1841, so that he could carry on with his improvements at Groundslow.[49]

Lewis continued to contribute advice and information about the estate, mainly the background to purchases, leases, and in one case a lawsuit. At the beginning of such a daunting job, Steward probably found this useful rather than an irritating interference, especially as the young man's first few months at Trentham were a baptism of fire.

We learn about the first problem in May, from a short letter from Lewis: Mr Steward had the measles.[50] He recovered well, so that in June his father in Morpeth could write a letter to Loch, thanking him for all his kindness to his son, who was now steward of Trentham. He obviously feared for him taking on such responsibilities at such a young age but was nonetheless immensely proud of his appointment.[51]

Mid-August brought another trial, however, which Lewis may well have felt relieved to have avoided. In the summer of 1842, North Staffordshire saw the outbreak of social unrest in the form of a strike by its colliers, who were roaming the streets and causing widespread disruption. The Potteries, already in the worst depression of the century, were in a state of great distress and tension. One of the local leaders of the Chartist movement addressed a public meeting in Trentham village itself, attacking both the monarchy and the Duke of Sutherland. By August bands of strikers had turned to violent conflict.[52]

In a series of letters beginning on 16 August 1842, William Steward reported to Loch that rioters in the Potteries were plundering and burning houses, and the Yeomanry had been called out. Steward was trying to get some soldiers to come and stay overnight at Trentham, but in any case he had kept some of the estate's own men in the yard all night. He succeeded in getting thirty-three soldiers from the Yeomanry the next night, but the night after that they were recalled back to Newcastle. There had been no outrages near Trentham – except one house in Trent Vale was set on fire – but the roads were all lined with colliers from Manchester and elsewhere, which was very threatening. He had got a magistrate to stay at Trentham each night, as he could not only read the Riot Act if necessary but had also sworn in as special constables all the reliable members of the Trentham workforce. The commanding officer of the Yeomanry had visited and advised him to send out scouts in all directions to give warning of any trouble, in which case he was to send for him and he would come immediately. Steward divided up all his workmen and appointed as leaders the departmental heads – the gardeners were under Fleming, the builders under Jenkins (the clerk of works), the park men under George Penson, and so on. They stood on duty around the site all night each night, rewarded by supper in the servants' hall with beer and a very little strong ale. This would continue until the whole affair was under control. He had taken it upon himself to tell Fleming he could not go on a proposed tour of the northern gardens as organised by the Duchess. Steward himself was very busy as the older Penson was laid up with rheumatism and Wood the farm bailiff had been called up to the cavalry, so he thus was doing their work himself.

The whole affair gradually quietened down when the striking miners went back to work ten days later. As all was quiet Steward felt it safe to go to Stittenham to collect rents although he had left strict instructions that one man should be left on guard every night in the park, one in the gardens and one near the buildings, in addition to the usual night watchman and the four or five men who slept in the hall yard. In the longer term, however, he had gratefully agreed with a letter from Earl Talbot, the Lord Lieutenant of the county, that the Roebuck Inn in Trentham be allocated as a temporary barracks for a troop of the Dragoon Guards over the next winter.

Clearly greatly relieved, Steward received letters from the Duke and Loch congratulating him on his actions. Steward said he had followed Loch's earlier instructions about special constables and was grateful to the magistrate who had stayed throughout most of the time. He had written to William Smith at Lilleshall recommending that he take the same action if it was ever needed there. Loch seemed very pleased with him, perhaps feeling he had at last a steadier hand on the tiller at Trentham than an easily panicked elderly William Lewis.[53]

William Steward stayed at Trentham for sixteen years. In the 1851 census he was single, living at Trentham with his widowed mother, one female servant and a groom. In 1858 he had left the

Sutherlands and moved to the much smaller estate belonging to the Bagots at Bithfield, where he was recorded in the 1861 census as still single, still living with his mother and a groom. By 1871 he had moved back to Northumberland and was obviously doing well, with a wife, two young daughters and three domestic servants; the daughters' birthplace was given as Lambton, their father's old workplace. His replacement as agent at Trentham in 1858 was the head gardener, George Fleming, who left in 1864.[54]

The last ten years

William Lewis himself settled down in retirement to a much quieter existence as tenant of Groundslow Farm, but his life was not without its grumbles. His relationship with the Duke cooled over a long-standing disagreement about the estate gamekeeper refusing to kill the hares in the park, which were proliferating and badly damaging Lewis's fencing. In the 1851 census William and Martha were still at Groundslow. He was described as a farmer of 475 acres, employing ten labourers and a sixty-year-old living-in farm bailiff, John Cameron. The latter had worked at Groundslow as a farm labourer for at least ten years, recruited from William's own homeland of Fife and no doubt promoted in responsibility as William's health deteriorated. Also working the farm was the younger son, twenty-year-old John Pearce, and there were two female domestic servants, both in their twenties.

Since the instructional letters about Boglilly to his brother ceased around the time of his first marriage, it seems that William did indeed relinquish his interest in the family farm, though his contact with his brother and family continued and visits were exchanged right until the end – William in fact died at Boglilly in May 1853, though his home address was still Groundslow Farm. The letters of administration of his will were granted to his younger son, John Pearce Lewis of Queensville, Forebridge, Stafford. The effects in the will amounted to between £500 and £1,000, so he was hardly insolvent. He left a legacy to the North Staffordshire Infirmary of £100. His wife Martha lived for a further seventeen years; upon her death in Wiltshire in 1870 her will, leaving more than £2,000, was administered by John Lewis, 'carpenter, son and one of the next of kin', presumably her youngest stepson, John Pearce Lewis.[55]

What happened to William's children?

Neither of William Lewis's sons had the sort of life their father might have hoped for them. The elder, Willie, eventually had his wish, but sadly not for long. In 1849 he married Anne Bright, the daughter of another land agent, John Bright, in Penkridge parish church. William Lewis was not one of the witnesses, so perhaps his disabilities had worsened by then. Two years later, according to the 1851 census, Willie and Anne were doing well, in a 300-acre farm at Dunston, near Penkridge. They had eleven-month-old twin girls, with a twenty-seven-year-old nanny and a twelve-year-old nurse girl, plus two other female servants and two farm servants living in. They were still at Dunston in 1855 when William advertised a reward for a stray calf.[56]

Ten years later their family had increased to six daughters and one son, two female servants and one manservant, with Anne's elderly father lodging with them; but then they were living in the town of Stafford, and Willie, though still only thirty-nine, was described as a retired farmer. At the next census he was described as an invalid, still with his wife and five children, one domestic servant and a lodger, though by then they have moved to Edgbaston in Birmingham. Ten years later they were still in Edgbaston, though at a different address; in the 1891 census William was still there with his wife, one daughter and one servant, but now described as 'paralysed'. Obviously his father's worries about his son's health had not been unfounded.

The younger son, John Pearce Lewis, remained on the farm at Groundslow until his father's death. What he did then remains obscure, though the address given on his father's letters of administration of the will is the same as that of his brother Willie, in Stafford. In 1861, aged thirty, he was visiting his uncle on his mother's side, George Pearce, the licensee of the Holly Bush Inn at Muxton, near Lilleshall, who lived in the pub with his wife and three daughters, all in their twenties. Two years later, in 1863, John Pearce Lewis married one of these girls, his first cousin Jane Pearce, in Lilleshall parish church. His marriage certificate shows he had taken the tenancy of a farm near Cheltenham. In the 1871 census, however, the couple were living at Hadley, Wellington, where he was working as a farm labourer. The burial of John Pearce Lewis, aged fifty, was recorded at Lilleshall in 1880.

What of William's only daughter, Helen? She was definitely still living at Groundslow when her stepmother died, but thereafter seems to disappear from view. It is possible she went to live at Boglilly with her father's brother's family.

William Lewis's genuine commitment and loyalty to the Sutherlands comes through in many of the letters to Loch. The Sutherlands were aware of this, especially in relation to his work at Tittensor, and rewarded him on several occasions, though towards the end of his tenancy the Duke was growing tired of Lewis's incessant requests for money for Groundslow, as shown by Loch's single-line note enclosed to Lewis: 'For God sake do not ask for any more money for Groundslow.' Duchess Harriet understood the defects of Lewis's character well, but she was also obviously distressed at seeing the state he was in after his stroke. Though Loch was sometimes exasperated by his agent's insecurity, he was clearly very fond of him and appreciated his energy and loyalty, towards the end trying to shield him from the Duke's impatience.

It is clear also that many people on the estate and elsewhere respected him, but even more than this they felt a real affection for him and for his very real kindness to those in poverty. The letter from Castle Howard written by John Henderson in reply to Loch's request for suggestions for a replacement for his old, esteemed and sincere friend is simple but heartfelt. Above all, though other agents followed after who were perhaps tougher in their physical and mental constitution, William Lewis must have made a significant contribution to the farming landscape of Trentham. Death notices are hardly the place for an objective view of a deceased's character, but in this instance whoever wrote the notice for the local newspaper did appreciate some of his true virtues:

At his brother's residence, Boglilly, near Kirkcaldy in Scotland, on the 11th instant, W. Lewis, Esq., of Groundslow Fields, in this county, of apoplexy. Mr Lewis had been for about forty years agent for the Duke of Sutherland's estates, and was extensively know in this county and in Scotland. He was much esteemed by his Grace, and by his Grace's predecessors ... He was a diligent and exact man of business, circumspect and careful, yet liberal to the tenantry with whom he had to deal, and always closely attentive to any representations they might have to make.

12

The Commissioner

'No Man of Straw'

James Loch was the *éminence grise* behind most of our stories. In his book on estate administration, David Spring described him thus: 'In cultivation he was his employer's equal; in business, his master and tutor.'[1] Eric Richard's verdict on him is no exaggeration: 'He was responsible for estate policies over large parts of England and Scotland, which made him remarkably influential in the improvement and modernization of agricultural and industrial property across Victorian Britain.'[2] For over forty years between 1812 and 1855 Loch's character imposed itself on the working life of Trentham, from the humblest cottage tenant or part-timer to the grandest house steward in the land. In no way does this short text attempt to encompass his general career and achievements, which have been researched and assessed by other scholars, particularly Eric Richards.[3] A short introduction to his family and public life would be useful, however, before turning to Loch as he appears in the correspondence on Trentham (see Illus. 32).

James Loch was born in 1780 at Drylaw, near Edinburgh, the son of a landowner, one of seven children who were all still very young when their father died. The Drylaw estate was sold in 1786, and James was brought up by his mother and later on his uncle's estate at Blair Adam, where he learnt the elements of estate improvement and supervision. He studied law at Edinburgh University and was called to the English bar in 1806, but soon embarked on a career in estate administration. He became the commissioner and chief agent to the 2nd Marquis of Stafford in 1812, aged thirty-two, at a salary of £1,000. His recruitment must have made a great impression on his employers, for the Marquess's sister-in-law complained on Loch's arrival that 'the Staffords seem to have turned their thoughts entirely to economy and the society of Scotch agents'.[4] Loch retained this position until his death in 1855, when he was succeeded in the post by his son George.

Loch had nine children, seven sons and two daughters, by his first wife, who came from Kincardineshire. He was widowed in 1842 and remarried a widow from South Staffordshire, who died two years later. He was a great believer in helping one's extended family and did so generously, expecting others to do likewise, as we saw with the Kirkbys. Throughout his career with the Leveson-Gowers he and his family were based in London, initially in Wimbledon and then in 12 Albemarle Street, the address where he kept his office.

Throughout his career with the Sutherlands he was also adviser to various other people and institutions. For the 1st Duke of Sutherland's second son, Lord Francis Edgerton (later to become the Earl of Ellesmere), he acted as supervising agent, as well as acting in various capacities to the Duke of Bedford, the Earl of Carlisle, the Earl of Dudley and Viscount Keith; he was also trustee and superintendent to the Bridgewater Canal. He held many public offices including the directorships of the Liverpool and Manchester Railway and the Birmingham and Liverpool Canal, and in Scotland he was a commissioner of Highland roads and bridges and of the Caledonian and Crinan Canals. He was one of the founder members of London University and MP for St Germains in Cornwall and later for Wick, as well as being one of the architects of the Reform Act of 1832. He was director of the English Historical Society, and in 1841 he was given an honorary degree by Jesus College, Cambridge. In short, he was generally regarded as 'the finest barrister-auditor of his day'.[5]

The Scottish Highland Clearances and social engineering

Given all these achievements it is as the architect of the Scottish Highland Clearances for which he is still remembered by many people. Yet as Eric Richards has shown, Loch was not the originator of the idea of relocating small-scale tenants off Highland crofts that could not support them onto coastal settlements where local fisheries and small-scale industries could be developed. He did, however, become one of its directors and an apologist on behalf of the prime mover on the Sutherland estates, Elizabeth, Countess of Sutherland, thereby bringing upon himself much public hatred and abuse. This was almost inevitable, tainted as was the whole Sutherland administration by the indictment in 1816 of Patrick Sellars, one of the estate sub-agents, for culpable homicide during evictions in Strathnaver. Though Sellars was acquitted, the bitterness remains even to the present day.

As Loch took over the management of the Clearances, correspondence shows that his instructions to his new agent Suther, moved to Scotland after three years at Trentham, were to use kindness in the evictions; yet the damning evidence of burnt-out houses is clear. Many evictions were precipitous and badly managed, and his assistants opinionated, stubborn and addicted to power. Loch's determined belief in 'improvement' – the rationalisation and technical development of agriculture and trade – led to policies of social control and inhumane treatment that were unacceptable even at the time and on a scale which was far larger than were originally envisaged.

The main body of clearances on the Sutherland estates was completed by 1820 but several smaller scale removals were carried out later, some of which were violent – one even requiring the presence of the Fusiliers and achieved only at the point of the sword. Reading through his correspondence with Lewis at Trentham around this time, dealing with anything from the design of drainage tiles to the requirements of a lease, it is sometimes difficult to keep in mind the context of the upheavals going on in the Highlands. Yet the same commitment to improvement can be seen in his work on the Trentham and Lilleshall estates as well as in the Highlands. Policies of eviction of undesirable beerhouse licensees, the amalgamation of tenancies into larger units, moving tenants around from one farm to another, rationalising field and farm layouts, encouraging grassland for livestock grazing at the expense of arable land, building new boundaries and new roads, underdraining and fencing heaths such Tittensor – all this can be seen as smaller, less aggressive versions of what was happening further north. Wordie has even described its effect on the Leveson-Gower's Midland estates as a new enclosure movement.[6]

Though obviously on a much smaller scale and with less extreme poverty and therefore less trauma inflicted than in the Highlands, nevertheless some individuals were subject to massive upheavals.

This was true of the cottagers and smallholders as much as the occasional farmer who was relocated. Thomas Bakewell, founder of the first lunatic asylum in Staffordshire and a man who described himself as long acquainted with human misery, was no lover of James Loch. In a public reply to Loch's pamphlet published in 1820 entitled 'An Account of the Improvements on the Estates of the Marquis of Stafford in Staffordshire and Shropshire and on the Estate in Sutherland', he heaped acid personal criticism on Loch. It was well known, wrote Bakewell, that the Marquess and his family were unpopular for their dealings with their tenants in Staffordshire and Shropshire as well as Scotland, but much of the odium must fall on Loch – odium which 'you may learn from every rustic and cottager in the county; you may hear it in the village meetings of Farmers, as well as in the polite assemblies of our gayest towns'. As an example of Loch's mercilessness in his dealings with delinquent tenants, Bakewell described an eviction of a poor man, his wife and six small children from a cottage in Tittensor, in the midst of winter, the wife recovering from recent childbirth. The cottage had originally belonged to the man but had been sold to the estate as part of the 'improvement' of Tittensor. The family could not afford regular payment of rent and rather than go into the workhouse they stayed put, only to be ejected by their new landlord. According to Bakewell, he 'found them encamped in the open air like a trio of gypsies'.[7]

Loch had a natural air of authority, even with his employers.[8] It is no surprise, then, that Loch's letters to tenants allowed of no misunderstanding, even when the payment of rent was not at issue, as we can see from his correspondence with George Pearce, the young licensee of the Holly Bush Inn at Muxton, Lilleshall:

It has been stated to me ... that your House in Muxton has been upon several Sundays the scene of very disgraceful and discreditable transactions and that every species of disorder has been permitted to go on in it.

At all times this is to be prevented but upon that day in particular and especially during divine service it cannot be tolerated ... I am given to understand that the disorderly state of things is produced ... by your underletting the tap which must not be continued ... I wish you to be here on Monday morning at ½ past 8 o'clock ... Mr Blunt has been asked to keep an eye on you.[9]

The Revd John Blunt, the vicar, was undoubtedly the complainant here, but the situation must have given Loch some slight embarrassment as George Pearce was in fact the brother of William Lewis's wife.

Loch's loyalty to the Sutherlands was practical; the experience of abuse they suffered in Scotland made him well aware of the need to nurse their reputations most carefully, for his own sake as well as for the family's. Partly for this reason he endorsed the practice in the Sutherlands' estates of under-renting – fixing rents slightly under the general average so 'the tenants should feel that they hold their lands on rather easier terms than their neighbours. It is fit and proper that those who hold of a great man should do so.'[10] What might appear as minor details in some of our stories show this concern with the family's public name. It is clear from William Smith's letters that part of Loch's concern about the Mrs Tungate affair was worry lest people ascribed blame to him or the family for making a poor old lady homeless. For the same reason, he was angry when the Lilleshall clerk risked public scandal for taking proceedings against the profligate James Penson, whom Loch preferred to bundle quietly off across the Atlantic. Again, after there had surfaced ample evidence that Mrs Doar had been stealing, his response was not to contact the police but simply to remove her from the premises as quietly and as soon as possible. The reputation of the family was indeed paramount in Loch's mind. No doubt the criticisms surrounding the clearances went deep into his memory, and there is no doubt they hurt him personally.

Loch's methods of land management continued to attract criticism during his later life and even beyond. As Richards has pointed out, one aspect which was most loathed was his attempt at social engineering by the insistence that once sons were married they should not share in the tenancy of their parents' holding, a practice which tended to encourage the sub-division of land. He persisted in this belief, and in 1842 a letter was published in several newspapers outlining his latest precept with respect not to the Highlands or even to the English estates belonging to the Duke but to the Bridgewater estate of Sir Francis Egerton, younger son of the 2nd Marquess, to whom Loch acted as adviser. Both Sir Francis and himself, the letter explained, were against 'ill considered marriages between very young persons ... marriages contracted without forethought, and without any consideration as to the means of future support', so that 'after Oct. 1 1842 no cottage tenant shall allow a married daughter or son to live in the house of their parents without leave in writing from agents, on pain of tenants being put under notice'.

Loch kept a wary eye on tenants' family sizes. This was perhaps a touch hypocritical given the number of his own children, but his reservations were all concerned with suitable means of support. One of his objections to James Penson was the size of his family in relation to his income, and certainly Walker, the house steward, must have been aware of Loch's opinion in this regard when he was setting on and asking for guidance over Trentham's first gas engineer, Abraham Derbyshire, as the only possible objection to Derbyshire was that he had already two children and that as he was young he was likely to have a large family.[11] Loch was a Malthusian, a firm believer that 'the natural tendency of population is to increase more quickly than the means of subsistence'.[12]

In an address to the House of Commons as late as 1845 he attempted to defend these and other aspects of the Sutherland management, only to be met by extreme vilification from the press, both in England and Scotland: 'When the real story [of the Strathnaver Clearances] is told, shame will burn on many brows, and round none more conspicuously than Mr James Property Loch.'[13]

Loch and Trentham

In the correspondence with William Lewis we can at times see a more human figure, sometimes exasperated, occasionally personal, exhausted and even intimate or apologetic. He could be forthright: describing how the frail 1st Duke caught what turned out to be his death of cold examining the new laundry at Dunrobin at three o'clock in the morning, he wrote to Lewis that he had 'objected to this sort of daftness before'. The Duke's death occasioned one of the few letters written by Loch which, while not exactly panicky, did show serious concern: to William his son, covering for him back in London, Loch described how they were searching Dunrobin for the Duke's will and could not find it. Could William look for it at Stafford House? The Duke's servant 'thinks that the will itself is lying on the shelf in the centre of the Bureau but that there is a codicil in the right hand upper drawer'.[14]

Loch could be curt with recalcitrant employees or tenants, too, but he was usually very patient with Lewis's touchiness, which became more marked in later years. He was obviously fond of

Lewis and put up with his faults, his nervousness, his hypochondria, his 'daftness', but was also aware that Lewis had nursed Trentham through difficult times and had made great improvements to the estate. That he had great patience in negotiation was noted by John Moss in 1836 when writing to him about the 'railway project': 'I wish I possessed a little more of your coolness. What seems to have no effect on you would drive me mad.'[15] He also had the largeness of heart to apologise, whether it was to admit that he was often confused over compass directions or that he was simply overwhelmed with work, as in the reply to a defensive letter from Lewis on the subject of John Penson.

This made Loch a good manager, as we see in the measured tones of his letter instructing Lewis how to deal with the Mrs Doar affair. He was careful to praise work well done, especially by one of his young protégées such as William Smith or William Steward. Smith, he wrote to Lewis, needed encouragement, 'for he is very modest'. What also emerges in the correspondence is Loch's own capacity for work, his grasp of the smallest detail and his ability to concentrate, which was phenomenal. Never is this seen more clearly than in his dealings with new agents or bailiffs. His vision in this as in so many areas was long-term. He wanted young men – in their twenties or early thirties – with a fair amount of experience but not so old that they were set in their ways and could not be moulded by himself; he wanted them full of energy, loyalty and integrity and with long-term ambition. For specific purposes he needed specific characteristics; for the collection of quit rents in Newcastle he told Lewis to find 'a pushing young man'. Above all he was prepared to put time and energy into their training. His delight in teaching the minutiae of management is one of his personal traits recognised by several writers – this and his capacity for work are the most important characteristic revealed by the Sutherland correspondence.[16]

James Loch's letter to Suther in 1817, during the latter's handover period to Lewis, is nothing if not detailed. Loch had asked Lewis to write him a report, which he subsequently corrected, not so much aiming at the content, of which he approved, but the writing style. His intention was to make Lewis feel 'comfortable and respectable in his situation' and, through Suther, he recommended him to practise every evening, by writing out a copy of text as quickly as he could, 'making his gs, hs, ls, ys etc as long as he can, taking pains to do it well'. He was to use the same sort of pen as Suther used and hold it longer, writing close to the edge of the paper without margins, except when laying out accounts or statements. He also corrected a few spelling mistakes and recommended him to use a pocket Johnson's Dictionary.[17]

Twenty-four years later he was still correcting his protégés' letters when he scolded William Steward's use of the word 'nice' when describing a man's character. Steward took the criticism with good grace, saying, 'I hope to be able to get rid of these North of England phrases in speaking, but <u>especially in writing</u>.'[18]

Loch's critique of the writing of the young Scotsman William Smith was very similar, but his advice on how Smith was to conduct himself generally was illuminating not only in relation to his expectations of Smith but also as far as his own approach to work was concerned. The points he raised over several letters were as follows:

1. Whenever he had any difficulties Smith was to consult Mr Lewis for his advice first. He was to remain with him some time at Trentham 'to see the ways of the people and of the country ... Open your mind freely to Mr Lewis, but in regard to everybody else keep your own counsel.'
2. He should 'Be civil and obliging to all, but take good care, and do not make promises. All men are apt to construe civility into what is favourable to themselves.'
3. He should 'mix intimately with those you have to deal with in the way of business, but have as little to do with their convivial parties as maybe – the more you dine at home by yourself the better. You will be much asked to dine by the tenants, but you will preserve your own independence by not doing so.'
4. He should 'Practice your writing as much as you can, and it is always safe to have a little English Dictionary along with you.'
5. Smith should keep a memorandum book, examining it every evening and crossing out those items he had attended to during the day. He should never let any business hang over unfinished or in arrears.

6. He was to examine carefully and patiently every matter brought to his attention and reply promptly, decidedly, firmly and clearly, in moderate and temperate language.

7. He should lose no time in learning all he could about the names and characters of all the cottagers so that he might answer any question put to him by his Grace.

8. Whenever his Grace, Mr Lewis or Loch addressed him, he should make some reply so that it was clear that he had understood what was said. If he agreed with the point made, he should say so, likewise if he wished to consider it further.

9. And a final warning: 'You will find a great jealousy of your country, which nothing but your own good conduct, prudence and reserve will enable you to get the better of.'[19]

Loch was especially concerned that his agents keep a social distance between themselves and the tenants and servants, because in the final analysis they were in control of them all. This, of course, was also one of the reasons why he recruited agents and sub-agents from Scotland or the North of England. It was not just that he thought education was better than in the south; he thought Northerners were more level-headed and with no local ties were able to stand outside the contentious issues on the southern estates. He warned his men that the tenants were apt to be jealous of each other and that they must beware of being drawn into such squabbles.

Clearly, his predilection for recruiting Scotsmen was not popular with the tenants of the Midlands of England. It is certainly true that under him the Sutherlands' administration was heavily weighted towards Scotland and the North, not just at the very top but from agents down to clerks, cashiers and porters, though this did not apply to the indoor domestic servants. Nevertheless, long-standing Staffordshire-born tenants and dependent families like the Pensons must have sometimes felt they had been invaded by a foreign force, which probably fed the local jealousies to which Loch referred.

Attitudes were even more complex than this, however, for on several occasions the Fifeshire-born Lewis betrayed to Edinburgh-born Loch an antipathy towards 'Highland emotion', especially in relation to

Mackay who hailed from Sutherland. In turn, Mackay's letters to the Duchess expressed in highly emotional terms his loyalty to the Sutherland family, formed by ancient clan ties which no one not born in the Highlands could understand, never mind emulate, and which meant he would work for them for no reward until death. Thus the Scots brought some of their own geographical divisions with them to Staffordshire.

Loch was also wary of mixing work with family life, as his advice to Henney with regard to taking work home showed. He certainly practised this himself but had the advantage of a large house and office area, where he often worked for several hours writing reports before breakfast.[20]

Since the men he recruited were usually single and often still in their twenties, for the first few months at least their lives in Staffordshire or Shropshire would be quite lonely, with Loch's advice to 'dine alone' ringing in their ears. This maybe partly explains why in the early years Lewis had time to involve himself in events at home in Boglily, and why the Kirkbys came to Trentham en masse. Nevertheless, almost all Loch's young men settled into their new home and in the space of a few years found suitable partners, mostly local girls, and married and had families.

Throughout most of his career Loch tried to keep stringent control over financial affairs of the estates – this despite the pressures of other work and the stresses of events in Scotland. The only time he distanced himself was in the early 1830s when he admitted that he had not wanted to interfere with the Marquess's running of Lilleshall. Within twelve months of starting his career with the Sutherlands in 1812, inspired by the economic principles of Adam Smith, he had introduced a new system of accounting on the estate. In a letter to Suther he explained that, from then on, each department should 'be paid for what they furnish exactly as if they had no connection with the family'; this did away with the confusing system, then common on landed estates, by which one set of accounts went in part payment of another set. In other words, Loch was introducing a system of cost centres.[21] He had also introduced a strict regime of monthly departmental abstracts and reports.

The bureaucratic dependence on paperwork and its centralisation on Loch was so great that it became another target for Thomas Bakewell's sarcasm: 'If an old wheel-barrow were broken down upon any of his Lordship's estates, Mr Loch must be written to for instructions as to whether it would be proper to have the old one mended or to get a new one.' With reference to Loch cutting the beer allowances, Bakewell accused Loch of bringing to the Marquess's household 'a sort of cheese-paring and candle-end economy, contemptible in any householder and much more so in one of the most opulent noblemen in Europe'.[22] Bakewell, of course, was a near neighbour of the Duke and had his own reasons for being antagonistic. He was also right in that Loch certainly took every opportunity to review expenditure, but, in fairness, once the guidelines were in position he seems to have expected people to get on with their work.

The 1st Duke's death in 1833 gave an opportunity, clearly long-anticipated, of embarking on a most detailed review of the administration of Trentham. Loch had already started on a strict regime of economy, doomed to failure in the long term given that the family was dependent on a level of spending which ate into even their enormous capital assets. The Marquess was well known for this extravagant addiction, summed up dryly by his sister-in-law Lady Granville in one of her letters: 'When will Lord Stafford buy the world?'[23] Matters were made much worse on his death by the unfortunate combination of the cessation of income from the Bridgewater Canal, under the terms of the Duke of Bridgewater's will, and the elevation to a dukedom with all its attendant social and financial implications.

At this point, therefore, Loch instructed that large parts of the gardens of Trentham were to be put down to grass (the Duke would not be coming to Trentham that year as he could not stand the long journey), and that Lewis himself must get rid of some of the casual workers, but this was to be done gradually and quietly. Loch confided in Lewis, 'We are much in want of money.' Now he looked carefully through the monthly reports and worked with Lewis and Woolley, the gardener, as well as the newly appointed house steward, Vantini. Although usually good at delegating responsibilities to his juniors, where financial scrutiny was involved no detail was too small for his personal attention, even to the point of asking for the wine cellar keys so that he could accompany a professional expert in carrying out a valuation. He also enquired as to how vegetables and fruit were brought to the house from the kitchen garden at Trentham. He instructed Lewis to keep separate books recording the production of each of the various centres – the garden, park, farm, and poultry yard – especially with regard to what they could supply to the house. The garden was especially important; Vantini was to keep duplicate books and ensure they were up-to-date. The same man should be used to take the produce to the house every day.[24] This was all to no avail in the long term: the family seemed to be on an unstoppable course of spending.

Given his comment on the 1st Duke's death following the cold caught at Dunrobin, and given that Loch must have attended more public occasions than most men, it is perhaps fitting that he himself died of pneumonia two months after catching a cold at the Duke of Wellington's funeral. Aged seventy-five, the stress had finally caught up with him in the form of recurring anxiety-related nightmares in which he was 'always striving to reach Tongue as the place in which he hopes to find quiet and repose'.[25] (Tongue is on the far north coast of Scotland, cut off from the south by the great mass of Ben Hope and Ben Loyal and surely one of the most beautiful and isolated spots in the kingdom.)

At his death his personal wealth amounted to £41,000. The administration of the Leveson-Gowers' estates passed seamlessly to his son George, who in any case had been heavily involved for many years, especially in the Sutherlands' railway interests. He followed in his father's footsteps for over twenty years.

The man who has studied Loch more than most has summed up his character thus: 'Upright, righteous, strong-principled, even puritanical – Loch was no man of straw.'[26] Though the press in general heaped vilification upon Loch, it is noticeable that his obituary in one Scottish newspaper in Wick, the area which he represented in Parliament, was generous: 'Locally, Mr Loch from his great influence, was the best representative that the burghs ever had or are likely ever to possess.'[27]

13

Finally ...

We have explored some of the topics with which I began, whether it be pensions, entitlement to accommodation, or the personal experience of working for the Sutherlands and its effect on serving families. From the few examples studied, the answers to my initial questions must be slightly mixed, subject as they are to the exigencies of the chance survival of material. We must not forget, however, those individuals in the background whose narratives may be very different.

On the whole, the Sutherlands emerge from these narratives as good employers. We can only judge events in the light of the mores and expectations of their day, not ours, and their day was a time when women expected to be paid lower wages than men, even for the same level of responsibility, when landowners could sack workers without notice or forcibly remove the fixtures from their homes. The Sutherlands' treatment of most of the servants whom they deemed worthy of their care was conducted with reasonable generosity and patience, though there seem to have been unfortunate exceptions, such as Woolley, and cases of sheer bad luck, such as James Kirkby and his mentally troubled wife. Some of this must have been the influence of their agents, Lewis in particular but also William Smith, both of whom seem to have been kindly men at heart. Loch's carefulness towards the staff was probably to some extent pragmatic – 'to make people honest and above suspicion they should have enough'. The family themselves, however, must have set the general standards of responsibility and behaviour, particularly when continued service over decades was concerned, and this was especially true of the 2nd Duchess. Some of this too will have been pragmatic; for very good reasons there was no family more aware of their public reputation.

Yet there is always a darker side. With a family that had such a huge self-regard and a clear awareness of their place in society, deference was always going to be at the heart of the relationship between man and master. We see this subservience clearly on the rare occasions when a middle-ranking servant wrote directly to the Duke or Duchess. No servant could afford to be found breaking the rules of the household, just as no one could ever take anything for granted, even Mary Penson who was as close to the Duchess as anyone could be, treading a fine line between discretion, honesty and intimacy.

In addition to the stories of individuals, there are wider narratives revealed. Generally, we see the importance of the collaboration between the administration of the various households, especially Trentham and Lilleshall. Housekeepers were switched or augmented in times of difficulty, garden produce was sent from one to the other as needed, the brewer worked at both, many outdoor workers were recruited from one to the other, and the clerks moved houses fairly regularly. This seemed to continue after the installation of the independent agent at Lilleshall, as Lewis and Smith worked well together.

The deliberate choice of a period when both family and national affairs were under enormous stress clearly results in a huge amount of correspondence and information, both at the level of the functioning of the administration and as regard individuals who otherwise might remain as unknown and unobserved. We see not only a family attending to its affairs, but a system of administration which is so huge as to be an elaborate business in itself. The Sutherland empire, with its estates both north and south, must have been one of the largest business administrations in the country, comparable to some of the extensive industrial enterprises which were then still embryonic. It is not merely the sheer size and complexity which is impressive, however. New systems for the management of manpower and departmental organisation may have been evolving as James Loch took over, but he professionalised the whole system into a business.

The numerous letters of the 1830s and the story of the separation of the two estates in particular reveals the extent to which national-scale financial distress impacted on the estates' staff on the ground in a way which is perhaps unexpected. Along with tenants and small-scale subtenants, the ground agent at Ketley found himself without income, deep in debt, and even without a chair to his name. The inability to keep rentals up-to-date was probably the root cause of Emery's as well as Henney's fall from grace, to say nothing of 'poor Plank'. Hardly spoken of was the laying off of indoor domestic staff at Trentham during its rebuilding, though this must have added to local economic depression as well the increased turnover in housekeepers.

In many ways, Trentham was an enclosed world of its own. Many of its employees were carrying out specialist jobs which had more in common with those of other great estates than locally. Servants in the lower ranks were deliberately limited in their time off and in their ability to socialise outside the house, though the porters' logbook no doubt recorded some of the occasions when young men in the house had to 'break-in' to get past the gatekeeper at night. Above all, perhaps, the parish records reveal the extent to which servants married into each others' families: the Wrights were connected by marriage to the Pensons and the Kirkbys, not once but many times. Ceremonies of marriage, christening and burial were often witnessed by fellow servants or their spouses. Certainly the two hierarchies of house servants and administrative staff worked as a team, especially during the rebuilding and in the family's absence, when Mrs Cleaver became such a good friend to the Lewis family.

As the Sutherlands gradually built and improved villages around them, such as Ash Green, Hanchurch and Tittensor, so contacts with the outside world widened. Lewis and those of the clerks who went out to collect rents obviously had regular contact with both tradesmen and tenants, rich and poor, throughout the county. The *Staffordshire Advertiser* bears testament to the frequency of notices and reports of short-term lettings, livestock for sale, and flower and vegetable shows held at and around Trentham (usually won by the Duke or one of his employees). Again, the parish registers reveal the role of clerks such as Kirkby, who by virtue of their estate employment were also parish clerks and overseers of the poor, whilst local bank records carry details of their jobs as secretaries and cashiers of the Trentham Savings Bank. Similarly, the housekeeper routinely came into contact with a large number of suppliers and tradesmen, either in her room at the house or in her travels around the nearest small town, Newcastle-under-Lyme. The people who remained somewhat isolated in the great house were the junior female servants. In many houses this was a deliberate policy to protect young girls. Yet many of these came from local families, were allowed out to visit them and themselves came into regular contact with casual helpers coming in to work in the house. In normal times they, along with the rest of the household, would be subject to the excitement of large numbers of much more sophisticated London servants arriving with the family, including foreign-born nannies, sewing maids and the house steward, and would be especially struck by the ebullience of the latter – very different from the usual run of English manservant.

Writing history is not just about answering questions: it always leaves new questions in its wake. Loch's frequent nagging about the urgency of making economies and earning more rental income from the estates draws our attention to the extravagant expenditure of a family that had just received a severe cut to its income. To what extent did this affect the family finances later in the century and the tragic fate of Trentham Hall? Presumably the depression of the 1830s created similar problems of tenant debt on other landed estates. Did their clerks and junior agents experience the same sort of stresses? In particular, the story of John Mackay and Ketley has only been summarised here, and although Barrie Trinder has written about the area during this period, it would be interesting to follow up the more personal aspects in greater detail. Similarly, the narrative of Zenon Vantini has been limited to his career with the Sutherlands. There is more to say and explore with regard to his other careers on Elba with Napoleon, and particularly his role in the development of railway hospitality and services both in England and France.

We have described James Loch's administration of the Sutherland empire as a huge business. Loch would not entirely have agreed with this; so let us allow him to have the last word, from his own summing up of his work which has been quoted elsewhere:

> The property of a great English Nobleman must be managed in the same principle as a little kingdom, not like the affairs of a little Merchant. The future and lasting interest and honour of the family as well as their immediate income must be kept in view – while a merchant thinks only of his daily profits and his own immediate life interest.[1]

APPENDICES

APPENDIX I

Members of the Household Mentioned in the Text

The Sutherland Family
George Granville, 2nd Marquess of Stafford (1803–1833) and 1st
  Duke of Sutherland (January 1833–June 1833)
Elizabeth Gordon, 2nd Marchioness of Stafford (1803–1833), 1st
  Duchess of Sutherland (January 1833–June 1833) and Duchess
  Countess (1833–1839)
George Granville, 2nd Duke of Sutherland (1833–1869)
Harriet Elizabeth Georgiana Howard, 2nd Duchess of Sutherland
  (1833–1868)
George Granville William, 3rd Duke of Sutherland (1869–1892)
Anne Hay Mackenzie, 3rd Duchess of Sutherland (1869–1892)

Duke's secretary
Henry Wright (1870s)
Thomas Jackson (*c.* 1833–1860s)

Duchess's lady's maid
Mary Penson (*née* Wright) (nanny by 1825; Duchess' lady's maid
  1840s–1865)

Chief agents
James Loch, chief agent (1812–1855)
George Loch, chief agent (1856–1877)

Trentham agents
William Lewis, agent of all English estates (1817–1834), Trentham,
  Wolverhampton and Stittenham agent only (1834–1841)
William Steward (1842–1859)

Lilleshall agents
William Smith (1834–1876)
John Mackay (Trentham clerk *c.* 1814; before 1820 went to Lilleshall; later became Ketley ground agent until 1851)

Clerks
Randal William Kirkby (Trentham *c.* 1810–1833; part-time until 1839)
Thomas Emery (Trentham *c.* 1820–1833)
William Henney (Trentham 1813–1822), Lilleshall (1822–1833), Trentham (1834–1845)
George Plank, borrowed from London (1833–1834)
William Day Kirkby (Trentham, part-time and casual 1830s–1839; full-time *c.* 1834–1880)

Trentham porters
Charles Kirkby (Trentham 1810–1854)
James Kirkby (Trentham *c.* 1817–1835)
Thomas Hemmings (Trentham 1864–?)

House stewards
Henry Prentice (1860s?–*c.* 1876)
Zenon Vantini (1833–1840)
Richard Walker (1840–1853)
John Whittaker (*c.* 1876–?)

Housekeepers
Dorothy Doar (London, casual *c.* 1818–*c.* 1823; Trentham 1832)
Martha Cleaver (London 1822–1832; Trentham 1832–1838)
Mrs Kirke (Lilleshall before 1830; Trentham 1838–1840; Lilleshall 1840–1840s)
Mrs Marsh (Trentham 1841–1853, then to London)
Sarah Tungate (London still-room maid before 1817; Lilleshall Old Hall housekeeper and brewer before 1822–1841)
Mrs Ingram (nanny by 1847, Trentham housekeeper 1861–1876)
Mrs Galleazie (London 1830s–?)

Head gardeners
John Woolley (Trentham 1826–1841)
John Beckie (Lilleshall ?–1839)

George Fleming (Lilleshall, ?–1841; Trentham 1841–1857; Trentham agent 1857–?)

Park and woodland keepers
John Penson, senior (Trentham, 1803–1840)
Reuben Penson (Trentham *c.* 1830; head 1840–1878)
James Penson (Lilleshall ?)

Baker/brewers
Robert Wright (Trentham under-baker *c.* 1819; baker/brewer 1831–after 1871)
Richard Wright (London 1820s–1838)

Groom
John Penson, junior (before 1821–1836)

Groom of the Chambers
John Wright (footman by 1821; groom of the chambers 1833; valet 1839–1853)

Duke's secretary
Henry Wright (1870s)
Thomas Jackson (1830s–40s)

Duchess's lady's maid
Mary Penson (*née* Wright) (nanny by 1825; Duchess's lady's maid 1840s–1865)

Sutherland Servant Households

Size of Sutherland servant households – indoor servants including coachmen and grooms (1839–40)

Households	Servants numbers			Annual wages		
	M	F	Total	M	F	Total
London – travellers	20	20	40	£830	£406	£1,236
London – resident Stafford House	6	6	12	£178	£101	£279
London – resident West Hill	2	5	7	£50	£96	£146
Trentham – resident	5	8	13	£157	£142	£299
Lilleshall – resident	3	7	10	£96	£128	£224
Total	36	46	82	£1,311	£873	£2,184

N.B. £s are rounded down to nearest £
(Source: SRO, D593/R/11/12, List of the Duke of Sutherland' Establishment 31st December–April 1st 1840

Notes

Abbreviations Used

SHRO – Shropshire Record Office
SRO – Staffordshire Record Office
VCH – Victoria County History of the County of Stafford, vol. XI, editor Nigel J. Tringham

Introduction

1. SRO, D593/R/4/9 List of servants and wages, nd, c.1817; D593/R/1/26/4 Statement of wages, 1822.
2. SRO, D593/ K/3/2/10 Lewis to Loch, 22 November and D593/K/1/3/18 Lewis to Loch, 29 November, both 1830.
3. SRO, D593/K/1/5/26 Loch to Lewis 2 December, 1830; D593/K/1/5/29 Loch to Lewis 10 July, 1833.
4. SRO, D593/K/1/3/28 Smith to Loch 12 May, 1840.
5. SRO, D593/K/1/3/29 Lewis to Loch 6 August, 1841; D593/K/3/1/27 Part 1 Loch to Lewis 4. August, 1841.
6. SRO, D593/K/1/3/29 Smith to Loch, 9 September, 1841.
7. SRO, D593/K/1/3/29 Smith to Loch, 11 September, 1841.
8. SRO, D593/K/1/3/29 Smith to Loch 17 August, 16 September, both 1841.
9. SRO, D593/K/1/3/29 Smith to Loch, 25 September, 1841.
10. SRO, D593/1/3/30 Smith to Loch, 23 December, 1842; Loch, J., *An Account of the Improvements on the Estates of the Marquess of Stafford*, 1820.
11. SRO, D593/K/1/3/30 Smith to Loch 20, 23, 31 December, 1842.
12. Hay, D., 'England, 1562-1875' in D. Hay and P. Craven, eds, *Masters, Servants and Magistrates in Britain and the Empire, 1562-1955*, (University of North Carolina Press, 2004).
13. Sambrook, P., *A Country House at Work: three centuries of Dunham Massey*, (London, National Trust, 2003).
14. Richards, E., *The Leviathan of Wealth: The Sutherland Fortune in the Industrial Revolution*, (RKP, London, 1973) p. 114.
15. Ibid. p. 16.

16. SRO, D593/K/1/3/18 Lewis to Loch, 11 December, 1830; Holland, M., *Swing Unmasked: The Agricultural riots of 1830 to 1832 and their Wider Implications*, (Family and Community Historical Research Society, Milton Keynes, 2005), pp. 62-85; Fyson, R, 'The Crisis of 1842: Chartism, the Colliers' Strike and the Outbreak in the Potteries' in *The Chartist Experience: Studies in Working Class Radicalism and Culture, 1830-60*, ed. James Epstein and Dorothy Thompson, (Macmillan, London, 1982), p. 205. See also Chapter 12.

17. For a discussion of the changes in tenant farm size see Wordie, J. R., 'Social Change on the Leveson-Gower Estates, 1714-1832' in *Economic History Review*, 2nd series, vol. 27, 4, 1974, pp. 593–609.

18. Richards, pp. 118–148.

19. Gower, R., *My Reminiscences*, vol. 1, (Trench and Co., London) 1883.

1 *The Servants of Trentham*

1. For a still-useful exposition of the structure of landed estate administration, including the difference between agents, commissioners, specialist agents, bailiffs and auditors, see Spring, D., *The English Landed Estate in the Nineteenth Century: its Administration*, (Baltimore, 1963) especially pp. 3–19.

2. SRO, 12 Albemarle Street is now the site of the Royal Arcade.

3. SRO, D593/N/2/8/5 Lodge book, 1818-1820; D593/K/3/5/5 Loch to Lewis, 26 November, 1817.

4. SRO, D593/R/11/12 List of the Duke of Sutherland's whole Establishment of Servants on 31 December 1839 to 1 April 1840.

5. Gerard, J. A., 'Invisible Servants: The Country House and the Local Community', *Bulletin of the Institute of Historical Research*, vol. LV11, No 136, November 1984, p. 180.

6. SRO, D593/K/1/3/21 English bundle, 8 November, 1833.

7. Campbell-Smith, D., *Masters of the Post: The Authorized History of the Royal Mail* (Allen Lane, London, 201), p. 126.

8. SRO, D593/K/1/3/32 Wm Steward to Loch, 15 April 15, 1844.

9. SRO, D593/R/11/12 List of the Duke of Sutherland's whole Establishment of Servants on 31 December 1839 to 1 April 1840.

10. SRO, D593/R/1/26/4B A Statement of wages paid at Stafford House and West Hill, 2 February 1832.

11. SRO, D593/K/1/3/29Walker to Loch, 25 January 1841.

12. SRO, D593/R/4/9 undated wage list but *c.* 1816.

13. Gerard, pp. 182, 185; D593/K/1/3/29 Henney to Loch, 31 September 1841.

14. SRO, D593/R/1/15/1 Cash Book, 1841.

15. Gerard, 'Invisible Servants, p. 184.

16. SRO, D593/R/5/1 Meals Book, 1850–53 for London, Lilleshall, Dunrobin and Tarbet; D593/R/5/3 Meals Book, 1867-73, as before, plus Trentham.

17. Sambrook, P., *A Country House at Work: three centuries of Dunham Massey*, (National Trust, 2003), chapter 3.

18. SRO, D593/K/1/3/30 William Smith to Loch, 22 June 1842.

19. For a good exposition of the demography of country house servants see Gerard, J., *Country House Life: Family and Servants, 1815–1914*, (Blackwells, Oxford, 1994), pp. 162–189.

20. SRO, D539/R/4/3 and /4 Wages Books, 1840–57.
21. *Oxford Journal*, Death notices, 27 February 1836.
22. Tudor, P. G., *The Domestic Establishments of His Grace the Duke of Sutherland* (private unpublished project report for Department of Adult Education, Keele University, 1995), p. 5.
23. SRO, D593/K/1/3/32 April 1844.

2 The Benefits of Serving the Sutherlands

1. SRO, D593/K/1/3/29 George Lewis to Loch, 2 August 1841.
2. SRO, D593/N/2/2/3/1(b) Reports on Cottages, 1835.
3. SRO, D593/K/1/3/24 Lewis to Loch, 24 September, 1836.
4. SRO D593/N/2/2/3/4 Notes on Fixtures in Properties, 1820–1840.
5. SRO, D593/K/1/3/26 Lewis to Loch 7 March, Smith to Loch 29 March, both 1839.
6. SRO, D593/K/3/2/8 Lewis to Loch, 18 November 1826.
7. SRO, D593/K/3/1/27 Part 1 Loch to Woolley, 4 August 1841.
8. SRO, D593/K/1/3/29Lewis to Loch, 6 August 1841.
9. SRO, D593/K/1/3/29 Henney to Loch, 23 August 1841.
10. SRO, D593/K/1/3/29 Henney to Loch, 24 August 1, 5, 13 September 1841.
11. SRO, D593/K/1/3/29 Woolley to Loch, 23 November 1841; D593/K/1/3/29 Lewis to Loch, 5 August 1841.
12. SRO, D593/K/3/2/8 Lewis to Loch, 18 November 1826.
13. SRO, D593/K/1/3/41 Jackson to Loch, 3 February 1853.
14. SRO, D593/K/1/3/29 Smith to Loch, 18 September, Henney to Loch, 28 September both 1841.
15. SRO, D593/K/1/3/29 Henney to Loch, 18 September 1841.
16. SRO, D593/K/1/3/29 Henney to Loch, 28 September 1841.
17. VCH Gregory, S., *A History of Staffordshire*, vol. XI, ed. Nigel Tringham, 2013, p. 242.
18. SRO, D593/K/1/5/182 George Loch's outletter book, 26 August 1876.
19. SRO, D593/R/10/3 George Loch to Mrs Ingram, housekeeper at Trentham.
20. SRO, D593/K/1/3/28 Mrs Galleazie to Loch, 7 January 1840.
21. SRO, D593/K/1/3/41Duchess to Loch, February 1853.
22. SRO, D593/R/10/2 Duchess to Mrs Ingram, nd.
23. SRO, D593/R/1/26/4b Statement of wages, 1832; D593/K/1/3/33 Culverwell (Loch's clerk) to Loch, 10 November 1845 and D593/K/1/3/44 Annuities in the Will of the late Duchess Countess, 1834–36.
24. SRO, D593/K/1/3/21 Lewis to Loch, 24 and 28 March, 24 May, all 1833. D593/K/1/3/24 Woolley to Loch, 8 June 1835.
25. SRO, D593/K/1/3/20 Kirkby to Loch, 14 March 1832.
26. SRO, D593/K/1/3/29 Mrs Kirke to Loch, 12 April 1841.
27. SRO, D593/K/1/3/29 Dudley and Tate to Loch, 1 November 1841.
28. SRO, D593/N/2/15/31 Nominations to North Staffordshire Infirmary.
29. SRO, D593/R/8, Vantini's letters, 30 April and 3 August, 1839.
30. SRO, D593/K/1/3/28 Duchess to Loch, 21 January, Lewis to Loch, 3 February, both 1840; D593/1/5/36 Lewis to Loch, 22 January 1840.

31. SRO, D593/K/1/3/20 Earl Gower to Loch, 26 February 1832; SRO, D4177/1-2 'A Daily Journal or Memorandum Book, by Thomas, Footman in the service of the 2nd Duke of Sutherland, 1838-9, Part 2'.
32. SRO, D593/R/4/9 List of servants and wages, nd *c*. 1816.
33. SRO, D593/K/1/3/24 Lewis to Loch, July 1836.
34. SRO, D593/K/1/3/29 Henney to Loch, 31 September 1841.
35. SRO, D593/L/1/32 List of Persons receiving perquisites at Trentham, 1817–18.
36. SRO, D593/K/1/3/22 Vantini to Loch, 11 December 1834.
37. SRO, D593/K/1/3/29 Walker to Loch, 25 January 1841.
38. SRO, D593/K/1/3/29 Walker to Loch, 25 January 1841.
39. SRO, D4177/1-2 'A Daily Journal or Memorandum Book'.
40. SHRO, 972/3/11/1 Vantini's Logbook 1833-1840 (microfiche only).
41. SRO, D593/K/1/3/29 Henney to Loch, 18, 28 September, 19 November, 31 December all 1841.
42. SHRO, D4177/1-2 ' Daily Journal or Memorandum Book'.
43. SRO, D593/K/1/5/36 Loch to Walker, 28 November 1840.
44. SRO, D593/K/1/3/23 Farrer to Loch, 6 March 1835.
45. SRO, D593/K/1/3/29 Mantell to Loch, 30 April 1841.
46. SHRO, D4177/1-2 ' Daily Journal or Memorandum Book'.
47. All the details of journeys which follow are in SRO, D593/R/1/25/7 Posting Book.
48. SRO, D593/K/1/3/28 Loch's clerk to E. Wright, July 1840.

3 Food and Drink

1. SRO D593/K/1/3/28 Walker to Loch 8, December 1840.
2. SRO D593/K/1/3/29 Walker to Loch 2, January 1841.
3. SRO D593/R/1/26/16/x Memoranda on domestic management, 1836–40.
4. SRO D593/K/1/3/28 Edward Wright to Loch, 25 November 1840.
5. SRO D593/K/1/3/28 George Readman to Loch, 25 November 1840.
6. SRO D593/K/1/3/28 William Hussey to Loch, 24 November 1840.
7. SRO D5678/11/201 153a Duchess to Loch, 1843.
8. SRO D593/K/1/3/32, Loch's inletters, April 8 1844.
9. SRO D593/K/1/3/32 Walker to Loch, May 8 1844.
10. SRO D593/R/1/19 Housekeeping Charges, 1873.
11. SHRO 972/3/11/1 Vantini's log book (microfiche).
12. SRO D593/K/1/3/29 Jackson to Loch, 12 October 1841.
13. SRO D593/K/1/3/29 Lewis to Loch, 19 May 1841.
14. SRO D593/K/1/3/32 Unkown to Loch, 23 December 1844.
15. SRO D593/K/3/1/27 Part 1 Loch to Lewis/ 22 August 1841.
16. Oglander, J., 'Rules of Husbandry' in *A Royalist's Notebook: the Commonplace Book of Sir John Oglander*, transcribed and edited by Francis Bamford, (London, 1936); Defoe, Daniel, *The Compleat English Gentleman*, 1728, later editions edited by Karl Daniel Bulbring, available as ebooks or print on demand.
17. See for example SRO D593/R/2/18/1 Grocery bills, 1838.
18. SRO D593/K/1/3/29 Smith to Loch, 21 August 1841.
19. SRO D593/R/1/14/1 Vantini's accounts, 1833–38.
20. SRO D593/R/1/26/21F List of tradesmen's accounts.

21. SRO D593/K/1/5/32 Loch to Woolley, 2 May 1836.
22. SRO D593/K/1/3/27 Henney to Loch, 20 March 1839.
23. Leveson-Gower, F., Vol. 1, p. 128.
24. SRO D593/K/1/3/20 Lewis to Loch, 17 March 1832.
25. SRO D593/K/1/3/27 Lewis to Loch, 25 October 1839.
26. SRO D593/K/1/3/27 Isaac Morley to Loch, 14 February 1839; D593/K/1/3/28 George Loch to James Loch, 4 January 1840.
27. SRO D593/K/1326 Jackson to Loch, 21 January 1838.
28. SRO D593/K/1/3/26 Lewis to Loch, 5 September 1838.
29. SRO D593/K/1/3/20 Lewis to Loch, 23 January 1832.
30. SRO D593/K/1/3 /27, 29 January; and 1 and 10 January, all 1839.
31. SRO D593/K/1/3/26 Jackson to Loch, 8 October 1838.
32. SRO D593/K/1/3/27 Fleming to Loch, 11 March 1839.
33. SRO D593/K/1/3/29 Lewis to Loch 7, March 1841.
34. SRO D593/K/1/3/29 Henney to Loch, 16 October 1841.
35. Mowl, T. and Parre, D., *The Historic Gardens of England: Staffordshire*, (Redcliffe, 2009).
36. SRO D593/K/1/3/29 Walker to Loch, 5 January 1841.
37. *Victoria County History of Staffordshire*, vol. 11, ed. Nigel Tringham, p. 241.
38. SRO D593/R/11/7 Brewer's reports, 1848.
39. For more detail about country-house brewing see Sambrook, Pamela, *Country House Brewing in England, 1500–1900*, (Hambledon Press, London, 1996).
40. SRO D593/K/3/9/80 George Menzies to the Inland Revenue, January 1897.
41. SRO D593/K/3/3/27 Kirkby to Lewis, 6 November 1832.
42. SRO D593/K/3/327 Kirkby to Loch, 6 November 1832.
43. SRO D593/K/1/3/27 Mrs Kirke to Loch, 21 March 1839.
44. SHRO 972/3/11/1 Vantini's log book; SRO D593/K/3/2/7 Lewis to Loch, 20 January 1825; D593/K/3/4/3 Lewis to Earl Gower, 7 February 1831.
45. SRO D593/K/1/3/21 Lewis to Duke, 3 May 1833.
46. SRO D593/K/1/3/27 Lewis to Loch, 20 March 1839.
47. SRO D593/K/1/3/32 Thurgood to Loch, April 25 1844.
48. SRO D593/K/1/3/32 Thurgood to Loch and Duchess to Loch, 10 December 1844.
49. SRO D593/K/1/3/32 Walker to Loch, 8 May 1844.
50. Yorke, J., p. 90.
51. SRO D593/R/6/2 Cellar Book, 1843–77.
52. SRO D593/Q/2/2/1 Loch to Henry Wright, 22, 25 February 1862, p. 39.
53. SRO D4177/1-2 'A Daily Journal or Memorandum Book, by Thomas, Footman in the service of the 2nd Duke of Sutherland, 1838-9, manuscript, Part 2.
54. Thanks to Alison Hirst for this information.

4 No Pressure ...?

1. SRO D593/R/1/26/4A-T, Item B, Wages at Stafford House and West Hill, c. 1822.
2. www.mkheritage.co.uk/hanslope.
3. SRO D593/K/1/3/20 Lewis to Loch, August 11, and Lewis to Lady Stafford, September 4 1832.

4. SRO D593/K/1/3/24 Lewis to Loch, 14 February 1836.

5. This was the farm which later became a listening post for Bletchley Park in World War II.

6. SRO D593/K/3/2/16 Lewis to Loch, January 9,11, 13, 23, 30, February 8, April 19 and D593/K/3/1/2 Feb, all 1836.

7. SRO D593/R/8 Lewis to Vantini, 1838, D593/K/1/3/26 Lewis to Loch, January 24, 28, May 8, all 1838.

8. SRO D593/K/1/3/26 Mrs Cleaver to the Duchess, May 16, Lewis to Loch, May 21, all 1838.

9. SRO D593/K/1/3/27 Mrs Kirke to Loch, 3 February 1839.

10. SRO D593/K/1/3/27 Mrs Kirke to Loch, 21 May, Mrs Kirke to Lewis, 10 May, 14 and 22 1839.

11. SRO D593/K/1/3/27 Jackson to Loch 13, July 1839; D593/K/1/3/30 Smith to Loch, 4 September 1842.

12. SRO D593/K/1/3/27, Loch's inletters, October 20th and November 20th, 1839.

13. SRO D593/K/1/5/36 Loch to Lewis, and Loch to Haldane and Rae, 3 January and 8 1840.

14. SRO D593/K/1/3/27 Mrs Kirke to Loch, 21 March 1839.

15. SRO D593/K/1/3/27 Mrs Kirke to Loch, 19 March 1839.

16. SRO D593/K/1/5/36 Loch to Mrs Douglas in Edinburgh, 16 January 1840.

17. SRO D593/R/11/12 List of the Duke of Sutherland's whole Establishment of Servants, 31 December 1839 to 1 April 1840; D593/R/4/3 Wages Book 1840–47.

18. SRO D593/K/1/3/29 Walker to Loch, 6 August 1841; D593/K/1/3/29 Lewis to Loch, 18 February 1841; D593/K/1/3/30 Smith to Loch, 4 September 1842.

19. SRO D593/R/11/12 wage list for 1839 and R/4/3, Wages Book 1840–47.

20. SRO D593/R/10/7 Sarah to Mrs Ingram, 29 May 1861.

21. SRO D593/R/10/7 Earl of Drogheda to Mrs Ingram, nd, and Earl of Wharncliffe to Mrs Ingram, 31 December 1875.

22. SRO D593/R/2/72/7 Mrs Ingram's book vouchers, D593/R/10/10/1 vouchers for 1870.

23. SRO D593/R/5/3 Meals book, 1867–73.

24. The following account is based on SRO D593/R/10/4 and 5 Henry Wright to Mrs Ingram, 30 May 30, 5 June and 5, 7, 30, July 13, 1872; D593/R/10/4 Henry Prentice to Mrs Ingram, 11 July 1872.

25. SRO D593/R/10/1 Duchess to Mrs Ingram, nd.

26. SRO D593/R/10/2 Duchess to Mrs Ingram, nd.

27. SRO D593/R/10/5 John Whittaker to Mrs Ingram, 26 April 1876.

28. SRO D593/R/10/7 John Reid to Mrs Ingram, 11 August 1875.

29. SRO D593/R/10/4 Henry Prentice to Mrs Ingram, nd.

30. Sambrook, P., *The Country House Servant* (Stroud, 1999) pp. 185–188.

5 The Public Face of the Sutherlands

1. SRO D593/K/1/5/36 Loch to Vantini, January 6 1840.

2. SHRO 972/3/11/1 Vantini's logbook; D593/N/2/8/5 Lodge Book, 1816.

3. Charles Kirkby's rental information taken from SRO D593/G/2/5/3, 4 and 5, 1815–51; D593/N/2/2/3/1(b) Reports on Cottages, 1835.

4. SROD593/R/4/9 List of Servants and wages, nd *c.* 1816.

5. WSL 92/2/64, Thomas Kirkby's Notebooks, 'Dele Ante del Vasajo', 1548.
6. Details of values of personal estates of Charles' sons from National Probate Calendar online database, 1858-1966, 1891, 1880 and 1900.
7. James Kirkby's rental information from SRO D593/G/2/5/4 Rent Book, 1833–34.
8. SRO D593/K/1/3/23 Lewis to Loch, March 30 1835.
9. SRO D593/K/1/3/24 Revd Vaughan to Loch, Oct 22,1836.
10. SRO D593/K/1/3/24 RW Kirkby to Loch, 2 and 25 November.
11. SRO D593/K/1/3/18 Revd Butt to Loch, July 20 1830; D593/G/2/5/3, Rent Book 1815–1833.
12. SRO D593/Q/2/1/1 Fleming to Duke, 16 December, and Fleming to Wright, 18 December 1863; D593/K/3/8/15 Fleming to Jackson, 7 January, Fleming to Duke, 21 January, Fleming to Wright 7 July, Fleming to Wright 10 July, all 1864.
13. SRO D593/N/2/8/1 Regulations for the Lodge-keeper at Trentham, 1810; D593/N/2/8/5 Lodge Book, 1816.
14. SRO D593/R/7/10B Inventory of the household furniture at Trentham, 1826.
15. SRO D593/K/3/7/20 Part 2, Night watchman's duties, March 1849.
16. SRO D593/N/2/8/11 Nightwatchman's book 1877–1880.
17. SRO D593/K/1/3/32 Anon, 15 May 1844.
18. SRO D593/K/1/5/45, Loch to Henney, 22 May 1844.
19. SRO D593/K/1/5/45 Loch to Henney 22, 23, 25 May 1844.
20. SROD593/K/1/3/32 Henney to Loch, 18 and 27 May; George Lewis to Loch, 22 May all 1844.
21. SRO D593/N/2/8/7 Lodge Bread and Beer book, 1848–67.
22. For details of endowed charities Trentham see VCH, 'History of Staffordshire, vol XI' p. 255.
23. SRO D593/L/1/32 List of Persons receiving perquisites at Trentham, 1817–18.
24. SRO D593/K/1/3/29 Jenkins to Loch, 21 August 1841.
25. SRO D593/N/2/8/5 Lodge Book 1816; D593/N/2/4/44 Milk Book 1823–30;D593//N/2/8/8/ Poor List, 1878.
26. SRO D593/N2/2/3/5 Weights Book, 1788–1804.
27. SHRO 972/3/11/1 Vantini's logbook (microfiche).

6 A Woman's Place

1. SRO D593/K/3/1/27 Part 2 Loch to Lewis, 5 February 1840.
2. SRO D593/R/1/13/1 Mr Lilley's Payments, 1805–1826.
3. SRO D593/R/1/12 Trentham Day Book, 1820-30; D593/K/4/1/24, Trentham accounts, June 1826.
4. SRO D593/K/1/3/18 Lewis to Loch, 24 November 1830.
5. SRO D593/K/2/12 Lewis to Loch, 1 January, 21 February, both 1832; D593/K/1/5/28 Loch to Lewis, 2 April 1832.
6. SRO D593/K/1/5/28 Loch to Lewis, 2 April, 1832.
7. SRO D593/K/1/3/20 Dorothy Doar to Lewis, 3 April 1832.
8. SRO D593/K/1/3/20 Lewis to Loch 4 April, 1832.
9. SRO D593/K/3/2/12, Loch to Lewis, 10,13 April 1832.
10. SRO D593/K/1/5/28 Loch to Mrs Doar, 10 April 1832.
11. SRO D593/K/1/5/28 Loch to Lewis, 7 April 1832.
12. SRO D593/K/1/3/20, Loch to Lewis, 9 May1832.

13. SRO D593/K/3/2/12, Lewis to Lady Stafford, 9 May 1832.

14. SRO D593/K/1/5/28, Loch to Lewis, 10 May 1832.

15. SRO D593/F/4/1/34, Draft accounts for Trentham, 1832.

16. SRO D593/K/3/2/12 Lewis to Loch, May 12 1832; D593/K/3/3/26 Pt 1of 3, Kirkby to Lewis, May 15 1832.

17. SRO D593/K/3/3/26 Pt 1of 3 Kirkby to Lewis, 15 May 1832.

18. SRO D593/K/3/2/12 Lewis to Loch, 17 May 17 1832.

19. SRO D593/K/3/2/12 Loch to Lewis, May 19 1832.

20. SRO D593/K/1/5/28, Loch to Lewis, 19 May 19 1832.

21. SRO D593/K/1/3/20 Lewis to Loch, May 22 1832.

22. SRO D593/K/1/3/20 Lewis to Loch, May 29 1832.

23. SRO D593/K/3/1/18, Loch to Lewis, 30 May 1832.

24. SRO D593/L/2/2/B Lewis's journal, 29 May 29 and 1 June 1832; D593/K/1/3/20, Lewis to Loch, 2 June 1832.

25. SRO D593/K/1/5/28 Loch to Lewis, 4 June 1832; D593/K/1/3/20 Lewis to Loch, 31 May 1832; D593/K/3/2/12 Lewis to Loch, 6 June 1832.

26. Adams, S. and S., *The Complete Servant* 1st pub.1825, new ed., Southover Press, 1989, p. 17.

27. SRO D593/F/4/1/34, Draft accounts for Trentham, 1832.

28. SRO D593/K/1/3/20 Lewis to Loch, May 9 1832.

29. Catherine Wilmshurst ran a school for young ladies at Hanford until 1843 when it moved to Standon, then back to Hanford in 1850 until 1860-63. VCH, vol XI, p. 254.

30. SRO D593/K/1/3/19 Lord Dover to James Loch, 2 December 1831.

31. SRO D539/R/4/3 and /4 Wages books, 1840–1850.

32. SRO D6578/11/201/1-80 Duke to Loch, 15 March 1843.

33. SROD6578/11/201/163 & 164 Duke to Loch, March 6 & 7 1842.

34. There was a long tradition of restrictions on servants' marrying. Women were automatically expected to give up their employment in a household when they married. Menservants were allowed to marry and remain in their posts if they were out of livery – i.e. at least a butler or underbutler. But if they were a liveried servant – footman, groom, or coachmen – they were expected to ask their employer for permission to marry. See P. Sambrook, *Keeping their Place*, (Stroud, Sutton, 2005) Chapter 9.

35. SROD593/K/1/3/33 William Wykes to Loch, November 1845; D593/R/4/3 & 4 Wages Books, 1840–54.

36. Barber, J., '"Stolen Goods": the Sexual Harassment of Female Servants in West Wales during the Nineteenth Century', in *Rural History*, Vol. 4, No. 2, Oct. 1993, pp. 123–136.

37. SRO D593/Q/2/2/1 Henry Wright to Duke, 5 February 1862.

7 The Incomer

1. SRO D593/R/1/26/15, package of accounts by Vantini, 1838–39.

2. SRO D593/K/1/5/29 Loch to Lewis, 7 October 1833.

3. SRO D593/K/1/5/29 Loch to Vantini, 5, 16 December 1833.

4. SRO D593/R/1/26/15c, Vantini to Loch, 22 April 1836.

5. National Archives of Scotland, Loch Family Papers, GD268/364 Duke to Loch, 21 April 1834; SRO D593/K/1/3/22 Duke to Loch, 22 April 1834; D593/R/11/2 List of Duke of Sutherland's horses in London, 1840.

6. SRO D593/R/8, Vantini's in letters, 25 October 1839.

7. SRO D593/K/1/5/32 Loch to Jackson, September 1836.

8. SRO D593/K/1/3/24 Jackson to Loch, September, Vantini to Loch, 27 September 1836.

9. SRO D593/K/1/3/26 Jackson to Loch, 11 August 1838.

10. SRO D593/K/1/3/26 Vantini to Loch, 8 October 1838; D593/K/1/3/27 Vantini to Loch, 8 September, 1839.

11. SRO D593/K/1/3/26 Vantini to Loch, 24 October 1838; D593/1/3/27 Jackson to Loch, 17 March 1839.

12. SRO D593/R/1/11/4 Vantini's accounts, 1836–40.

13. SRO D593/R/1/3/29 Smith to Loch, 17 January1841.

14. SRO D593/R/1/3/28 Vantini to Loch, 2, 5, 7, 9 March 1840.

15. SRO D593/K/1/3/28 Vantini to Loch, 18, 28 July 1840.

16. SRO D593/K/3/1/27 Part 2 of 5 , Loch to Lewis, Dec 31, 1840.

17. Sykes, C. S., *Private Palaces: Life in the Great London Houses*, (Viking, New York, 1985) p. 260.

18. SRO D593/K/1/3/28 Officer of the Birmingham Railway Company to Loch, 15, 28 August 1840; 593/R/8 Vantini's in letters, 26 September 1839; D593/K/1/3/27 Vantini to Loch, 30 November 1839.

19. Keele University Library, Sneyd Papers, SC13/138 Duchess Harriet to Ralph Sneyd, 8 July 1844.

20. SRO D593/K/1/3/28 Vantini to Loch, nd September 1840.

21. SRO D593/K/1/5/36 Loch to Walker, 19 September 1840.

22. SRO D593/K/1/3/29 Vantini to Loch, 24 January 1841.

23. SRO D593/K/1/3/29 Walker to Loch, 17, 20 January 1841.

24. Curtis, B., *The Golden Dream: the Biography of Sir Peter Hesketh-Fleetwood, Bart., and the founding of the town of Fleetwood*, (Manchester, 1997) p. 79; *Manchester Courier and Lancashire General Advertiser*, 3 June 1843, p. 1; and 9 July 1842, p. 1.

25. *Preston Chronicle*, 12 June 1841, p. 3.

26. Beechey,Canon St Vincent, *The Rise and Progress of Rossall School: a Jubilee Sketch*, Skeffington, 1894, p. 5.

27. Curtis, p. 80; *Manchester Courier and Lancashire General Advertiser*, 9 July 1842, p. 1 ; 5 July, 1842, p. 11; 16 July, p. 2; 30 December 1843 p. 1 and *The Cheltenham Looker On*, 23 June 1894, p. 585.

28. SRO D593/Q/1/1/1 Duke to Jackson, 20 March 1844.

29. Curtis, p. 91.

30. Monday, *Birmingham Gazette*, 28 July 1845, p. 1.

31. *Northampton Mercury*, 2 December 1843.

32. Vajda, J., *Les Pereire and Nagelmackers, promoteurs du transport ferroviaire et du réseau hôtelier parisien, 1855-1900*, pp. 27–44.

33. Beechey, p. 3.

34. www.gerard.hilbert.free.fr/saga_vantini.

35. *Almanac Impérial* [Official Directory of the French Republic], 1812,p. 84 and 1814, p. 70.

36. www.elbalink.it/infotourist/napoleon, p.7;Christophe, Robert, *Napoleon on Elba*, (translation London, 1964) p. 73.

37. Christophe, R.,*Napoleon on Elba*, Transl edition, (London, 1964) pp. 105–8; Mackenzie, N., *The Escape from Elba: the Fall and Flight of Napoleon, 1814-1815*, (Oxford, 1982), pp.112, 119, 224.

38. *Newcastle Courant*, Saturday, 2 March 1895.

39. Bourrier, M., *François Filidoro, le capitaine du port de l'Isle d'Elba: tribulations et jours de gloire d'un Corse né en 1766*, (1978), p.179; Lentz, T., 'Les Cent-Jours' vol. 4 of *Nouvelle Histoire du Premier Empire*, (Paris, 2002-10) p. 190; advice from Malcolm Crook of Keele University to whom I am grateful for help with this whole subject.

40. Bertrand, H., *Cahier de Sainte-Helene*, Jan 1821–May1821 (Sulliver, 1949).

41. www.g.hilbert.perso.informe.fr 20,000fr was perhaps around £800 at that time, the equivalent of 8 years of Vantini's salary with the Sutherlands or in terms of purchasing power equivalent to perhaps £40,000 to £50,000 in 2013.

42. http://stsepulchres.org.uk/burials/blott_alfred.html .

43. *Dorset County Chronicle and Somersetshire Gazette*, 11 April, 1867; *Salisbury & Winchester Journal and General Advertiser*, 4 May 1867; *ibid.* 28 August 1869; *The Western Gazette*, 6 August 1880; Kelly's *Directory, Sherborne, Dorset*, 1880, p. 935.

44. Beechey, p. 5.

45. Richards, *Leviathan*, pp. 85–148 .

46. Semmel, s., *Napoleon and the British*, (Yale UP, 2004), pp. 176–226.

47. SRO D593/K/1/3/28 Vantini to Loch, 8 October 1840.

8 Staying for the Long Term

1. SRO D593/L/2/1 Loch's Notebook 1817-42, taxables for 1825, pp. 267–273.

2. John Penson sen.'s rental information taken from SRO D6578/11/89 List of Tenants, 1843 and D593/G/2/5/2, 3 and 4 Rent books 1803-1848; D593/K/1/3/29 Lewis to Loch, 5 August 1841.

3. For example, Lady Blanche's funeral. SRO D593/K/1/3/20 Lewis to Loch, March 3 1832.

4. SRO D593/K/1/3/21 Anon to Loch, May 24 1833.

5. SRO D593/K/1/3/21 Lewis to Loch, May 30 June 1, 1833.

6. *Staffordshire Advertiser*, Saturday 14 July 1838.

7. SRO D593/K/1/3/19 Loch's in letters, 28 January 1831, Lewis to Loch, 28 January.

8. SRO D593/K/1/5/27 Loch to Lewis, 1831.

9. SRO D593/K/1/5/32 Loch to Smith May 18, 1836.

10. SRO D593/K/1/3/19 Blunt to Loch, 31 May 1831.

11. SRO D593/K/1/5/27, English estates, Loch to John Penson, 6 June, 1831.

12. SRO D593/K/1/3/19 Mackay to Loch 3 July, and Lewis to Loch, 5 July 1831.

13. SRO D593/K/1/3/20 Loch's in letters, 15, 28 June, 20 July 20, 18 August 1832.

14. SRO D593/K/1/3/22 Lewis to Loch, 8 March 1834.

15. Though Penson is not an unusual name in the area, the identification of James and Ann and their family is secure due to names ages and birthplaces of both them and their children, eight in total.

16. SHRO 972/3/11/1 Vantini's log book; SRO D593/L/2/L Loch's notebook, 1817–1842; D593/K/1/5/29 Loch to Lewis's 18 June 1833; D593/N/2/2/3/1b Reports on cottages starting 1835.
17. SRO D6578/11/89 List of Tenants, 1843.
18. SRO D593/K/3/2/16 Lewis's out letters, 7 June 1836.
19. SROD593/K/3/1/2 Lewis's in letters from Loch, June 7th, 1836. D593/K/3/2/16 Lewis's out letters June 14, 1836. D593/K/3/1/2 Lewis's in letters from Loch, June 15, 1836.
20. SRO D593/K/3/1/2 Lewis's in letters from Loch, 10 June 1836; D593/K/3/2/16 Lewis's out letters, 11 June 1836 D593/K/3/1/2 Lewis's in letters from Loch, 16 Jun 1836.
21. SRO D593/K/3/2/16 Lewis's copy outletters, 4, 17 June 1836 and D593/K/3/1/2 Lewis's in letters 7, 18, all 1836.
22. SRO D593/R/8 Penson to Vantini, 3 May 1838.
23. SRO D593/K/3/4/5 Lewis to Duke, 20 March 1840.
24. SRO D593/K/3/1/27 Part 2 of 5, Lewis's inletters from Loch, 31 March and 6 April 1840.
25. *Staffordshire Advertiser*, 20 February, 1841. For John Penson jun. rent details see D593/G/2/5/4 Rent books, 1833–1848.
26. SRO D593/K/1/3/31 Lewis to Loch, 5 May 1843 and Penson to the Duke, 11 May 1843.
27. SRO D593/K/1/5/41 Loch to William Steward, 15 May 1843.
28. SRO D593/K/1/3/31 Lewis to Loch, 17 May 1843.
29. SRO D593/K/5/41 Loch to Steward, 22 May 1843.
30. SRO D593/K/1/3/32 Duchess to Loch, 31 March, 1844; D593/K/1/5/43 Loch to Duchess, 4 April 1844.
31. SRO D593/K/1/3/32, Steward to Loch, 28 April 1844.
32. SRO D593/K/1/5/45 Loch to Steward, 29 April 1844.
33. SRO D593/K/1/5/45 Loch to Steward, 4 May, 1844. George Samuel Fereday Smith was deputy superintendent of the Bridgewater Canal Trust from 1837 to 1887.
34. SRO D593/K/1/5/45 Loch to Steward, 11 June 1844.
35. SRO D593/K/1/5/45 Loch to Steward, 12 September 1844.
36. SRO D593/K/3/1/32 Duchess to Loch, 10 December 1844.
37. SRO D593/K/1/5/45 Loch to Steward, 14 December 1844.
38. SHRO 972/3/11/1 Vantini's log book: SRO D593/R/11/12 Wages list 1839–40; D593/R/4/3 and 4 Wages lists 1840–54.
39. Lord Ronald Gower, *My Reminiscences*, vol. 1, Kegan Paul, Trench and Co., 1883, pp. 216–7.
40. National Probate Calendar online database, 1858–1966, 1865.

9 Keeping the Records Straight

1. McBride, T., *Social Mobility for the Lower Classes: Domestic Servant in France,* in Journal of Social History, 1974, 8, p71..
2. D593/N/2/8/5 Lodge Book, 1816.
3. Census Henderskelf, Yorkshire, 1851–1881.
4. D593/K/1/3/18 Kirkby to John Smith, Loch's clerk, 7 February, 1830.

5. D593/K/1/3/18 Revd Butt to Loch, 20 July, 1830.
6. D593/K/1/3/20 Lewis to Loch, March 3 1832.
7. D593/K/1/5/29 George Loch to Lewis, Oct 14, 1833.
8. D593/K/1/3/19 Kirkby to Loch Feb 2.
9. D593/K/1/3/20 Lewis to Earl Gower, Aug 9, 1832.
10. D593/K/13/19 Lewis to Loch Sept 3, 1831; D593/K/1/5/29 Loch to Lewis, Oct 9, 1833.
11. D593/K/1/3/19, RWK to Loch, Feb 2, Sept 4 1831.
12. D593/K/1/3/19 Loch to RWK, July 8, 1831.
13. D593/K/3/3/26 Pt 1of 3, Lewis's miscellaneous inletters, Jan-June 1832,May 15, Kirkby to Lewis.
14. D593/K/1/3/19 Kirkby to Loch 2 February 1831.
15. D593/K/1/3/21 Emery to Lewis, Feb 2, 1833.
16. D593/K/1/3/21 Emery to Lewis, Feb 3, 1833.
17. D593/K/1/3/21 Lewis to Loch, Feb 4 x 2 1833.
18. D593/K/1/5/29 Loch to Lewis, Feb 9 1833.
19. D593/K/1/5/29 Loch to Lewis, Feb 14, 1833.
20. D593/K/1/3/21 Emery to Loch, Feb 15, 1833.
21. D593/K/1/3/21 Lewis to Loch, Feb 16, 1833.
22. D593/K/1/3/21 Lewis to Loch, March 18, March 20, 1833.
23. D593/K/1/3/21 Lewis to Loch, March 18, 1833.
24. D593/K/1/5/29, Loch to Lewis, 18, 28 June 1833.
25. D593/K/1/3/21, Emery to Loch, Aug 13, 1833.
26. D593/K/1/3/22 Lewis to Loch Jan 6, 7, 15, Feb 2, May 31;Henney to Loch Jan 16, 1834.
27. D593/K/1/3/22 Plank to Loch July 16, 1834.
28. D593/K/1/3/22 Lewis to Loch July 28, Butt to Loch July 28,Plank to Lewis July 18, 1834.
29. D593/K/1/3/22 Davidson to Loch July 27, 1834.
30. D593/K/1/3/22 Mackenzie to Loch July 31, 1834.
31. D593/K/1/5/30, Loch to Lewis, Aug. 1, 1834.
32. D593/K/1/5/30 Loch to Wm Adam Loch, Aug 2, 1834.
33. D593/K/3/1/1/1 Loch 1813.
34. D593/K/1/3/18 Revd Butt to Loch 20 July, 1830; D593/N/2/17/1/1 Savings Bank Minute Book; D593/G/2/5/3 Rent Books 1815-1833; D593/K/1/3/8 Lewis to Loch 1, 19 April and 2 May, 1820.
35. D593/K/1/3/18 Lewis to Loch, 22, 26 May, 1830.
36. D593/K/1/5/27 Loch to Raikes June 8, 1831; D593/K/1/5/30 Loch to Bank of England April 6, 1834.
37. D593/K/1/3/18 Henney to Loch Nov 8, 1830.
38. D593/K/1/5/27 Loch to Mrs Henney Jan 3, 1831.
39. D593/K/1/5/27 Loch to Lewis April 21, 1831.
40. D593/K/1/5/27 Loch to Lewis June 27, 1831.
41. D593/K/1/3/19 Lewis to Loch Oct 6, Nov 8, 1831.
42. D593/K/1/5/29 Loch to Henney March, 1833.
43. D593/K/1/3/21 Lewis to Loch March 14, 19, 23, 24, 1833.
44. D593/K/1/3/22 Henney to Loch April 1, 7, 1834.

45. D593/K/1/5/30 Loch to Lewis Feb 15; Loch to Henney March 30, June 25; Loch to Duke April 7, July 7, all 1834.
46. D593/K/1/3/22 Henney to Loch April 1, July 17, 1834.
47. D593/K/1/5/30 Loch to Lewis Aug 8, 1834.
48. D593/K/1/3/22 Henney to Loch Aug 12; Lewis to Loch Aug 14, both 1834.
49. D593/K/1/3/22 Henney to Loch Dec 12, 1834; D593/K/1/5/23 Lewis to Loch Jan 17, 1835.
50. D593/K/1/3/18 Lewis to Loch Dec 16 and 22, 1830.
51. D593/K/1/3/27, Lewis to Loch Jan 14, Feb 2, Feb 4, 1839.
52. D593/K/1/3/22 Lewis to Loch May 24, 31 1834.
53. D593/K/1/3/30 George Kirkby to Loch 1 April 1842.
54. D593/K/1/3/27 letters between Lewis, Hathorn, Fenton and W. D Kirkby April 26, 29, May 1, 6, 12, 18, Nov 28, all 1839.
55. D593/K1//3/27 W. D Kirkby to Loch 12 March, 1839.
56. D593/K/1/3/30 George Kirkby to Loch 1 April, 1842.
57. 593/K/1/3/8 Lewis to Loch 26 January, 1820.
58. Emery's rental information taken from D593/G/2/5/2, 3, 4, Rent Books, 1815–48.
59. D593/N/1/1/37 Valuation Survey of the North Staffordshire Estate, 1840–52.
60. D593/H/14/3/18A, Survey of Trentham Hall Estate, 1859; Henney's rental information taken from D593/G/2/5/4 and 5, Rent Books 1833–1850.

10 The Parting of the Ways

1. For their whole background, see: 'Victoria History of the County of Shropshire: vol. 11, Telford' ed. G. C.Baugh and C. R. Elrington (London 1985), pp. 266–269; Trinder, B., 'The Open Village in Industrial Britain', in *The Industrial Heritage: the Third International Conference on the Conservation of Industrial Monuments, Sweden, 1978*, Nisser, M. (Stockholm, 1981), pp. 374–5; Loch, J., *An Account of the Improvements on the Estates of the Marquess of Stafford*, 1820.
2. SRO D593/G/2/5/2 Rent Book, 1803–15.
3. SRO D593/K/1/5/27 Loch to Lord Gower, 28 January 1831.
4. SRO D593/K/1/3/18 James to Loch, 11, 29 December, 1830.
5. SRO D593/K/1/5/27 Loch to Mackay, June 20; D593/K/1/3/19 Mackay to Loch, 3 July; Lewis to Loch, June, all 1831.
6. SRO D593/K/1/5/29 Loch to Mackay,9,16 March 1833.
7. SRO D593/K/1/3/21 Mackay to Loch, 13, 31 March, 21 April 21 1833.
8. SRO D593/K/1/3/22 Lewis to Loch, 17 February 1834.
9. SRO D593/K/1/3/21 Dr. Webb to Loch, 21 April 1833.
10. SRO D593/K/1/5/30 Loch to Lewis, 16 December 1834.
11. SRO D593/K/1/3/22 Mackay to Loch, 12 April 1834.
12. SRO D593/K/1/3/22 Mackay to Loch, 3 January, 12, 13 April 1834.
13. SRO D593/K/1/3/22 Mackay to Loch, 18 April 1834.
14. SRO D593/K/1/5/30 Loch to Lewis, 16 December 1834.
15. SRO D593/K/1/3/22Lewis to Loch, 19, 27 May 1834.
16. SRO D593/K/1/3/22 Lewis to Loch, 11 December 1834; Lewis to Loch, 21 January 1835.

17. SRO D593/K/1/3/23 Lewis to Loch, 21 January 1835.
18. SRO D593/K/1/3/23 Mackay to Loch, 19, 21 January 1835.
19. SRO D593/K/1/3/23 Mackay to Loch, 19, 20 January 1835.
20. SRO D593/K/1/3/23 Lewis to Loch, 5 January 1835.
21. SRO D593/K/1/3/23 Mackay to Loch, 29 June 1835.
22. SRO D593/K/1/5/30 Loch to W. Smith May 20, 1834.
23. SRO D593/K/1/3/23 Lewis to Loch, 26 May, 8 July 1835.
24. SRO D593/K/1/3/24 Smith to Loch, 23 May, 18 June 1836.
25. SRO D593/K/1/3/22 Mackay to Loch, 3 January 1834.
26. SRO D593/K/1/3/24 Memorial to His Grace the Duke of Sutherland, 26 May, 1836.
27. SRO D593K//1/3/24 Webb to Loch, 31 May 1836.
28. SRO D593/K/1/3/24 Kirkby to Loch, 3 June 1836.
29. SRO D593/K/1/5/32 Loch to Mackay, 8 June 1836.
30. SRO D593/K/1/3/24 Smith to Loch, 18 June, 1836.
31. SRO D593/K/1/3/24 Smith to Loch, 6 September, 1836; D593/K/1/3/25 Smith to Loch, 6 September 1837.
32. SRO D593/K/1/3/29 Mackay to Duke, forwarded to Loch, 4 January 1841.
33. SRO D593/K/1/3/29 Smith to Loch, 8 February 1841.

11 The Agent

1. SRO D593/K/1/3/14 Lewis to Loch, 11 March 1826.
2. All the following section on Lewis family is based on SRO D593/K/3/5/3 Lewis's private correspondence, 1817–1819.
3. SRO D593/K/1/3/26 Lewis to Loch, 24 February 1838.
4. SRO D593/K/3/5/5 Loch to Lewis Memorandum, 1817–? .
5. SRO D641/5/E(C)/20 Ford to Fitzherbert, 27 September and 26 October 1836.
6. Wordie, Ross, 'Estate Management in 18th century England', Royal Hist Soc. London, 1982, pp. 64–66.
7. Spring, p.105.
8. SRO D593/K/1/3/8 Lewis to Loch 7 February 1820.
9. SRO D593/K/1/3/19 Lewis to Loch, 16 February, 1831.
10. SRO D593/L/2/2b Lewis's Memorandum Book, February 1835.
11. SRO D593/K/1/5/29 Loch to Lewis, 13 May, 1833.
12. SRO D593/K/1/3/20 Loch to Lewis, 10 and 26 July 1832; D593/K/1/3/21 Lewis to Loch, 11, 13, 19, 20 May 1833; D593/K/1/5/29 Loch to Lewis, 13 May 1833; D593/K/1/5/27 Loch to Lewis, 10 June, 1831; D593/K/1/3/21 Kirkby to Loch, 13 October 1833; D593/K/1/5/29 Loch to Lewis, 14 October 1833; D593/K/1/3/20 Lewis to Loch, 14 April 1832.
13. SRO D593/K/1/3/21 Lewis to Loch, 5 January 1833.
14. SRO D593/K/3/5/3 William Lewis to George Lewis, 12 November 1818.
15. SRO D593/K/1/3/18 Lewis to Loch, 9 February 1830.
16. SRO D593/K/1/3/18 Lewis to Loch, 5, 6, 11, 15 December 1830; D593/K/1/3/26 Lewis to Loch, 11 July 1838.
17. SRO D593/K/1/5/29 Loch to Lewis, 7 February 1833.
18. SRO D593/K/1/3/26 Lewis to Loch, 24 February 1838.

19. SRO D593/K/13/22 Lewis to Loch, 28 February 1834.
20. SRO D593/K/1/3/29 Lewis to Loch, 14 March 1841.
21. SRO D593/K/1/3/18 Lewis to Loch, 28 December 1830.
22. SRO D593/K/1/3/18 Lewis to Loch, 22, 28 December 1830.
23. SRO D593/K/1/5/29 Lewis to Loch and Loch to Marquess, 18 and 20 April 1833.
24. SRO D593/K/1/3/21 Lewis to Loch, 3 May 1833.
25. SRO D593/K/1/3/22 Lewis to Loch, 17 January 1834.
26. SRO D593/K/1/5/27 Loch to Marquess 9 January, Loch to Lewis 28 January, 1831.
27. SRO D593/K/ 1/3/19 Kirkby to Loch 2 February, 1831.
28. SRO D593/K/1/5/32 Loch to Bakewell 14 January, 15, 16 June, 1836.
29. SRO D593/K/1/5/27 Loch to Lewis 30 September, 1831.
30. SRO D593/K/1/5/27 Loch to Lewis 8 August, 30 September, 1831; D593/K/1/3/21 Lewis to Loch 10 January, 9 and 24 June, 1833.
31. SRO D593/K/1/3/21 Lewis to Loch 5 February, 26 September, 1833; D593/K/1/5/29 Loch to Lewis 29 September, 1833; D593/K/1/3/22 Lewis to Loch 29 April, 1834.
32. SRO D593/K/1/3/27 Lewis to Loch 26 June, 1839.
33. SRO D593/K/3/1/27 Loch to Lewis 27 July 1839; D593/K/1/3/27 Lewis to Loch , 26 June, 29 July, 1839.
34. SRO D593/K/1/3/27 Lewis to Loch 7 March, Henney to Loch 2 and 30 May, 6 June , 6 and 29 June, all 1839.
35. Extracts about Mrs Lewis's illness are from SRO D593/K/1/3/27 Lewis to Loch, nd March, 30 March, 6 June all 1839.
36. Extracts commiserating with Lewis are from SRO D593/K/3/1/27 Part3, Loch to Lewis 7 March, 14 June, Mrs Loch to Lewis 19, 27 March all 1839.
37. SRO D593/K/3/3/42, Part 1, Thomas Cleaver to Lewis May 11, 1840.
38. SRO D593/K/3/1/28 Lewis to Loch 17 June, 1840; D593/K/3/1/27 Part 2 of 5, Loch to Lewis June 18, 1840.
39. SRO D593/K/1/3/27 Lewis to Loch 29 January, 28 June, 1839; D593/K/1/3/28 Lewis to Loch 21 September, 12 November 1840; D593/K/1/3/28 Lewis to Loch 5 and 9 December, 1840.
40. SRO D593/K/1/3/29 Lewis to Loch, 5 August, 1841.
41. SRO D593/K/1/3/29 McKenzie to Loch 8 and 29 August, Smith to Loch 9 August, Broomhall to Loch 21 August, Lewis to Loch 10 November, all 1841.
42. SRO D593/K/1/3/29 Henney to Loch 17 November, 1841.
43. SRO D6578/11/201, 5a Duchess to Loch 3 January, 1842.
44. SRO D6578/11/201, 10-11c and 13 Duke/Duchess to Loch 7 and 8 January, 1842.
45. SRO D593/K/1/3/30 John Henderson to Loch 20 January 1842.
46. SRO D593/K/1/3/29 In letter to Loch, 19 November 1841.
47. SRO D593/K/1/ 3/30 Morton to Loch, 19 January 1842, Ogilvie to Loch, 10 January 1842.
48. SRO D593/K/1/3/30 Steward to Loch, 16 and 19 February 1842.
49. SROD593/K/1/3/30 Lewis to Loch, 23 March, 11, 20, 27 April 1842.
50. SRO D593/K/1/3/30 Lewis to Loch, 9 May 1842.

51. SROD593/K/1/3/30 Richard Steward to Loch, 15 June 1842.

52. For a detailed account of both the colliers' strike and the Chartist movement in the Potteries see Fyson, R., 'The Crisis of 1842: Chartism, the Colliers' Strike and the Outbreak in the Potteries' in *The Chartist Experience: Studies in Working Class Radicalism and Culture*, eds., Epstein, James and Thompson, Dorothy, (London, Macmillan 1982), pp 194–220.

53. SRO D593/K/1/3/30 Steward to Loch, 16, 17, 18, 22, 24, 25, 28 August, 4 and 22 September, 1842.

54. VCH p. 247.

55. National Probate Calendar, Index of Wills and Administrations, 1858–1966; *Staffordshire Advertiser*, 3 November, 1855. Annual meeting of the North Staffordshire Infirmary.

56. *Staffordshire Advertiser*, 10 February, 1855.

12 The Commissioner

1. Spring, David, *The English Landed Estate in the Nineteenth Century: its Administration* (Baltimore, 1963) p. 96.

2. Eric Richards, 'Loch, James (1780-1855)', *Oxford Dictionary of National Bibliography*, (Oxford University Press, 2004) [http://www.oxfordddnb.com/view/article/16883, accessed 1 December 2015].

3. Eric Richards, *The Highland Clearances: People, Landlords and Rural Turmoil*, (Birlinn, 2008); Eric Richards, 'The Leviathan of Wealth* (London, 1973) pp. 19–34; *The John o' Groats Journal*, 6 July, 1855.

4. Leveson-Gower, F., *Letters of Harriet, Countess Granville*, vol. 1 (London, 1894) p. 39.

5. Spring, pp. 95–96.

6. Wordie, J. R., *Social Change on the Leveson-Gower Estates, 1714–1832*, Econ. Hist. Rev., 2nd series, vol. 4, 1974, p. 603.

7. Thomas Bakewell, 'Remarks on a Publication by James Loch Esq. (Agent to the Marquis of Stafford) entitled "An Account of the Improvements on the Estates of the Marquis of Stafford in Staffordshire and Shropshire and on the Estate in Sutherland"' 17 May, 1820.

8. Spring, p. 95.

9. SRO D593/K/1/5/27 Loch to Lewis, 5 January 1831.

10. Richards, *Leviathan of Wealth*, p.29.

11. SRO D593/K/1/3/29 Walker to Loch, 30 January 1841.

12. Richards, *Leviathan of Wealth*, p. 31.

13. See for example 'The London Evening Standard, 18 August, 1842 and 'The Northern Warder and General Advertiser' for the counties of Fife, Perth and Forfar' 10 July, 1845; The Fife Herald, 24 June, 1845.

14. SRO D593/K/1/5/29 Loch to Lewis, 10 July; Loch to William Adam Loch, 1 August, both 1833.

15. Richards, E. S., 'James Loch and the House of Sutherland, 1812–55, Ph.D. thesis, University of Nottingham, 1967, p. 126.

16. SRO D593/K/1/5/30 Loch to Lewis, 25 June1834. See Potter, J., 'The Training and Early Career of James Loch of Drylaw, 6 May 1780-28 June 1855', MA thesis, Keele University, 1995.
17. SRO D593/K/3/5/5 Loch to Suther, 26 November 1817.
18. SRO D593/K/1/3/30 Steward to Loch, 19 February 1842.
19. SRO D593/K/1/5/30 Loch to Smith, 20 May, 25 June, 8 December, 1834.
20. SRO D593/1/5/30 Loch to Duke, 2 April 1834.
21. SRO D593K/1/5/29 Lewis to Loch and Loch to Marquis, 18 and 20 April 1833; D593/3/1/1/1 Loch to Suther, 1813.
22. Bakewell *op. cit.*
23. Leveson-Gower, F., vol. 1, p. 437.
24. SRO D593/K/1/5/29 Loch to Lewis, 23 January, 7, 13 February, 7 October, 5, 16 December 1833.
25. Checkland, S. G. in *Leviathan of Wealth, p. Xviii.* Tongue was one of the Sutherland's houses on the far northern coast of Scotland.
26. Richards, *Leviathan of Wealth*, p. 34.
27. *The John o' Groats Journal,* 6 July 1855.

13 Finally ...

1. Richards, *Leviathan of Wealth*, p. 26.

Bibliography

Adams, S. and S., *The Complete Servant* 1st pub. 1825, new ed. (London, 1989)

Barber, J., '"Stolen Goods": the Sexual Harassment of Female Servants in West Wales during the Nineteenth Century', in *Rural History*, Vol. 4, No. 2 (Oct. 1993)

Bertrand, H., *Cahier de Sainte-Helene, Jan 1821–May 1821* (1949)

Bourrier, M., *François Filidoro, le capitaine du port de l'Isle d'Elba: tribulations et jours de gloire d'un Corse né en 1766* (1978)

Campbell-Smith, D., *Masters of the Post: The Authorized History of the Royal Mail* (London, 2001)

Christophe, R., *Napoleon on Elba*, trans. edition (London, 1964)

Defoe, D., *The Compleat English Gentleman*, 1728, later editions edited by Karl Daniel Bulbring, available as ebooks or print on demand.

Fyson, R., 'The Crisis of 1842: Chartism, the Colliers' Strike and the Outbreak in the Potteries' in *The Chartist Experience: Studies in Working Class Radicalism and Culture, 1830–60*, ed. James Epstein and Dorothy Thompson (Macmillan, London, 1982)

Gerard, J. A., 'Invisible Servants: The Country House and the Local Community', in *Bulletin of the Institute of Historical Research*, vol. LV11, No. 136 (November 1984)

Gerard, J., *Country House Life: Family and Servants, 1815–1914* (Oxford, 1994)

Gower, R., *My Reminiscences*, vol. 1 (London, 1883)

Hay, D., 'England, 1562–1875' in D. Hay and P. Craven, eds, *Masters, Servants and Magistrates in Britain and the Empire, 1562–1955* (University of North Carolina Press, 2004)

Holland, M., *Swing Unmasked: The Agricultural Riots of 1830 to 1832 and their Wider Implications* (Milton Keynes, 2005)

Lentz, T., 'Les Cent-Jours', *Nouvelle Histoire du Premier Empire*, vol. 4 (Paris, 2002–10)

Leveson-Gower, F., *Letters of Harriet, Countess Granville*, vol. 1 (London, 1894)

Loch, J., *An Account of the Improvements on the Estates of the Marquess of Stafford*, 1820.

Mackenzie, N., *The Escape from Elba: the Fall and Flight of Napoleon, 1814–1815* (Oxford, 1982)

McBride, T., 'Social Mobility for the Lower Classes: Domestic Servant in France', in *Journal of Social History* (1974, 8)

Potter, J., *The Training and Early Career of James Loch of Drylaw, 6 May 1780–28 June 1855*', MA thesis, Keele University (1995)

Richards, E., *The Leviathan of Wealth: The Sutherland Fortune in the Industrial Revolution* (London, 1973)

Richards, E., 'Loch, James (1780–1855)', in *Oxford Dictionary of National Bibliography* (Oxford, 2004)

Richards, E., *The Highland Clearances: People, Landlords and Rural Turmoil* (Edinburgh, 2008)

Sambrook, P., *Country House Brewing in England, 1500–1900* (London, 1996)

Sambrook, P., *The Country House Servant* (Stroud, 1999)

Sambrook, P., *A Country House at Work: three centuries of Dunham Massey* (London, 2003)

Spring, D., *The English Landed Estate in the Nineteenth Century: its Administration* (Baltimore, 1963)

Sykes, C. S., *Private Palaces: Life in the Great London Houses* (New York, 1985)

The Victoria History of the Counties of England, A history of the County of Shropshire: Telford', vol. XI, ed. G. C. Baugh and C. R. Elrington (London, 1985)

The Victoria History of the Counties of England, A history of Staffordshire, Audley, Keele and Trentham', vol. XI, ed. Nigel J. Tringham (London, 2013)

Trinder, B., 'The Open Village in Industrial Britain', in *The Industrial Heritage: the Third International Conference on the Conservation of Industrial Monuments, Sweden, 1978*, Nisser, M. (Stockholm, 1981)

Tudor, P. G., 'The Domestic Establishments of His Grace the Duke of Sutherland', unpublished project report for Department of Adult Education, Keele University (1995)

Wordie, J. R., 'Social Change on the Leveson-Gower Estates, 1714–1832' in *Economic History Review*, 2nd series, vol. 27, 4 (1974)

Wordie, Ross, *Estate Management in 18ᵗʰ century England* (London, 1982)

Index